IMAGES
of America

CRANSTON

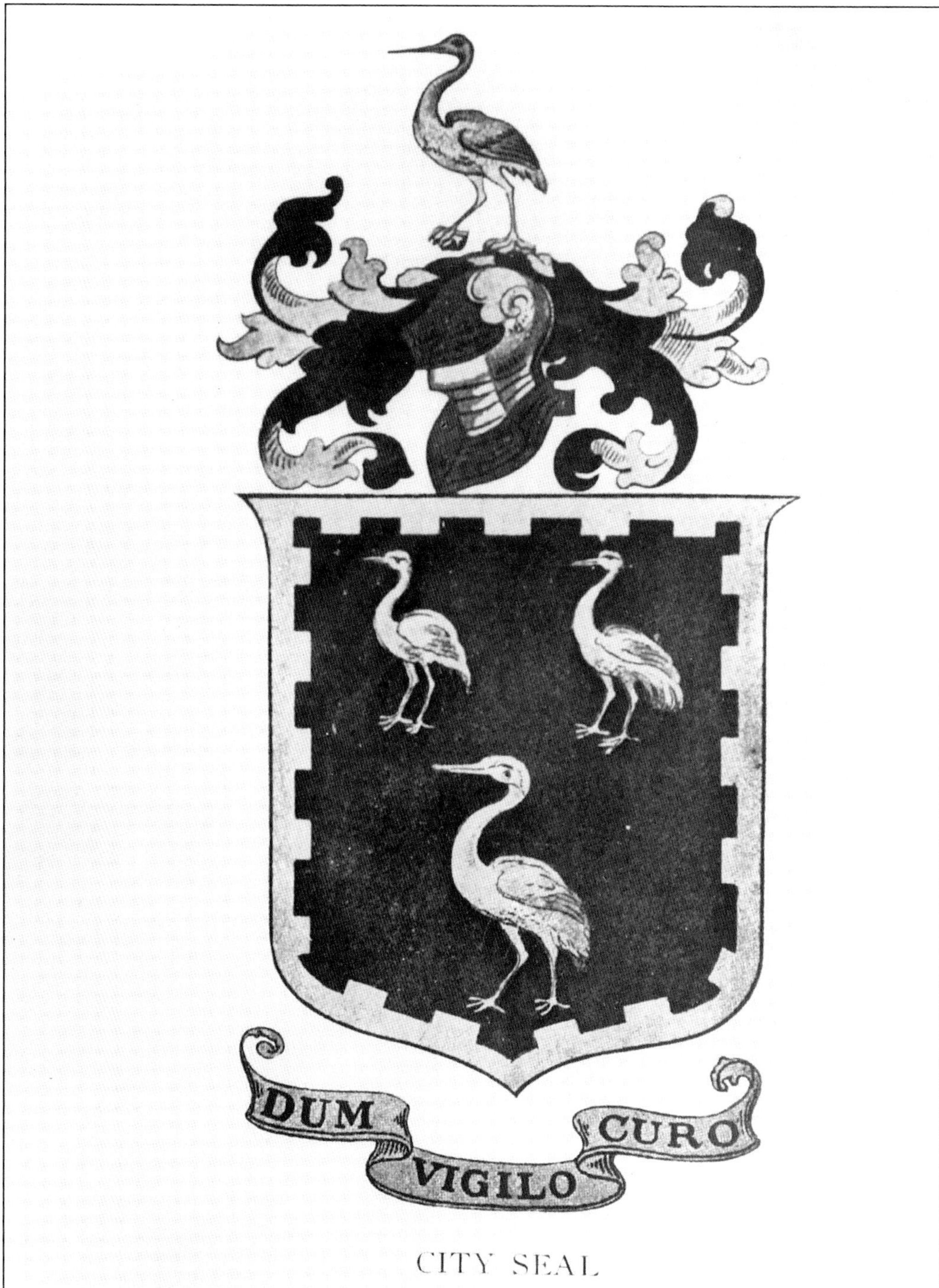

THE COAT OF ARMS OF GOVERNOR SAMUEL CRANSTON. Cranston, incorporated in 1754, was named for Governor Samuel Cranston, who was governor from 1698 to 1727. His family's coat of arms consists of three silver cranes on a red shield with a silver border. The motto "Dum Vigilo Curo" has been translated as "While I watch, I care."

IMAGES
of America

CRANSTON

Lydia L. Rapoza and Bette Miller

ARCADIA
PUBLISHING

Copyright © 1999 by Lydia L. Rapoza and Bette Miller
ISBN 978-0-7385-0158-1

Published by Arcadia Publishing
Charleston, South Carolina

Printed in the United States of America

Library of Congress Catalog Card Number: 99-62235

For all general information contact Arcadia Publishing at:
Telephone 843-853-2070
Fax 843-853-0044
E-mail sales@arcadiapublishing.com
For customer service and orders:
Toll-Free 1-888-313-2665

Visit us on the Internet at www.arcadiapublishing.com

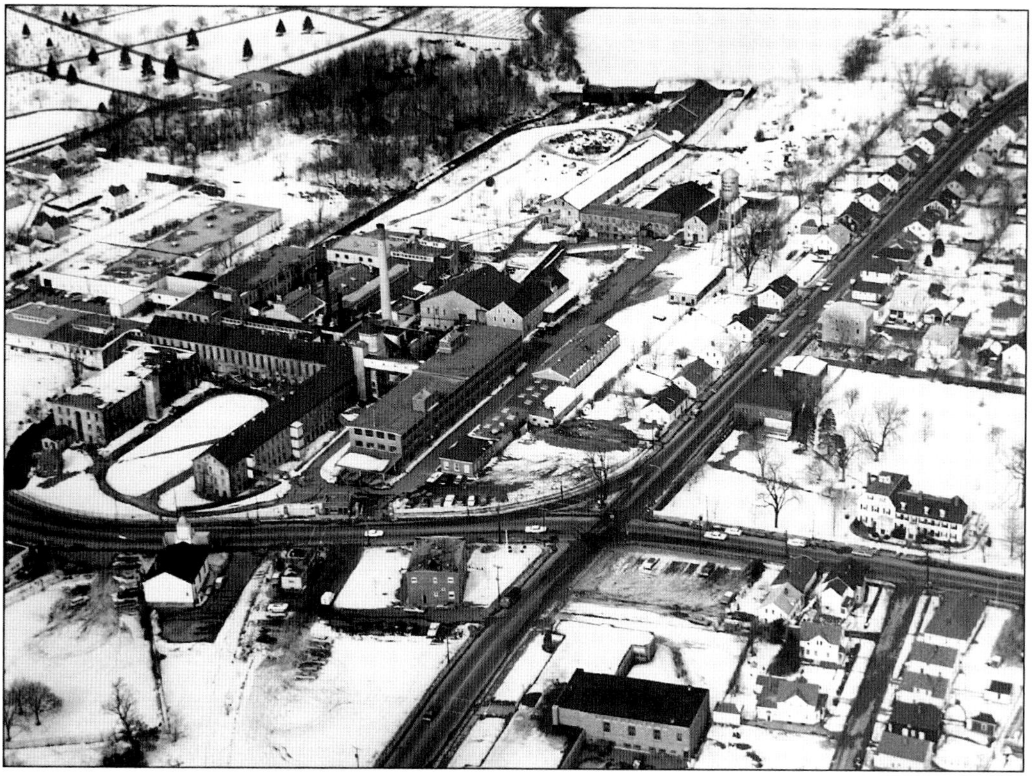

SPRAGUEVILLE ON DYER AVENUE AND CRANSTON STREET, C. 1963. From the cupola of the Sprague Mansion the Sprague family could see all they owned. A small city within Cranston, Sprague's Village had its own water and gas systems, steam fire engine company, and farms for raising cattle, sheep, and poultry. The city government was established here. The town clerk's office was behind the Sprague's company store.

Contents

This work is dedicated to the memory of Mrs. Amasa Sprague (formerly Harriet Bryon Sprague), the daughter of Byron and Harriet Comstock-Sprague and the wife of Amasa Sprague II. Her generosity to the Cranston Historical Society has afforded us the opportunity to preserve and share the history of the Sprague family.

INTRODUCTION

Cranston's beginnings can be traced back to the 1638 Pawtuxet Purchase by Roger Williams from the Narragansett sachems Canonicus and Miantinomi. William Arnold, the father of Benedict (who became the first governor of Rhode Island under the Royal Charter of Charles II), accompanied Roger Williams in his flight from Massachusetts and established the first permanent settlement in Pawtuxet, which was incorporated as Cranston in 1754. Eleven days after the town's incorporation, the Caleb Arnold Tavern in Knightsville was chosen by lottery to be the meeting place for the first town council.

In the 19th century, William Sprague II and his descendants made Cranston and the Sprague Mills the richest textile mills in the United States, outproducing all the other mills in the U.S. combined. The immigrants who worked in the Sprague Mills along the Pawtuxet River settled in little mill villages that still exist with their ethnic diversity intact today. After the decline of the Sprague fortune, the Knight Brothers carried on the textile industry with their Fruit of the Loom mills.

Linked forever in Rhode Island history are a young Irish immigrant, John Gordon, and Amasa Sprague. Gordon changed Rhode Island jurisprudence when he was convicted and executed for the murder of the wealthy and powerful Amasa Sprague, partner in the A&W Sprague Manufacturing Company. Gordon's conviction may have been fueled by the prejudice of the local newspapers, which covered every word of the trial. It was a sensational case that sold papers, and the news media took full advantage of it. The aftershocks of Gordon's execution are still felt in Rhode Island today, more than 150 years after the fact.

Other important people of the area in the 19th century included Nehemiah Knight, William Sprague III, Eliza Harris, William Sprague IV, and Henry Howard, native sons of Cranston who governed Rhode Island. Roby Wilbur, an Oak Lawn woman, started the New England tradition of annual May Day breakfasts in 1868 as a way to raise funds for the Benevolent Baptist Church. The Budlong family, with their market gardens, supplied many New England and New York families with fine produce. Their farms in Eden Park hired so many Swedish immigrants that the community was fondly called Sweden Park.

In the 20th century the area continued to thrive as it had in the 19th. Edward Sullivan, a young man from Knightsville, was elected the first mayor when Cranston became a city in 1910. John M. Dean, with his model community in Meshanticut, gave families a chance to have a home on the installment plan and at affordable rates. Julia Lippett Moran, a gentlewoman farmer from Western Cranston, made her own history by being the first woman granted a driver's license. Dean, Budlong, Sullivan, Knight, and Sprague were some well-known names of Cranston; however, there are others, not so well known, who were just as important in forming the cornerstone of Cranston. Names like Bigbee, Haven, Latham, Westcott, and Williams belonged to early civil servants, pioneers who paved the way for today's fine public service people. Slocum and Dolan were Auburn druggists at a time when soda fountains were popular and pharmacists used mortars and pestles to make up prescriptions. Like trolley lines in Cranston, these names belong to history.

Despite modern progress in Cranston, which is now one of the major commercial and industrial areas of the state, the Sprague Mansion, the Cranston Print Works, the Knightsville Meeting House, Oak Lawn's historic district, Pawtuxet's Baptist Church, and the Joy Homestead, witnesses to the march of history, survive. As we journey into this pictorial history of Cranston, remember that when this book is closed, we return to the present—which will soon be our history.

Author's Note: All photographs and items unless otherwise noted belong to the Cranston Historical Society. Proceeds from the sale of this book go to the Cranston Historical Society to support the maintenance of the Joy Homestead and the Governor Sprague Mansion.

One

Arlington and Spragueville

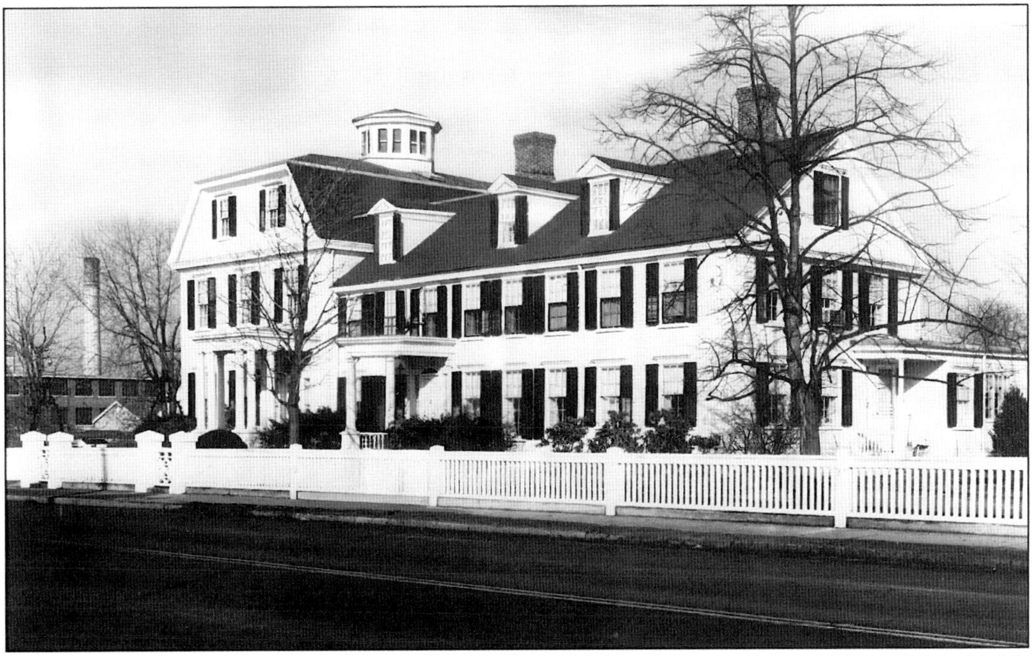

The Governor Sprague Mansion, Cranston and Dyer Streets, c. 1790, 1808, 1864. This 28-room house was nearly destroyed in 1966 to build a supermarket on the property. The birthplace of two Rhode Island governors and the site of landmark judicial history, the house is now owned by the Cranston Historical Society and is a National Historical Landmark intended to be enjoyed by everyone. Many events are held at the mansion, including the annual open house held in December, which gives visitors and guests the opportunity to see beautiful furnishings in an historic setting.

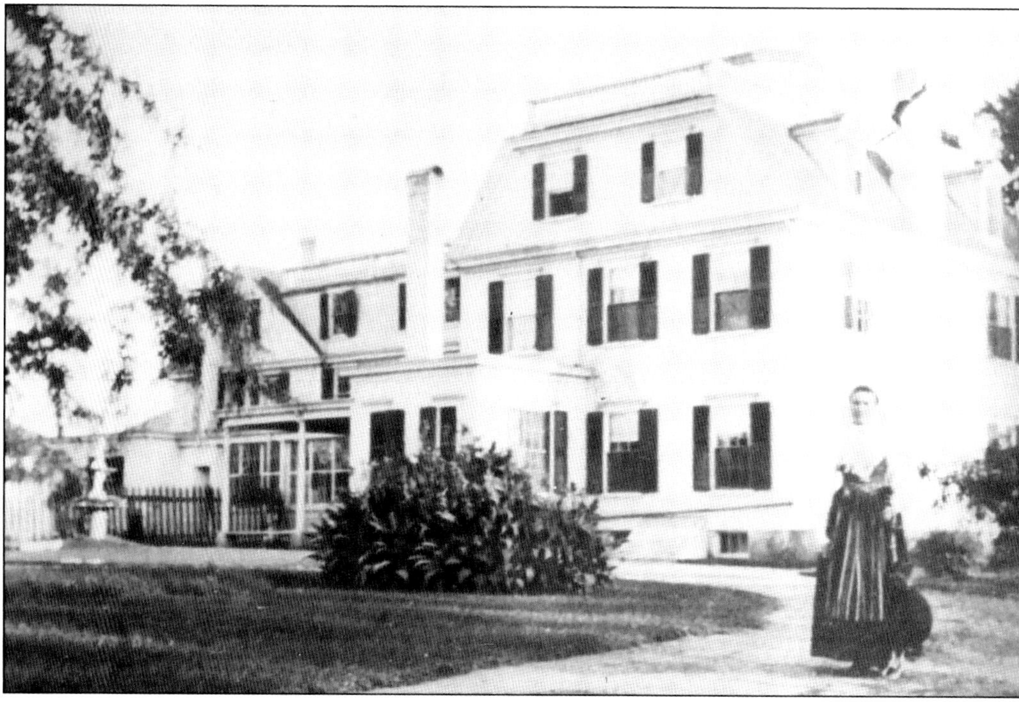

A Rear View of the Sprague Mansion, c. 1910. In 1863, when Amasa Sprague II added this new section to the house, a gasometer was installed, which furnished fuel for lights in the Sprague Mansion. In the mahogany-paneled ballroom he included an Italian marble fireplace. The lady in the photo is Margaret Danielson Bornander.

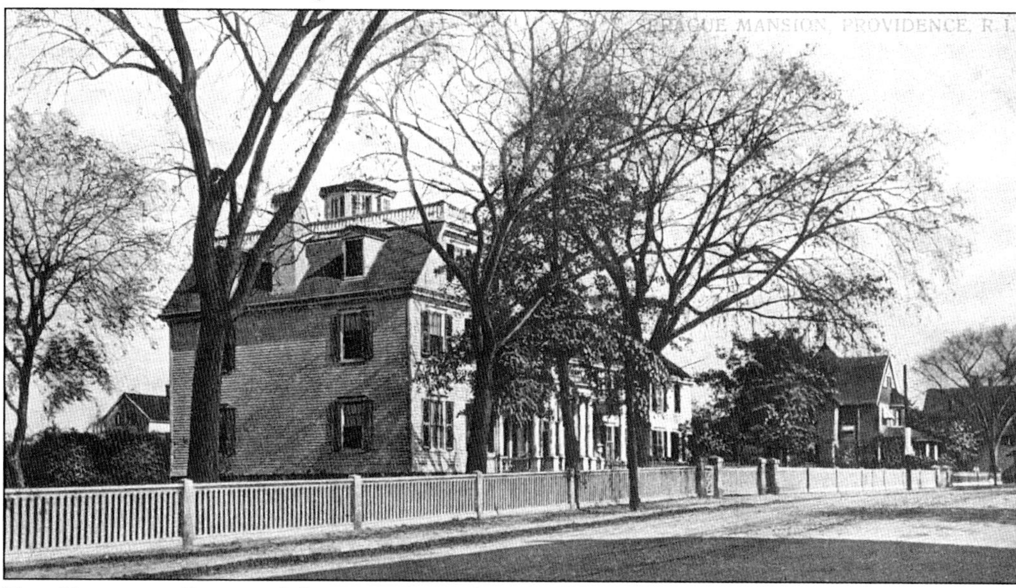

The Governor Sprague Mansion, 1351 Cranston Street, c. 1908. Through the years the Sprague family grew as did their financial empire and their house. The old part of the home was built by William Sprague II during the 1790s. The addition and carriage house were added by Amasa Sprague II in 1863. Two Rhode Island governors, William Sprague III and his nephew, William Sprague IV, were born in this house.

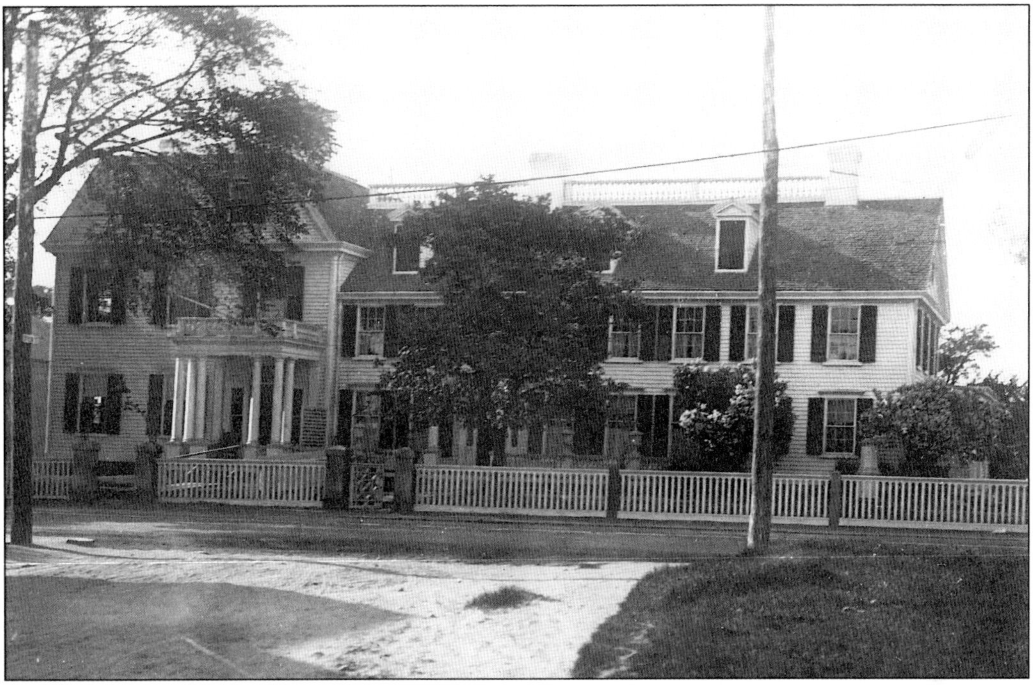

The Sprague Mansion, c. 1910. After the Spragues lost their fortune in 1873, the new owners of the Print Works used the mansion as housing for the superintendents of the mill until 1967.

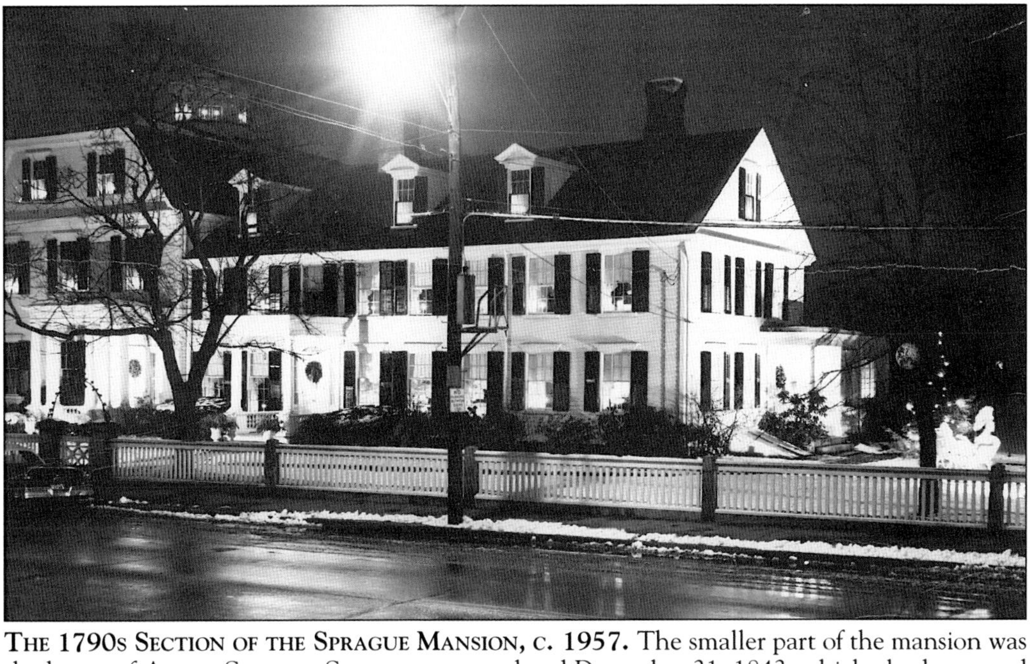

The 1790s Section of the Sprague Mansion, c. 1957. The smaller part of the mansion was the home of Amasa Sprague. Sprague was murdered December 31, 1843, which also happened to be the birthday of his wife, Fanny Morgan Sprague. Fanny and Amasa were also celebrating their 26th wedding anniversary with their four children, Almira, Amasa, Mary Anna, and William IV.

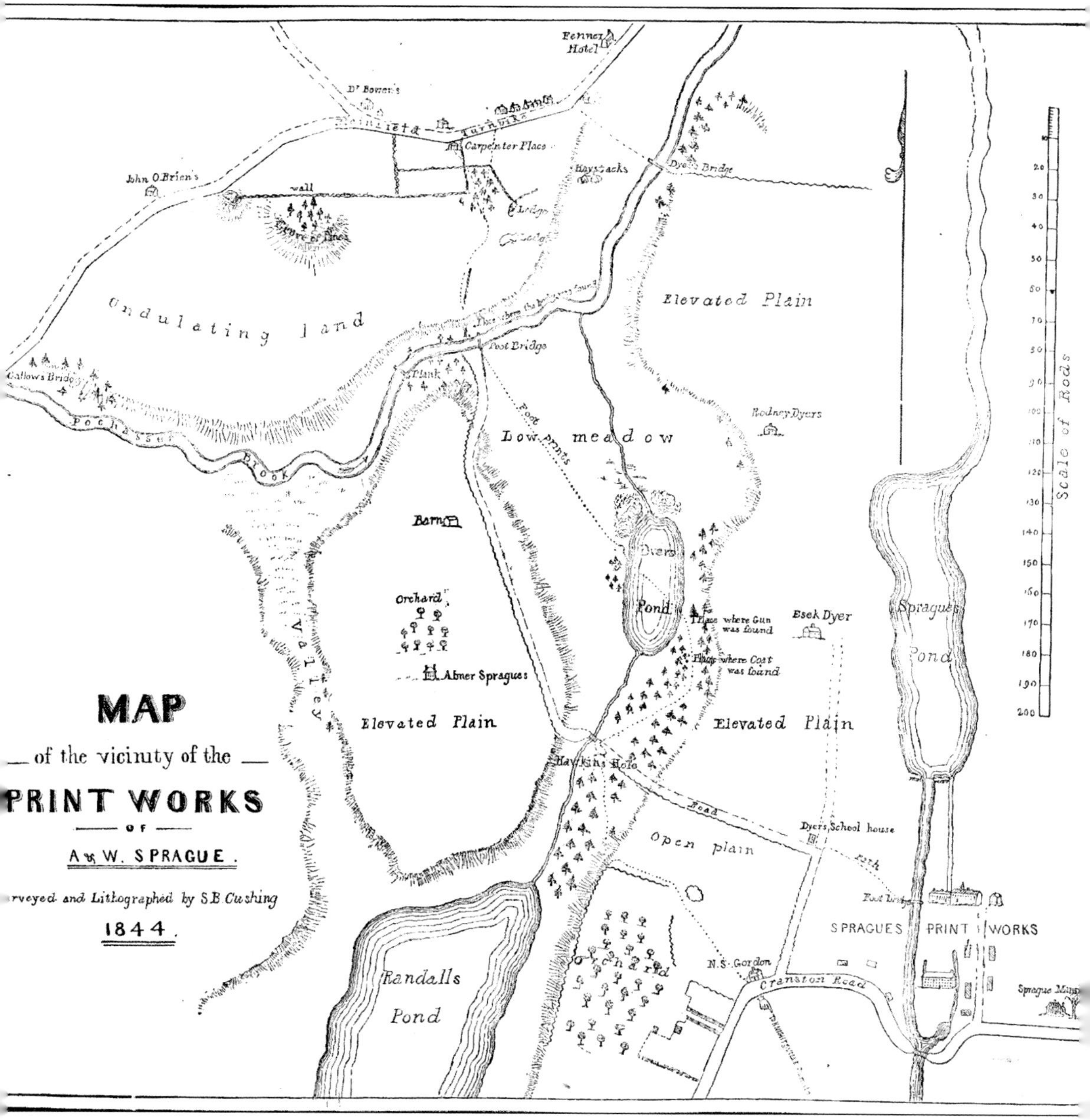

A Map Drawn on January 9, 1844, by Surveyor S.B. Cushing. This map was used as evidence in the murder trial of John and William Gordon. It displays the place where the beaten body of Amasa Sprague was found on December 31, 1843. Footprints in the snow indicted that the murderer or murderers went back to the home of Nicholas Gordon. Witnesses recalled that Sprague and Gordon had some bitter words over Sprague using his influence with the town council to have Gordon's liquor license revoked. Other circumstantial evidence also pointed to Gordon. His entire family was arrested on January 1, 1844, including his mother, sister, two brothers (John and William, who had arrived from Ireland in July), and the family dog. In the days following the murder, prejudiced feelings ran high. Local newspapers told of nativism and prejudice and by January 3 had found the Gordon brothers guilty long before they were brought to trial.

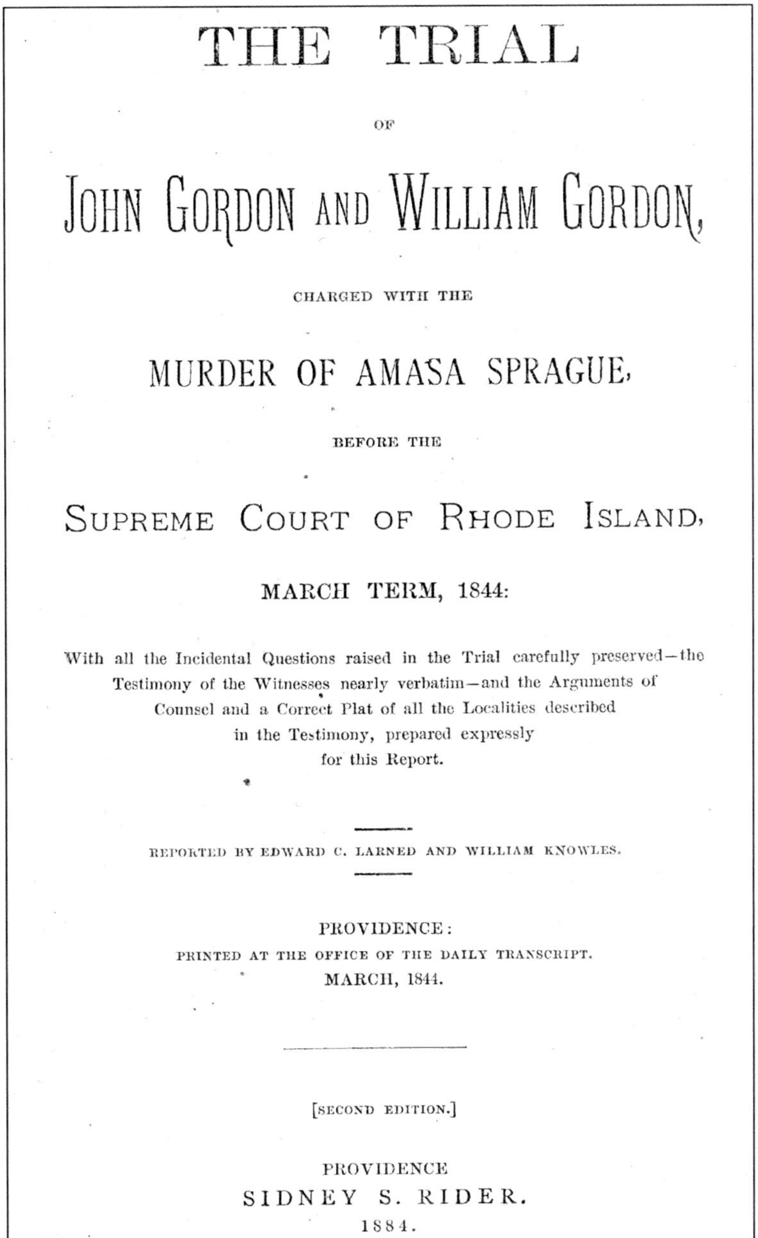

THE TRIAL

OF

JOHN GORDON AND WILLIAM GORDON,

CHARGED WITH THE

MURDER OF AMASA SPRAGUE,

BEFORE THE

SUPREME COURT OF RHODE ISLAND,

MARCH TERM, 1844:

With all the Incidental Questions raised in the Trial carefully preserved—the Testimony of the Witnesses nearly verbatim—and the Arguments of Counsel and a Correct Plat of all the Localities described in the Testimony, prepared expressly for this Report.

REPORTED BY EDWARD C. LARNED AND WILLIAM KNOWLES.

PROVIDENCE:
PRINTED AT THE OFFICE OF THE DAILY TRANSCRIPT.
MARCH, 1844.

[SECOND EDITION.]

PROVIDENCE
SIDNEY S. RIDER.
1884.

A TRANSCRIPT OF THE TRIAL. Chief Justice Job Durfee called the court to order on April 8, 1844, in the old State House on North Main Street, Providence. Nicholas Gordon was charged with being an accessory before the fact and was tried separately. Both of his trials ended in mistrials. John and William Gordon were charged with the murder of Sprague. The Irish Catholic community rallied around the Gordons and raised the funds for a defense team. The trial was over April 17; the jury deliberated for an hour and 15 minutes, finding John guilty but William, because he had an alibi, not guilty. John's appeals for a new trial were dismissed and he was sentenced to hang. Claims of new evidence did not reprieve him, and he was hanged in the state prison yard on February 14, 1845. In 1852 the Rhode Island General Assembly abolished the death penalty. No one ever confessed to the murder of Sprague.

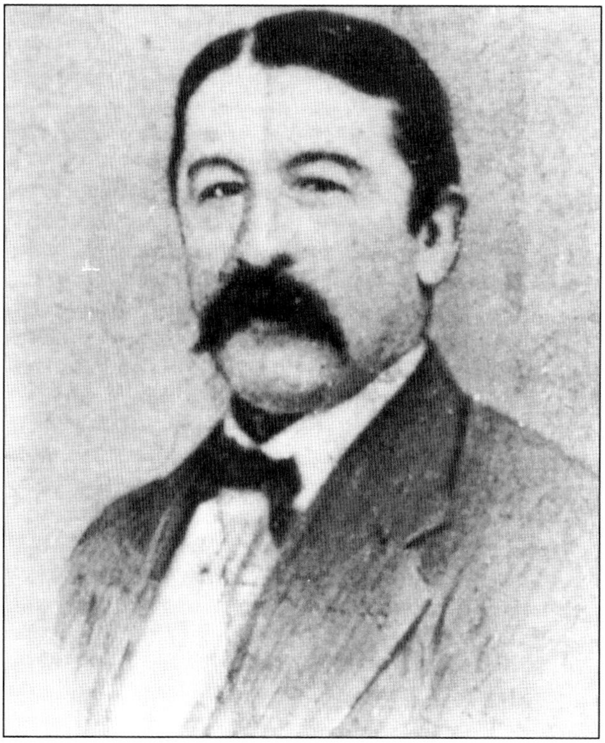

AMASA SPRAGUE. Sprague was 45 years old when his severely battered body was found lying by a footpath near Pocasset Brook on December 31, 1843. He was in charge of the Print Works while his brother, Senator William Sprague III, was in Washington, D.C. After the death of Amasa, William resigned and ran the mills. Amasa's sons William IV and Amasa II took over the mills after the death of William III.

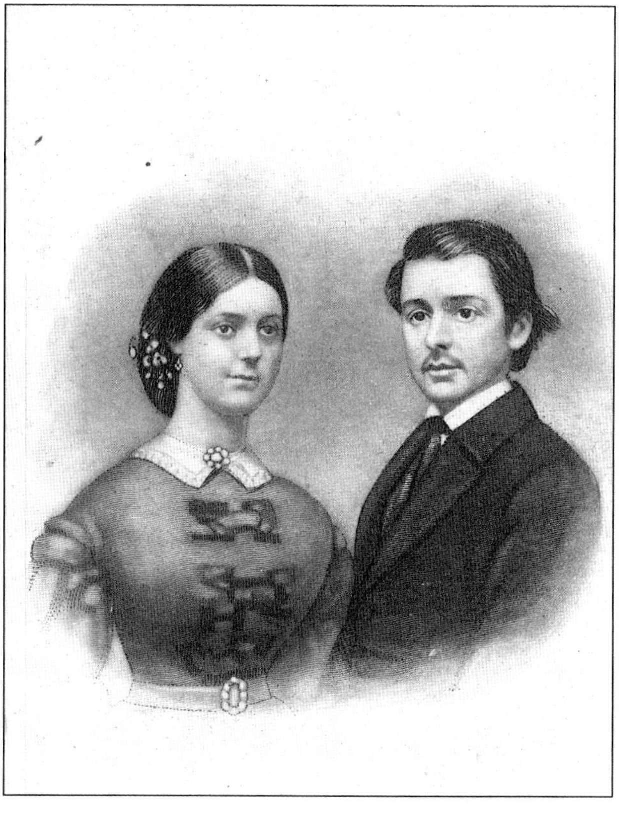

SENATOR WILLIAM SPRAGUE IV AND HIS WIFE, KATE CHASE, C. 1863. On November 12, 1863, when he married Kate Chase, daughter of Treasury Secretary Salmon P. Chase, Senator William Sprague IV, the youngest son of Amasa Sprague, was the wealthiest man in America. That wealth was estimated at $22 million. (Lydia Rapoza Collection.)

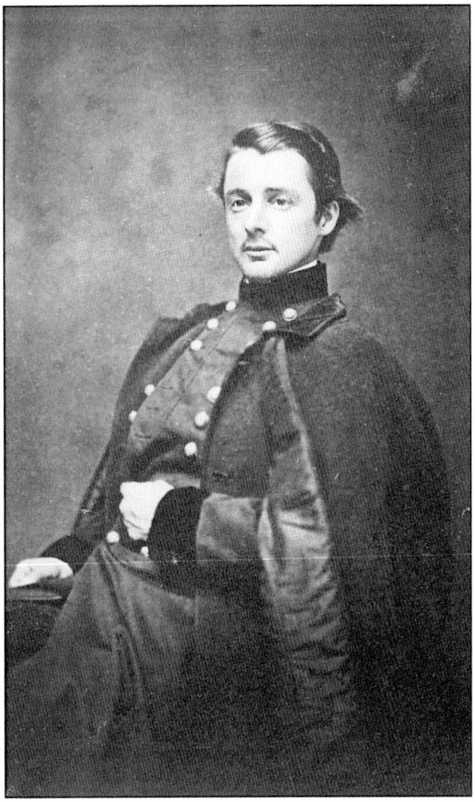

GOVERNOR SPRAGUE, C. 1861. Sprague was the first governor to volunteer his state's militia to President Lincoln to defend Washington in the early days of the Civil War. Sprague mills furnished cloth for the uniforms of the troops and money for equipment. Sprague himself was with his troops at the first Battle of Bull Run, July 21, 1861. (Lydia Rapoza Collection.)

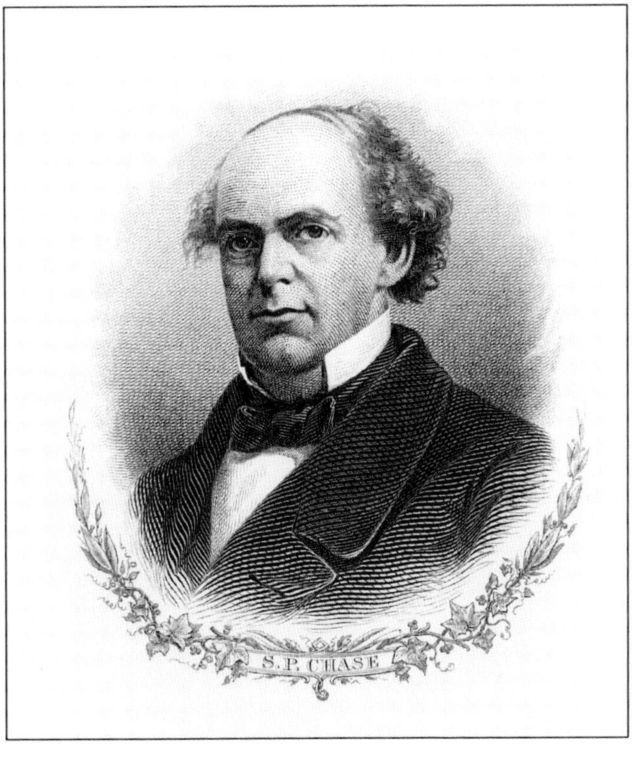

WILLIAM SPRAGUE'S FATHER-IN-LAW, HONORABLE SALMON P. CHASE, SECRETARY OF THE TREASURY, C. 1861. Chase was appointed in 1863 as chief justice of the Supreme Court by President Lincoln. In 1868, he presided over the impeachment trial of President Andrew Johnson. Despite his father-in-law's strong opposition to the conviction of Johnson, Senator Sprague and his colleague from Rhode Island, Henry B. Anthony, both voted to remove the President from office. (Lydia Rapoza Collection.)

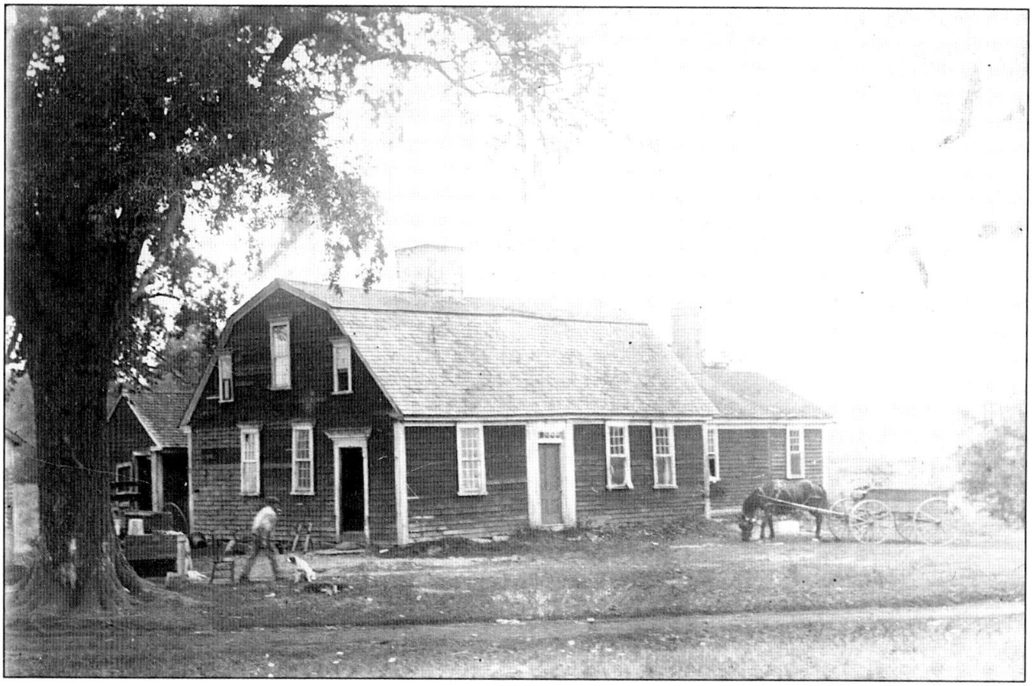

The Old Dyer Homestead, c. 1736. Descendants of Mary Dyer, the martyred Quaker, lived in this house. The last descendant, Rodney Dyer, sold his property to the A&W Sprague Company. The house was used as a schoolhouse and a church in 1843. People attending a church service at this house were the last to see Amasa Sprague alive on the afternoon of December 31, 1843. The house was later destroyed by fire.

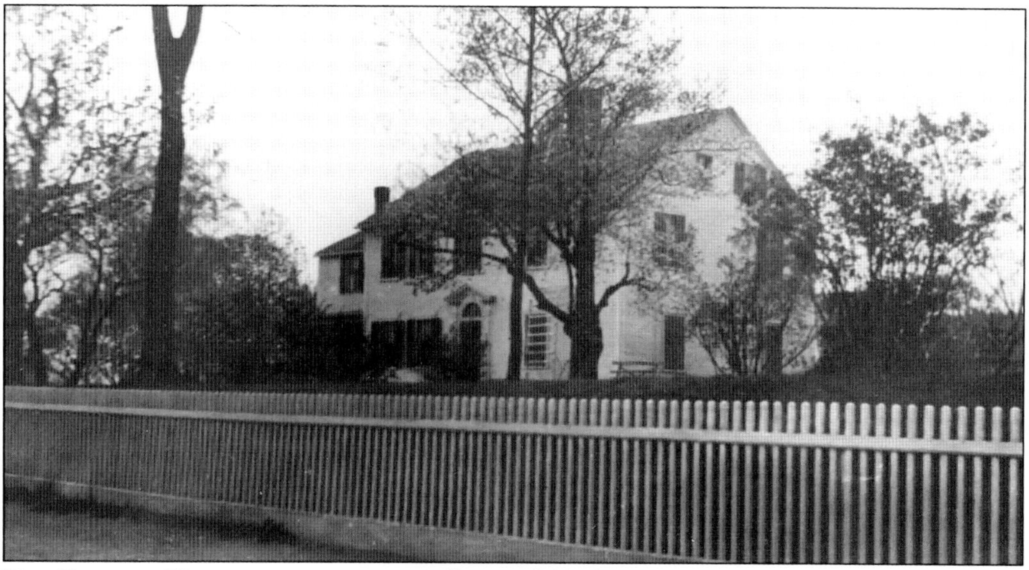

The Randall Homestead, c. 1920. Sally Randall, the widow of John Smith, sold her land to Amasa Sprague with the provision that he would have the house moved to a hilltop. The house was moved, despite the Spragues' financial difficulties, to a site by a pond that became known as Randall's Pond. It was torn down in 1935 to make way for the building of St. Mary's Church.

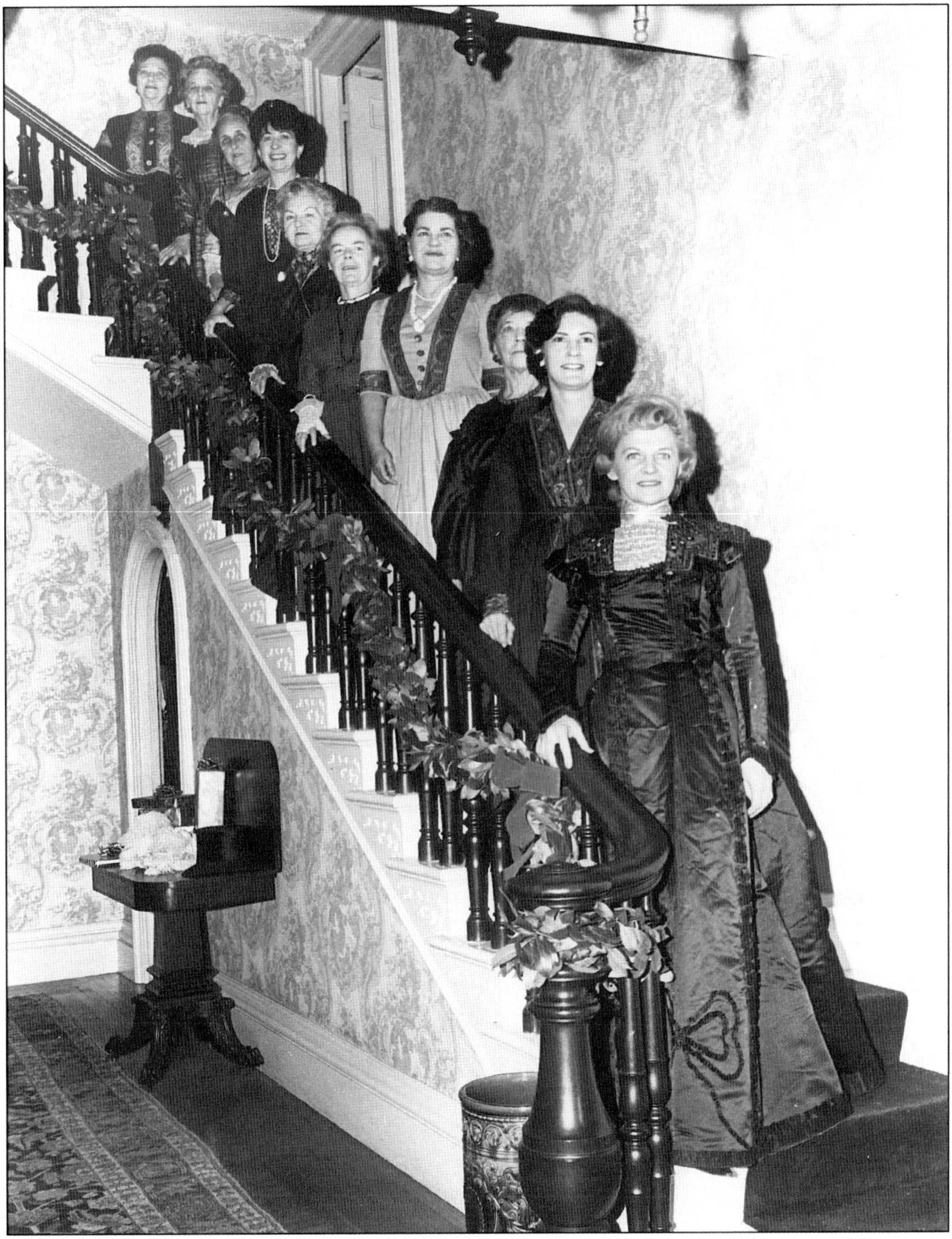

The First Annual Christmas Open House in December 1967 at the Sprague Mansion. Proudly showing off the mansion that they helped to save with the "Save the Sprague Mansion" campaign, these members of the Cranston Historical Society welcomed guests to the first annual Christmas Open House in December 1967 at Sprague Mansion. They are, from front to back, Mrs. Viola Lynch, Mrs. Ruth Vallone-Hollingworth, Mrs. Gladys Brayton, Mrs. Elsie Williams, Mrs. Alice Baxter, Mrs. Roberts, Mrs. Longo, Mrs. Frances Chartrand, Mrs. Marguerite Smythe, and Mrs. Martha Walker.

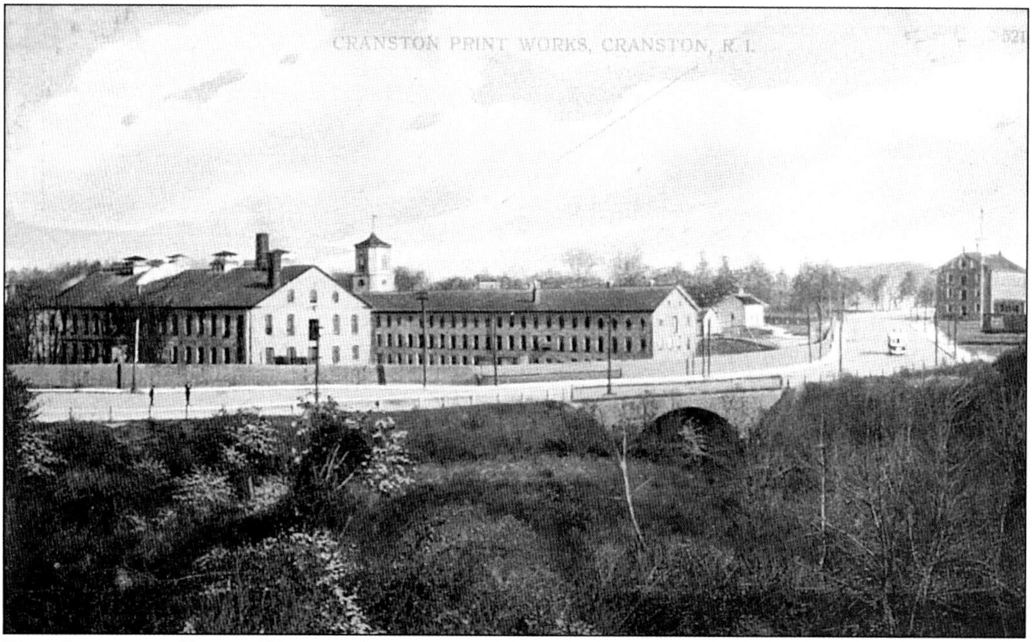

THE CRANSTON PRINT WORKS, CRANSTON STREET, C. 1900. William Sprague II converted a gristmill into a small cotton mill for carding and spinning in 1808. In 1813, after his mill burned to the ground, William II built this new mill out of stone. The company employed 22,000 employees in their cotton manufacturing plants, and it was said that "Whenever you saw smoke in Rhode Island it belonged to the Spragues."

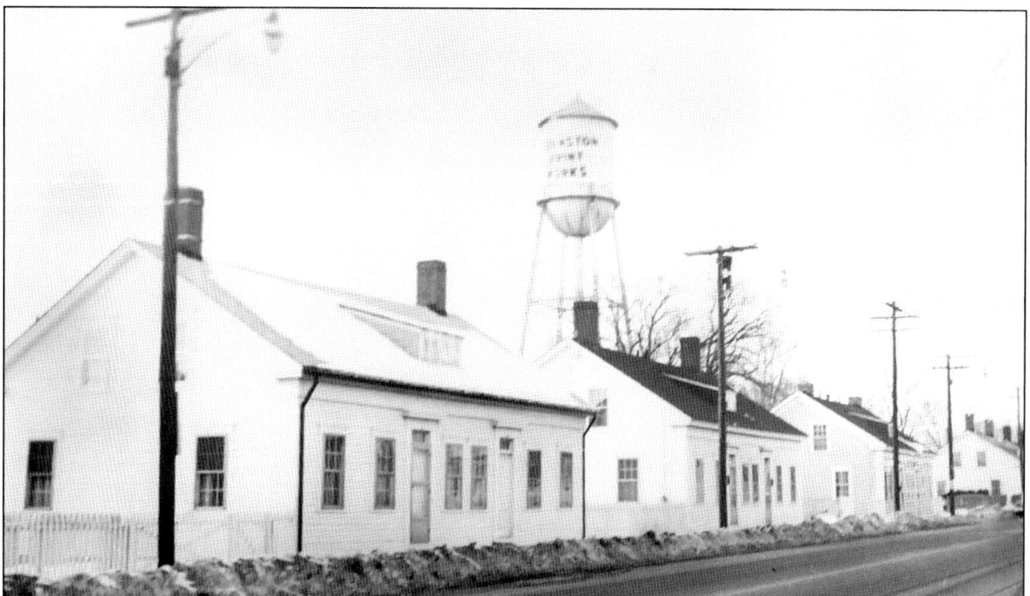

DYER AVENUE, SPRAGUE'S VILLAGE, C. 1950. Built in 1844, these double cottages housed workers of the A&W Sprague Manufacturing Company. Of the many homes, only three were single-family houses—the rest were double cottages divided in the middle. One outhouse was provided for every four houses. Today the homes, some of which are privately owned, represent the classic 19th-century mill village.

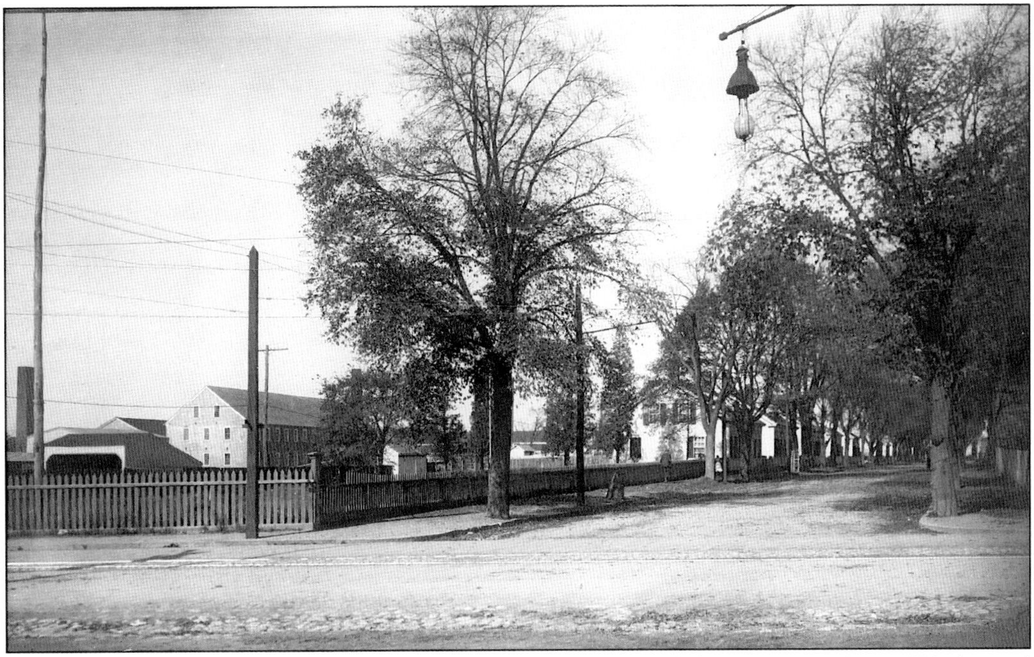

Cranston and Dyer Avenue, c. 1900. This is a view of the Cranston Print Works and Sprague's Village. Many of the trees that lined the street were planted by William Sprague IV on the advice of his mother, Fanny Sprague, to make the village more appealing. The trees and quaint street light are gone.

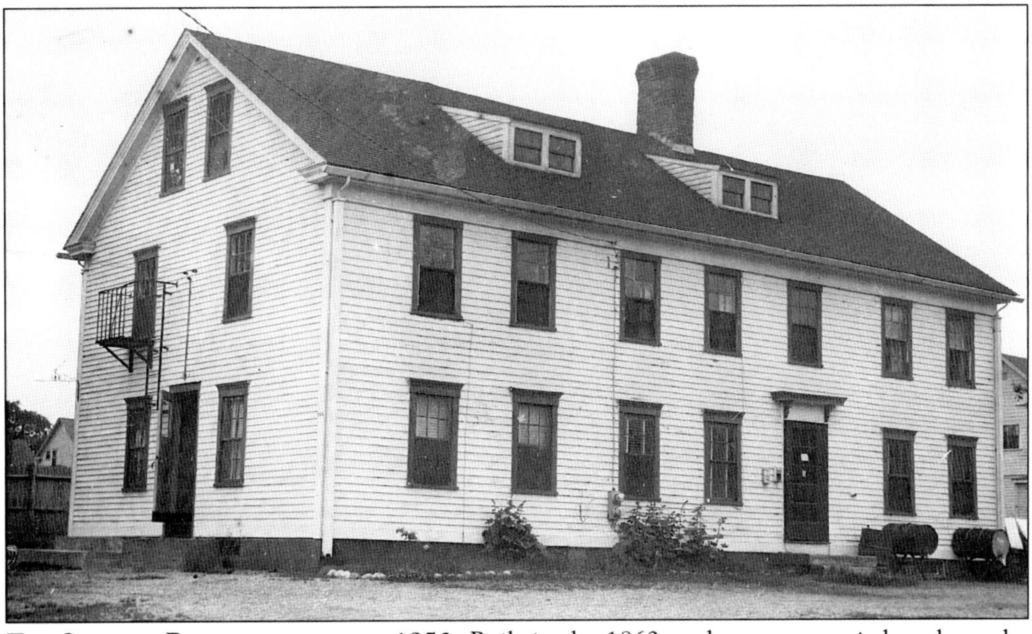

The Sprague Boardinghouse, c. 1950. Built in the 1860s to house unmarried workers, the boardinghouse was originally an L-shaped building with 99 small rooms, nearly the size of cells. Boarders had to be in the house by 10 p.m. and were not allowed to gamble or drink on the premises. The boardinghouse was located on Cranston Street about where St. Ann's School was later built.

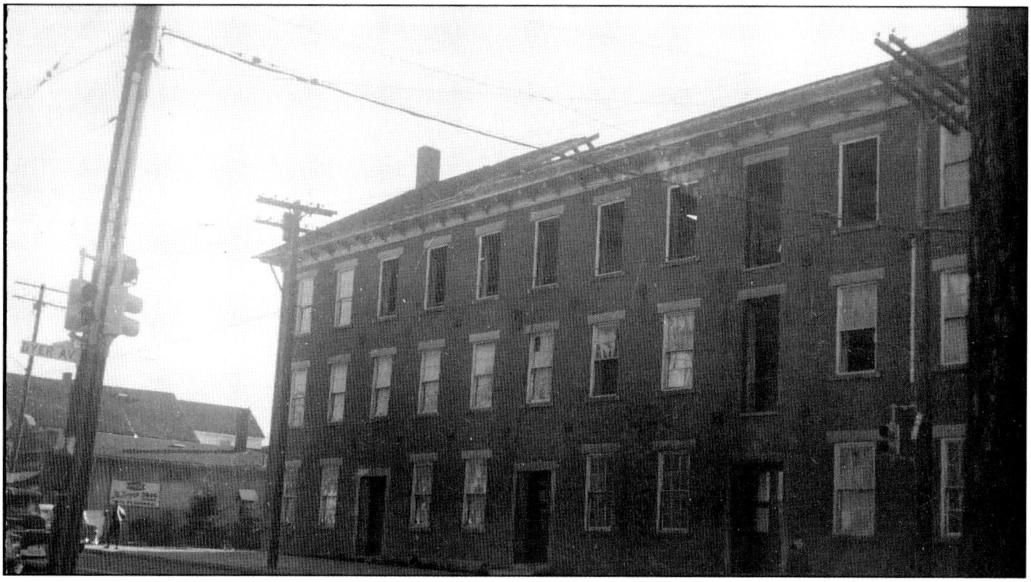

THE BRICK STORE, THE SPRAGUE COMPANY STORE, C. 1962. Wages at the A&W Sprague Company ranged from $2.50 to $5 a week. Being paid once a month, workers many times would owe the company store more than their pay for the supplies purchased during that month. The store was built in 1858; it is shown being demolished in 1962.

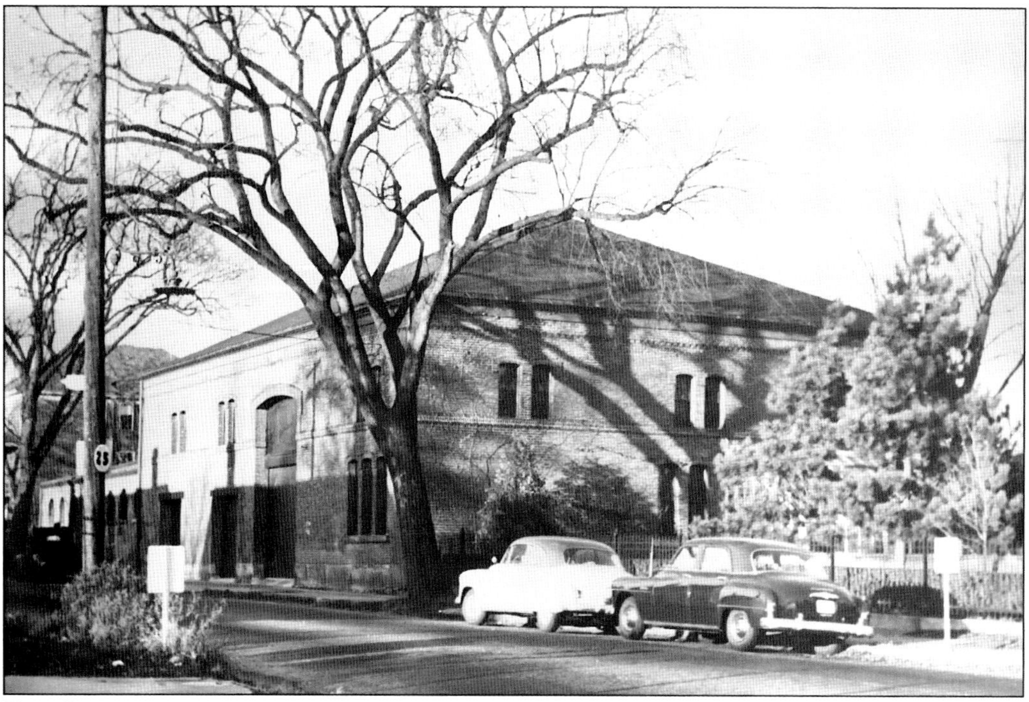

THE SPRAGUE MANSION CARRIAGE HOUSE, DYER AVENUE, C. 1948. Amasa Sprague II, a widower, married his second cousin, Harriet Byron Sprague, in 1873. In that year he had the addition to the mansion and this carriage house built. Colonel Sprague was known in horse breeding circles for quality horses. His famous trotting horse "Governor Sprague" sold for $25,000, which was a considerable amount for a horse in the 19th century.

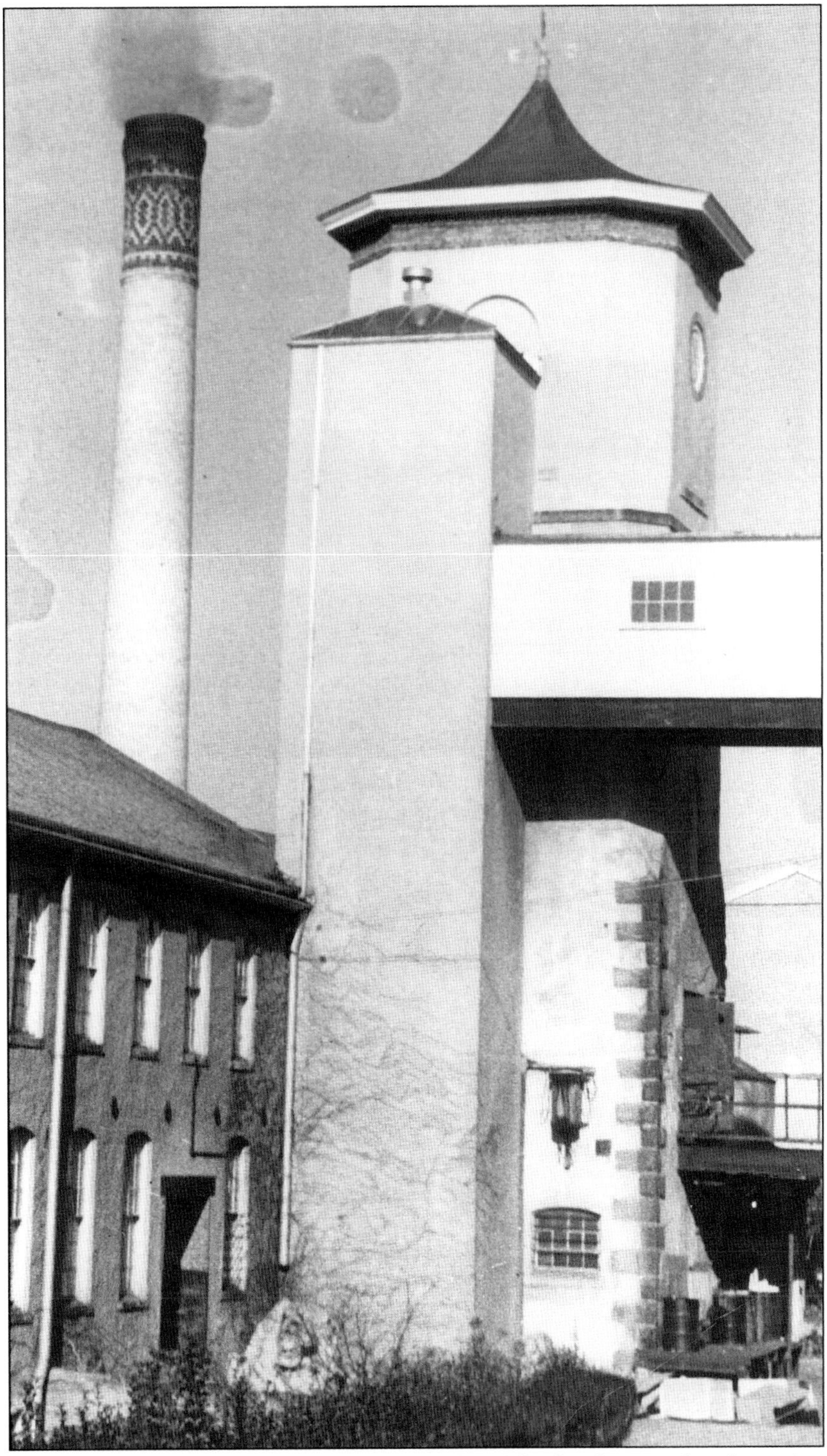

The Cranston Print Works Tower, c. 1950. In 1864 the Sprague brothers, Amasa II and William IV, expanded the Print Works by building a large four-story mill that included this 90-foot bell tower and chimney, still standing tall in the Print Works yard on Cranston Street.

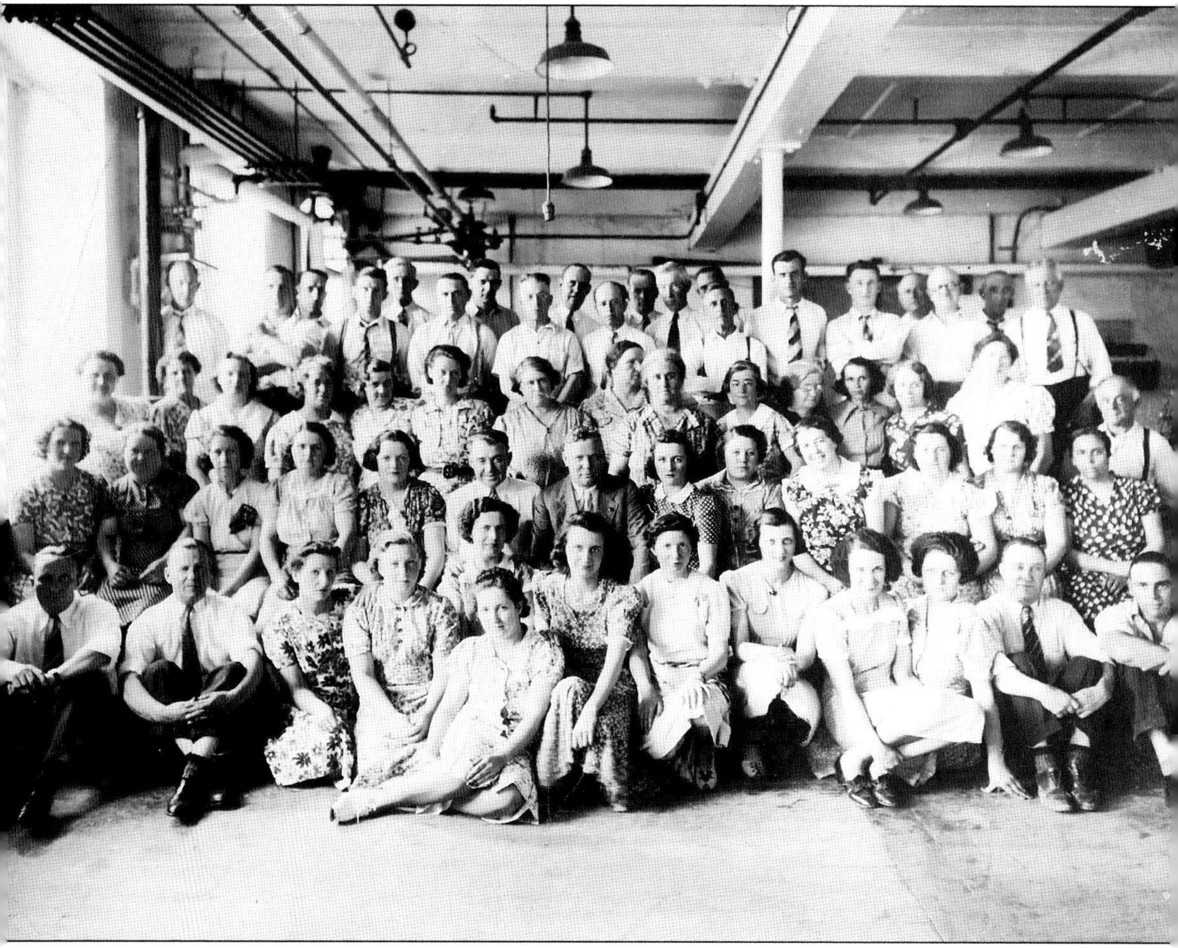

EMPLOYEES OF THE CRANSTON PRINT WORKS IN THE FOLDING ROOM, 1938. From left to right are as follows: (front row) Roy Lewis, Ted Murphy, Germaine Doucette, Anges McNabb, Antoinette Fischer, Rolande Duby (in front of Antoinette), Pat Davis, Lorette Gowdy, Irene McGinty, Evelyn Bromley, Ethel Hazerman, Walter Whiting, and Ray Stone; (second row) Helen Enright, Sadie Anderson, Alice Gomes, Etta Evans, Germaine Stone, Sam Johnson, Ray Crompton, Dea Kelly, Marion Wisherm, Esther Nelson, Babe Johnson, Stella Madden, and Liz Desesarl; (third row) Rose Perry, Emily Christopher, Maggie Johnson, Mae Ouimette, Ruth Grandchamp, Alice Cowsill, Mame (Mumford Kennedy?), Mae Richards, Anna Rhode, Anna Martin, Mrs. Perry, Dot Bowen, Kitty Murphy, Gladys Krause, and Louie (the Man!!) McKay; (back row) Jack Prior, Geo Fugere, Ralph Misto, Buck Herman, Bob Hannon, Bud Budlong, Bill Schintze, Bill Prior, Ray Page, Harold Sheffel, Harold Petling, Frank Dodd, Jimmie Hurley, Harry Erickson (in back of Hurly), Bill Glendenning, Ed McCann Sr., Charlie Legacy, Frank Conley, Bob Suiter, and Pat Kelly.

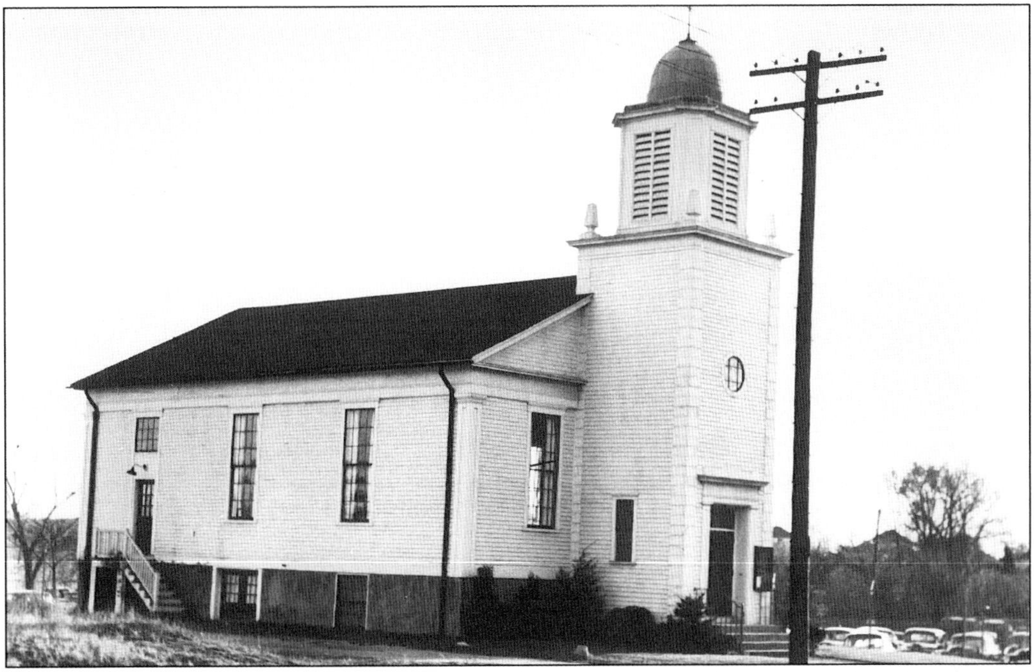

The Sprague Meeting House, c. 1950. Also known as St. Bartholomew's Church, this plain New England-style church was built with the contributions of local residents on land donated by William Sprague II in 1825. It was moved to its present location in 1864 when Dyer Avenue was straightened to allow for expansion of the Print Works. The belfry was added during that reconstruction.

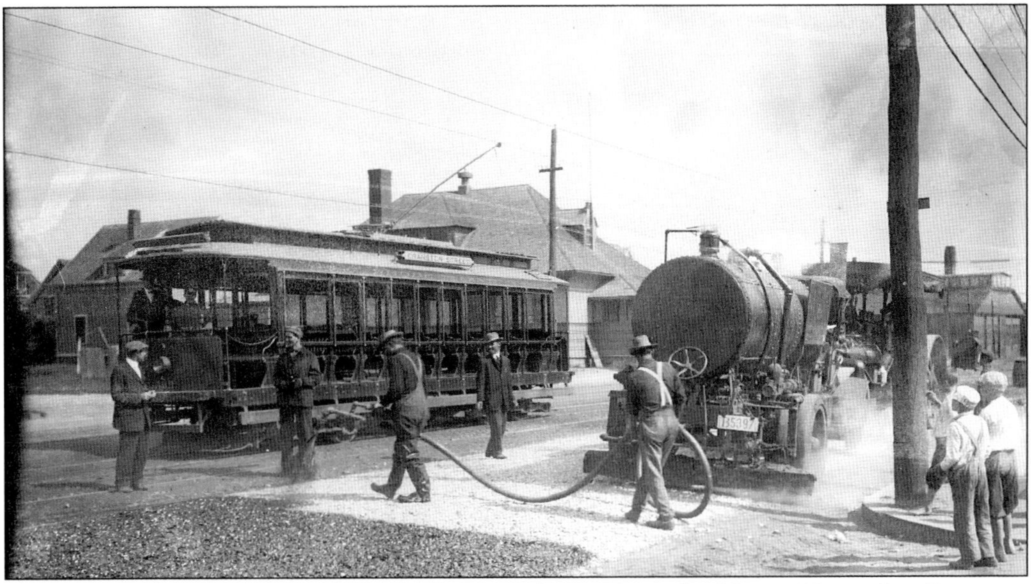

The Cranston Street Trolley, c. 1900. A far cry from the Union Horse Car Company operated by the Spragues in 1865, the trolley lines made mass transportation cheaper, faster, and more convenient. Mill owners and organizations rented entire cars for their employees and members for special days out on the town to events at such places as Rhodes on the Pawtuxet and Roger Williams Park.

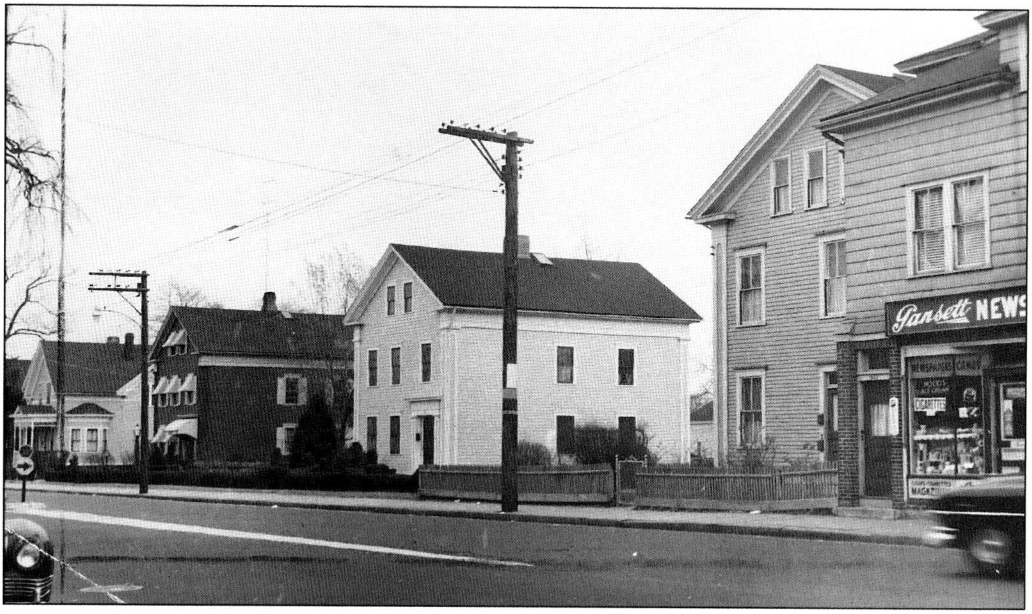

Cranston and Howard Streets, c. 1950. Bull Town begins approximately at Cranston and Howard Streets and ends near Gansett Avenue. These homes were built for the managers and heads of the A&W Sprague Company. Many of the supervisors of the mills were from England at the time, and the neighborhood came to be called Bull Town.

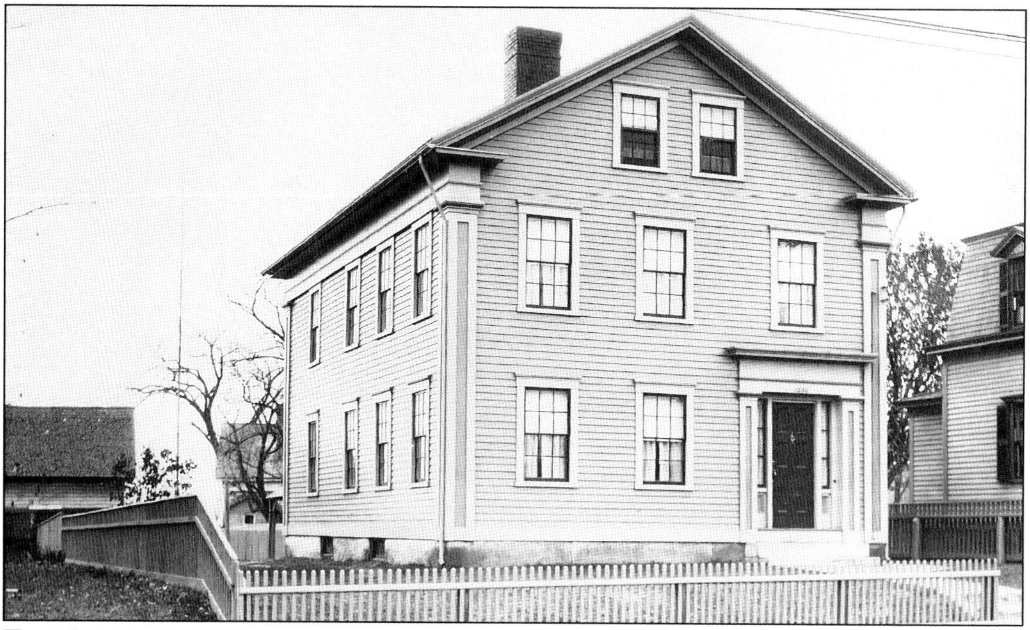

The Home of John Hamilton, 1230 Cranston Street, c. 1950. This house and four others similar to it originally housed supervisors of the A&W Sprague Company. In later years it became the home of John Hamilton. Named overseer of the poor in 1909, Hamilton held that post for over 43 years. In 1915 Mr. Hamilton was also appointed juvenile probation officer for the Eighth District Court.

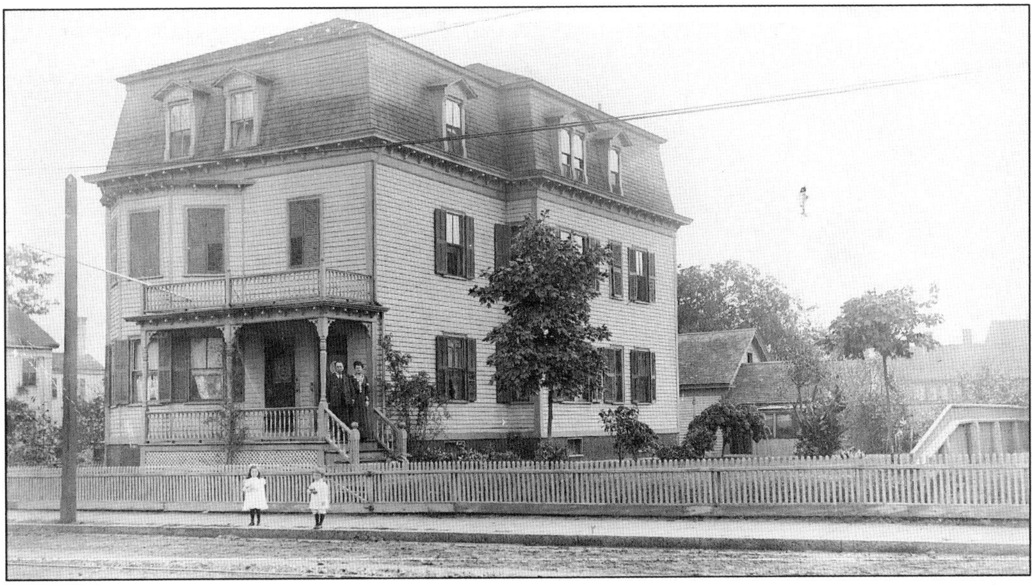

The Bigbee House, 1224 Cranston Street, c. 1900. Grace and DeForest Bigbee are standing on the sidewalk as their parents, John and Elizabeth Bigbee, stand on the porch. John Bigbee was the town sergeant, Cranston's first chief of police and overseer of the poor. Elizabeth Bigbee managed the Sprague boardinghouse.

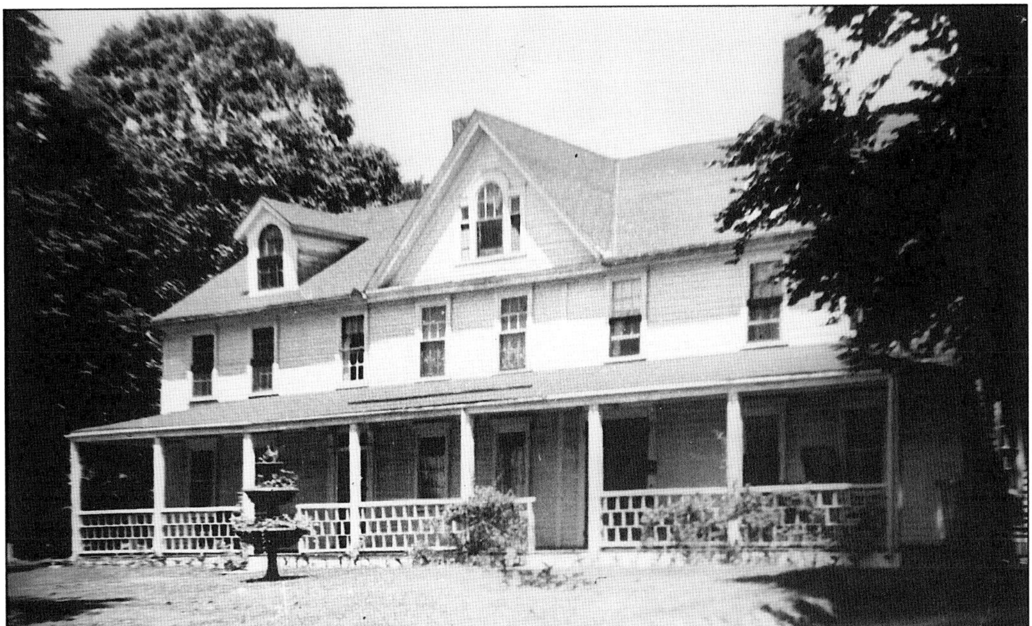

The Dyer Mansion at Pocassett Cemetery, c. 1940. In 1732 Charles Dyer built a stone end house that became the core of the Dyer Mansion. His son Nathan added a much larger addition in 1800. The mansion was located on the property of the Pocassett Cemetery, and is no longer standing. The farm was referred to as Cabbage Neck because of its large fields of cabbages.

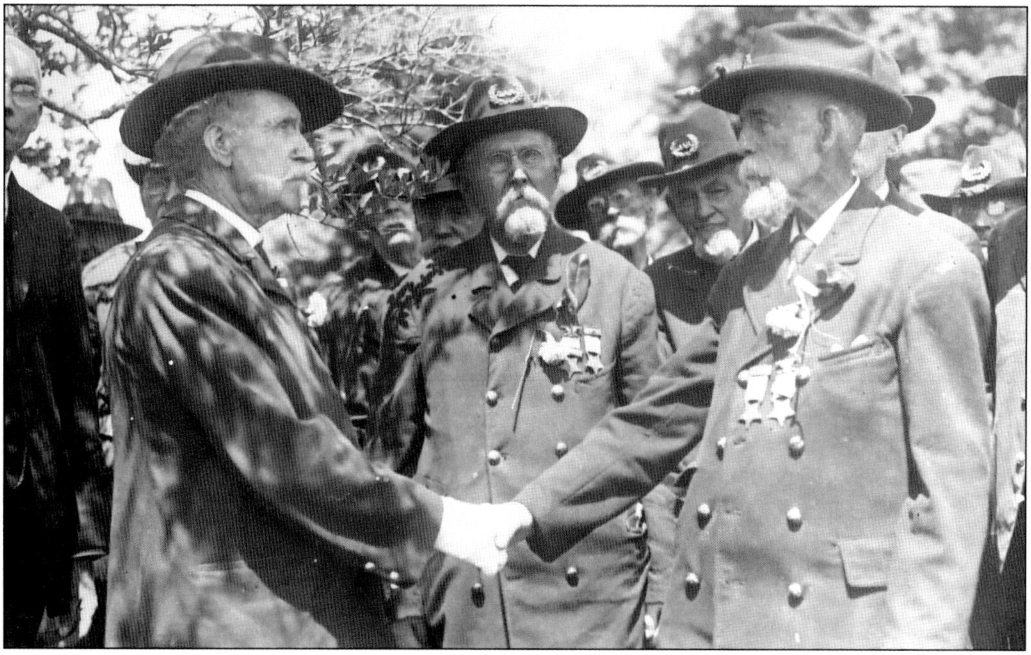

DECORATION DAY AT POCASSETT CEMETERY, C. 1940. Honoring the memory of the 300 or more Rhode Island Civil War veterans who rest in Pocassett Cemetery, these members of the Grand Army of the Republic met for annual observances held on Memorial Day. When President Abraham Lincoln called for troops during the Civil War, 23,778 Rhode Islanders answered the call.

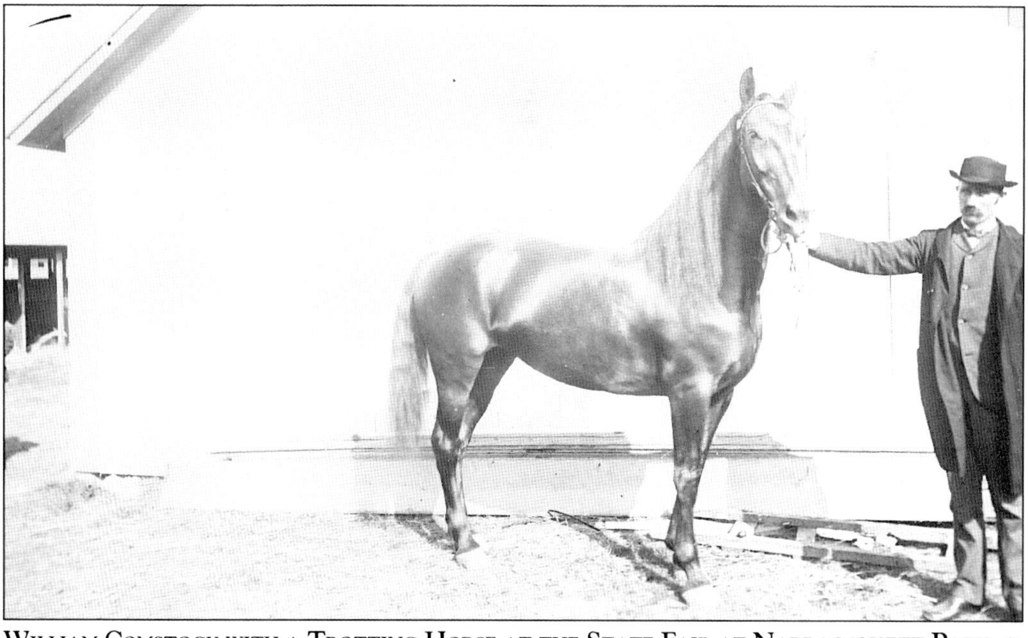

WILLIAM COMSTOCK WITH A TROTTING HORSE AT THE STATE FAIR AT NARRAGANSETT PARK, C. 1895. Comstock owned a stable of trotting horses located in the vicinity of 1140 Park Avenue. Amasa Sprague II financed the building of the Narragansett Trotting Park. Cornelius Vanderbilt and J.P. Morgan attended the opening of the park on July 31, 1867.

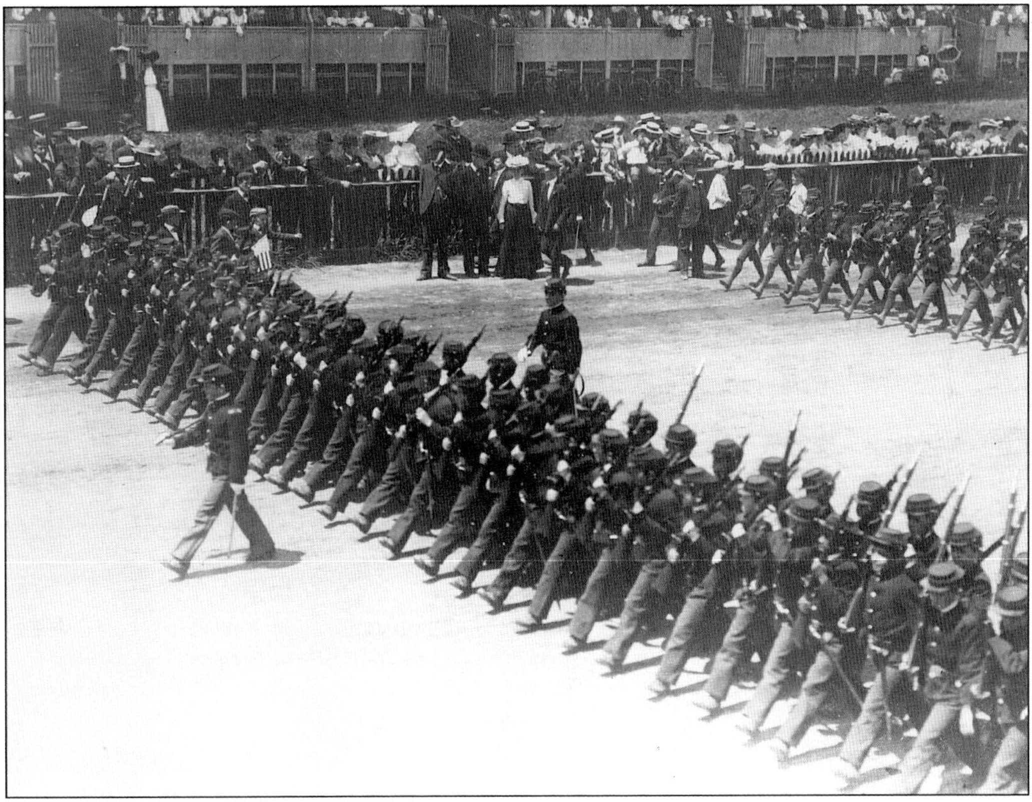

The Narragansett Trotting Park, 1904. Cadets from the Sockanosett Military Battalion are shown marching in the parade marking Cranston's 150th anniversary. Early in 1886 the RI Society for the Encouragement of Domestic Industry purchased the Old Narragansett Trotting Park for the State Fair grounds. Races of all types were held at the park, including foot races, trotting races, and bicycle races, which were a big favorite.

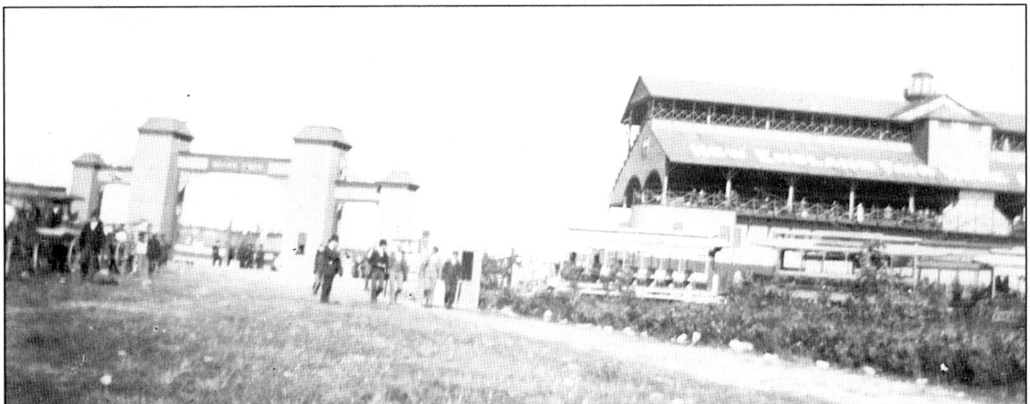

The Narragansett Park Gates, 1904. Cranston marked its 150th anniversary at the Narragansett Trotting Park with a parade nearly a mile long. A firemen's muster between Cranston's five volunteer fire departments ended with the Fire King Company of Pawtuxet winning the event. Speakers topped off the day; among them was former governor William Sprague IV, who was greeted with a tremendous cheer at the close of his speech, bringing a smile to his 74-year-old face.

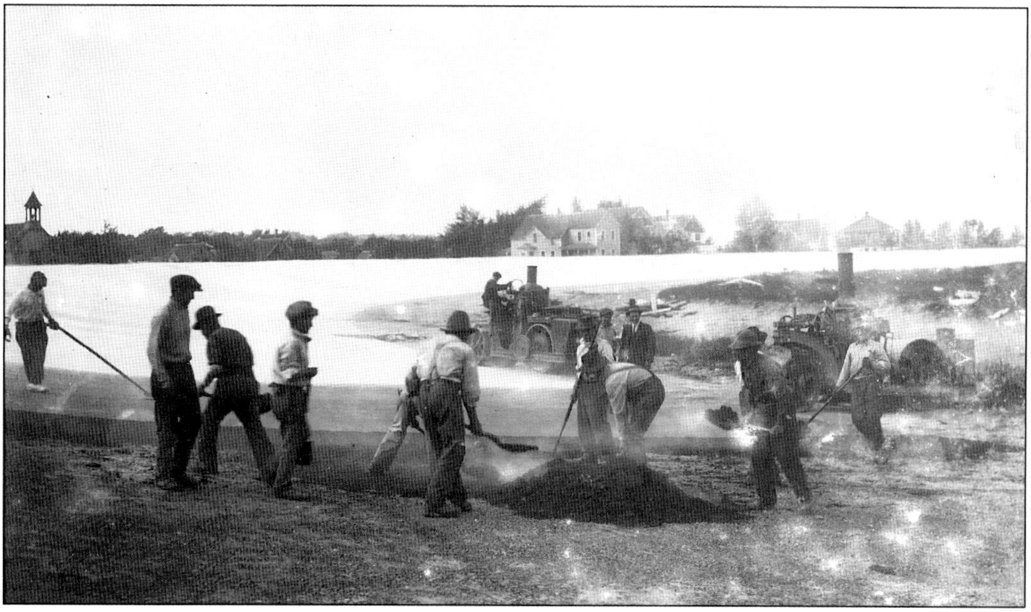

Narragansett Park, c. 1928. These men are building the track for the Narragansett Speedway at the former Narragansett Trotting Park. The first event held was a motorcycle race, which drew over 4,000 spectators. In 1929 the park was sold to developers and was renamed the Speedway Plat. As a reminder of the area's past, many of the streets nearby were named for automobiles that raced at the track.

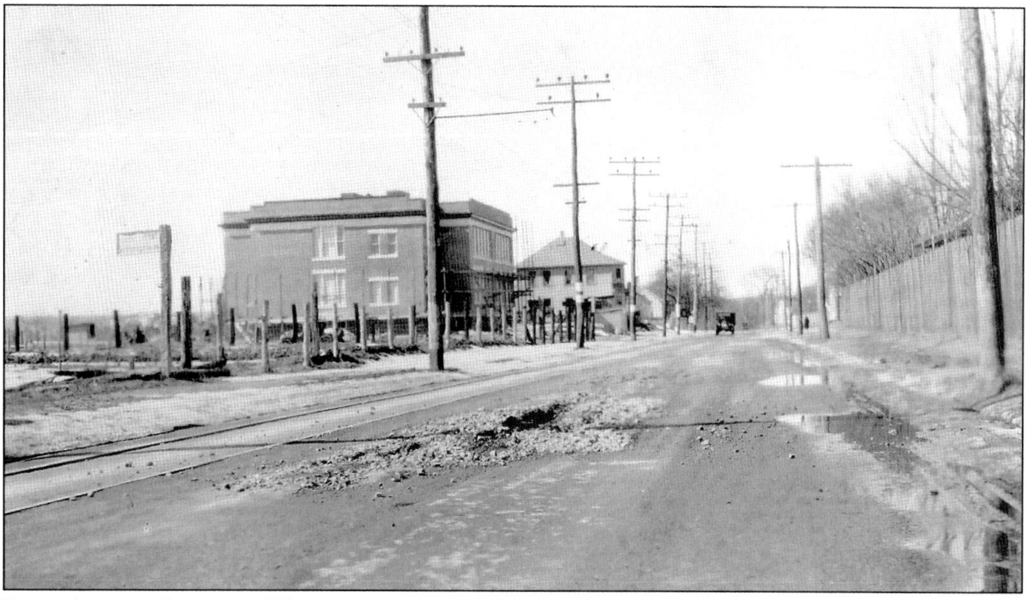

Park Avenue Looking West toward the Horton School, c. 1928. The fence on the right borders the Narragansett Speedway. Trolley car lines ran along the left side of the street. During the glory days of Narragansett Speedway Park, trolleys brought spectators right to the gates of the park.

ARLINGTON BAPTIST CHURCH, C. 1950. Originally built in the spring of 1876 on new Depot Avenue, the church building was moved to Lincoln Avenue in 1881 when a nearby coal yard made the building unsuitable for worship. Reverend Arthur Given welcomed parishioners on October 28, 1881, when the church reopened.

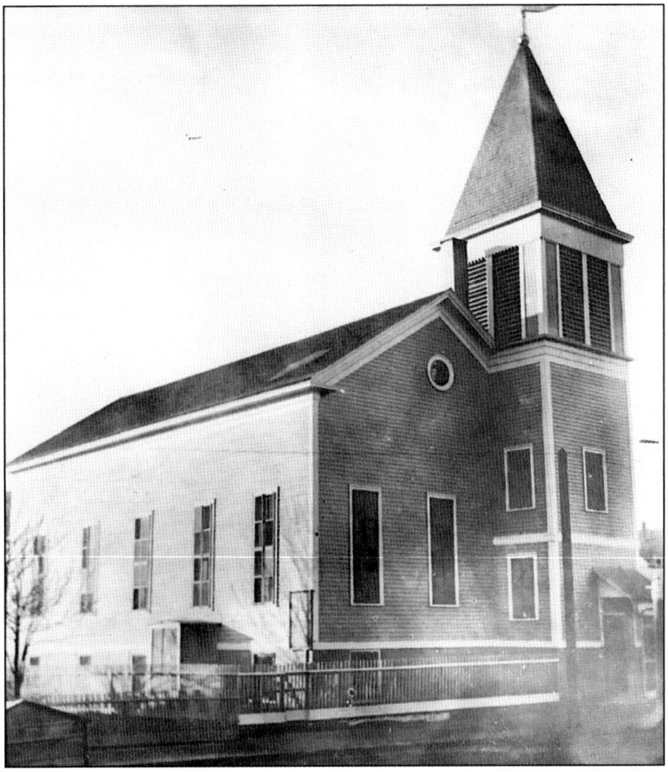

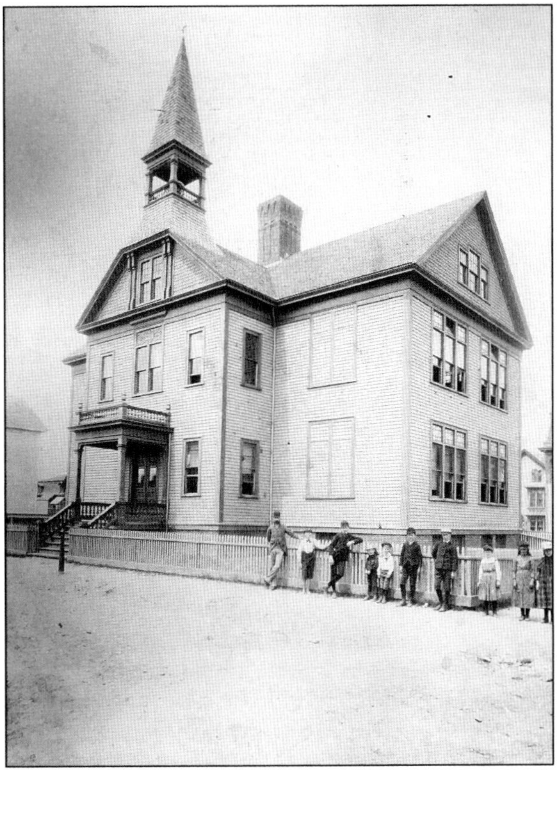

THE ARLINGTON GRAMMAR SCHOOL, WHIPPLE AVENUE, C. 1888. In 1891 the high school in Providence refused to admit more non-resident students due to a lack of space, so Cranston had high school classes conducted by grammar school principals in the Arlington Grammar School. James Earle was principal of the school at the time this photograph was taken.

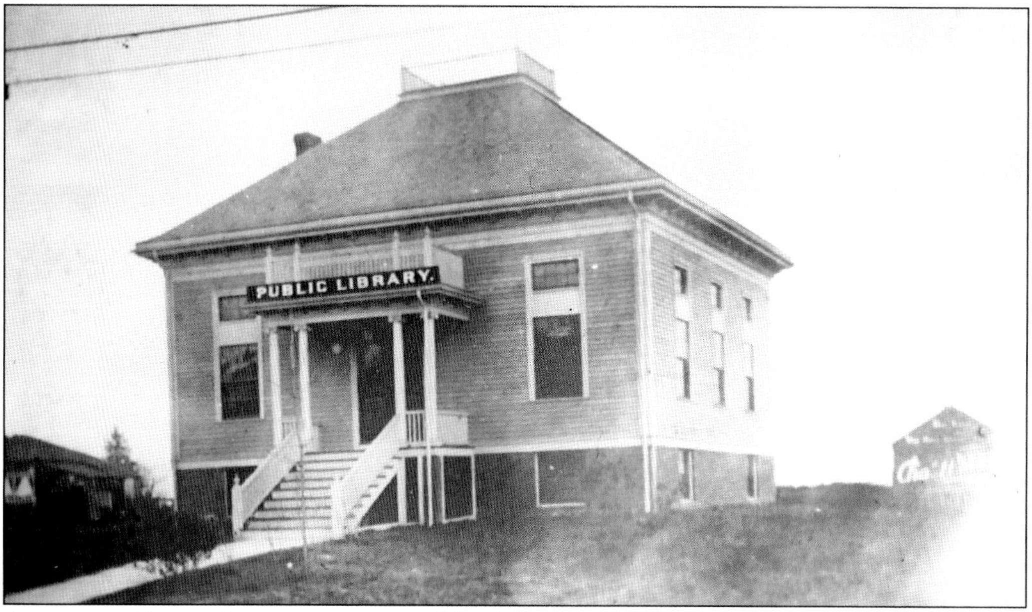

Arlington Public Library, c. 1906. The Arlington Improvement Association began their undertaking to establish a public library in Arlington in 1894. In 1906 the trustees moved into this new building on the corner of Cranston and Oneida Streets. Jannis Arnold, Georgina Field, Mary Walker, Mrs. Bennis, and Margaret Knox are former librarians of the Arlington Library.

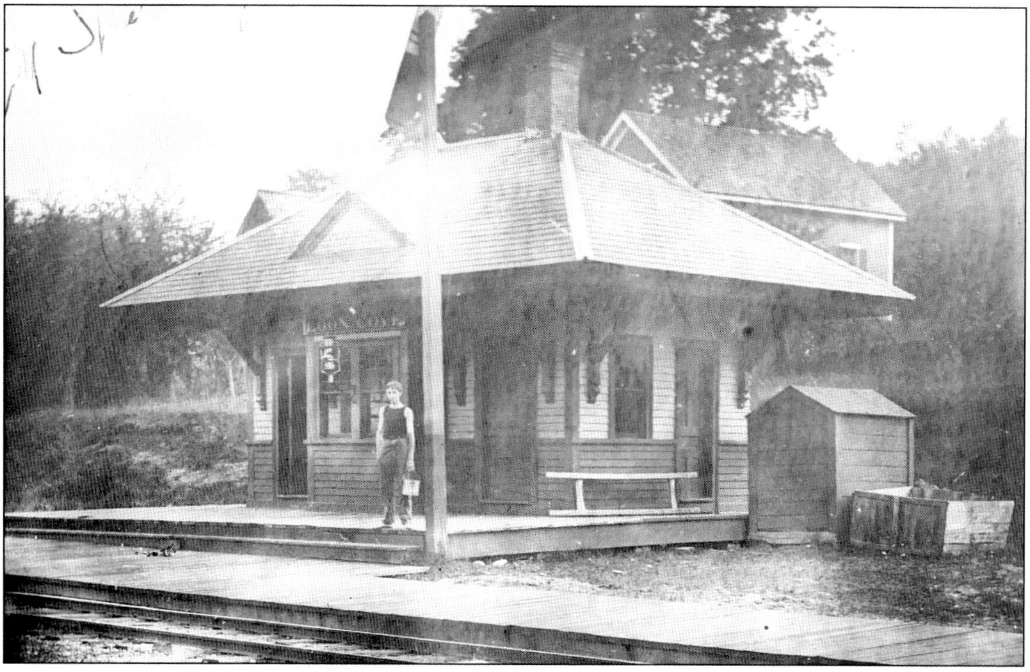

The Arlington Railroad Station on Depot Avenue, c. 1900. The Arlington depot was one of the whistle stops that vice-presidential candidate Teddy Roosevelt stopped at one Saturday morning during the McKinley-Bryan election of 1900. Roosevelt was on his way from Connecticut to Providence on the Willimantic branch of the New Haven Railroad.

Two

AUBURN

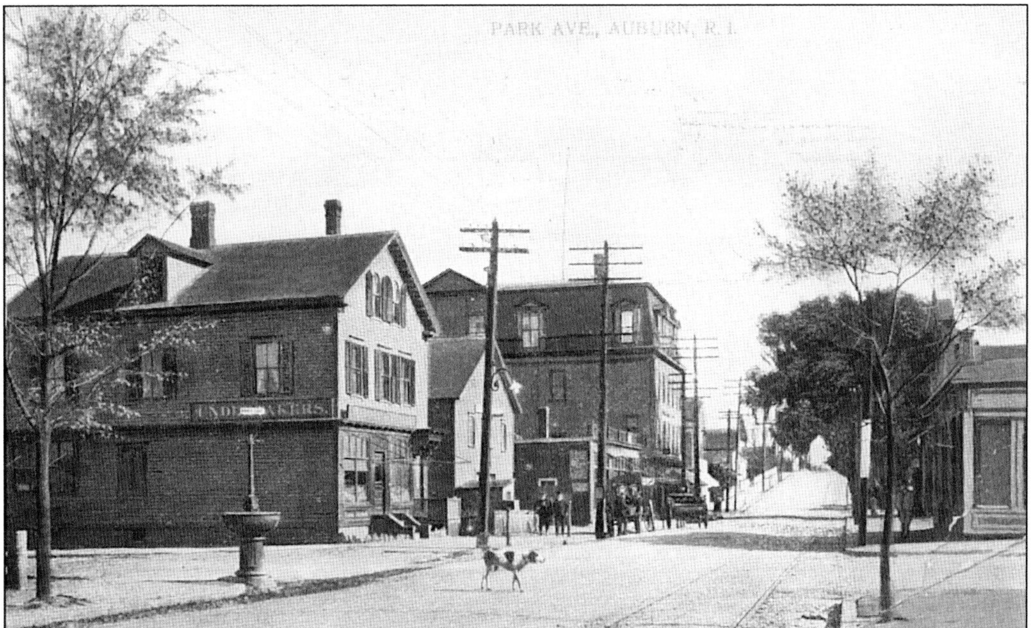

AUBURN, C. 1894. This was a time when cows roamed freely just as long as they had a collar and a tag identifying their owners. Auburn center was the typical small town. It had everything a person living in the surrounding area might need. There was Slocum's apothecary shop, Bagley's variety store, Hoyle's Market, and the forerunner of the modern department store, McGuigan's. For needs of another kind there was Whipple and Fuller, undertakers and embalmers.

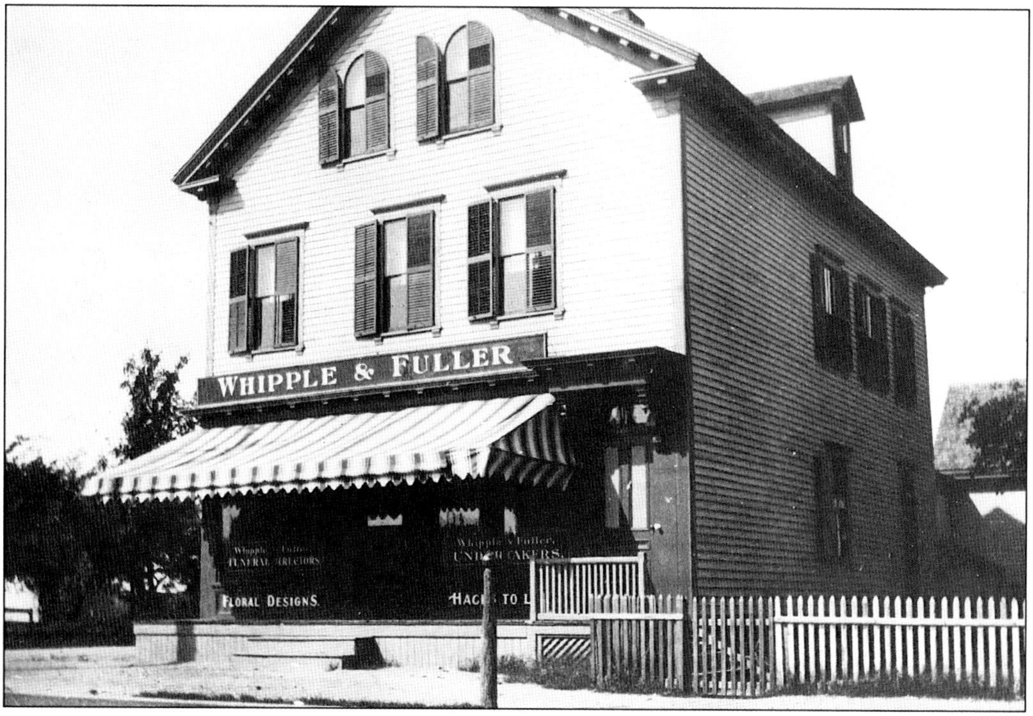

WHIPPLE & FULLER, FUNERAL DIRECTORS AND EMBALMERS ON THE CORNER OF DORIC AND PARK. Later the establishment moved to the corner of Cross and Station Streets. In 1902 the cost for a coffin and interring for an infant was $10.50. Removal of the body was priced at $4, an outside box at $2.50, the grave was $2, and a marble headstone was also $2.

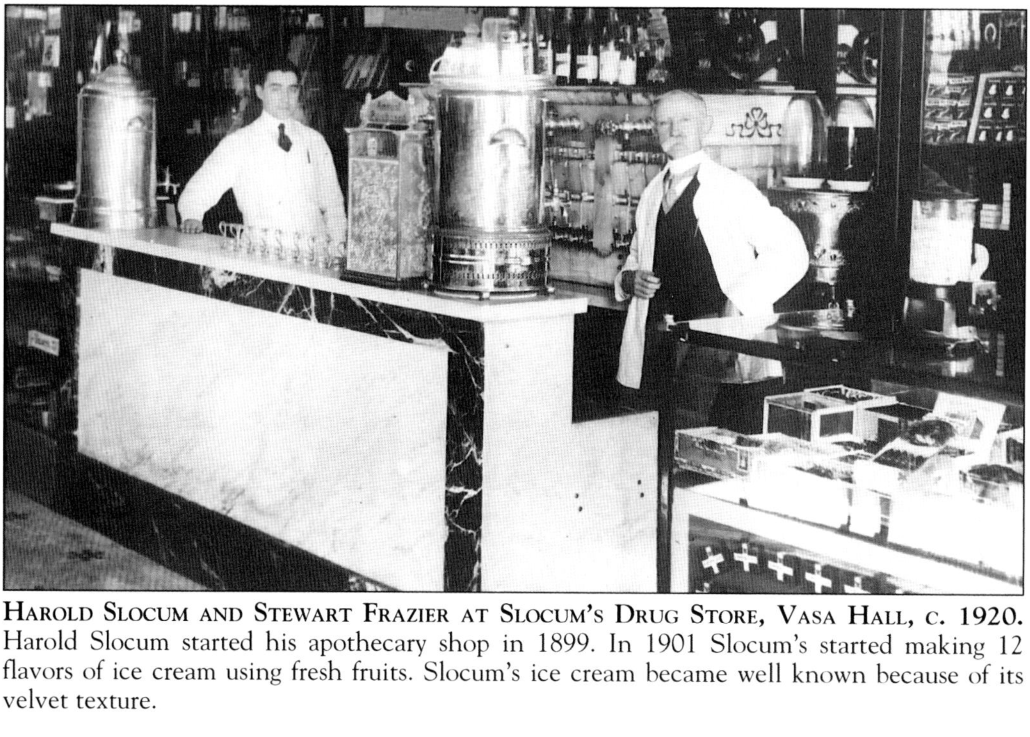

HAROLD SLOCUM AND STEWART FRAZIER AT SLOCUM'S DRUG STORE, VASA HALL, C. 1920. Harold Slocum started his apothecary shop in 1899. In 1901 Slocum's started making 12 flavors of ice cream using fresh fruits. Slocum's ice cream became well known because of its velvet texture.

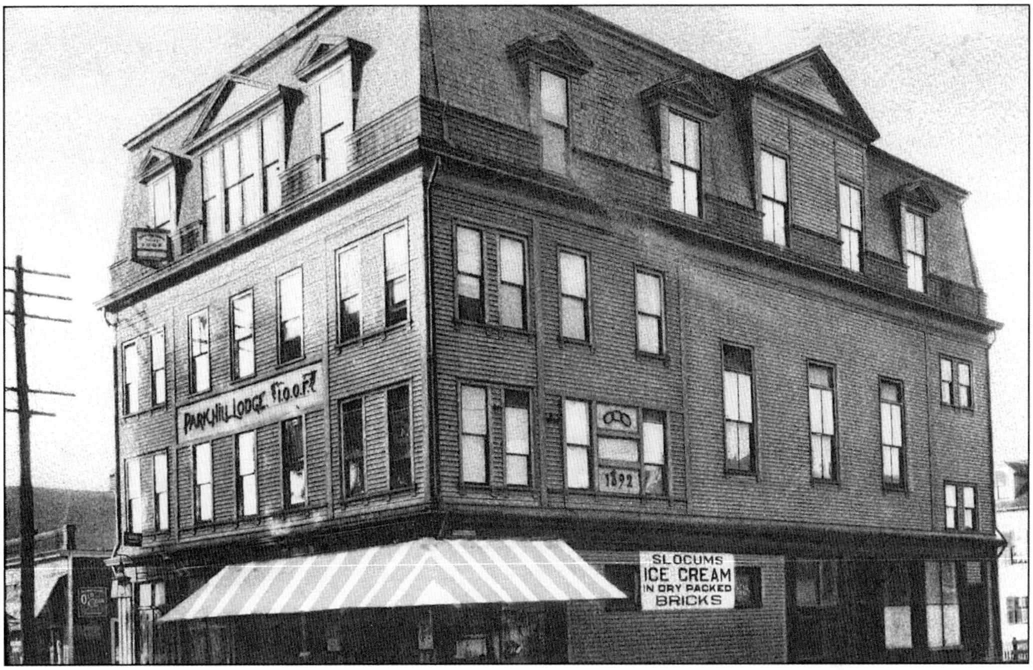

Vasa Hall, c. 1894. Located near the corner of Park and Wellington Avenues, Vasa Hall was the place to be for all the social events of the community. Slocum's Drug Store was located on the ground floor of this four-story building; note the Slocum's ice cream sign by the canopy.

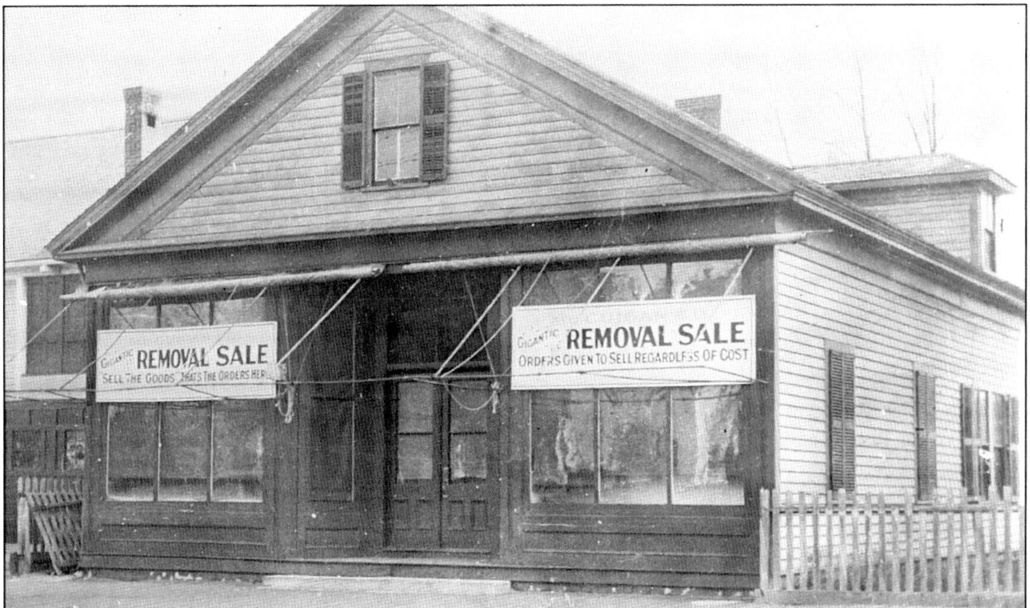

McGuigan's Store, c. 1894. McGuigan's was the type of store that everyone liked to visit. It carried almost everything people of the area wanted when they needed dry goods and all kinds of accessories.

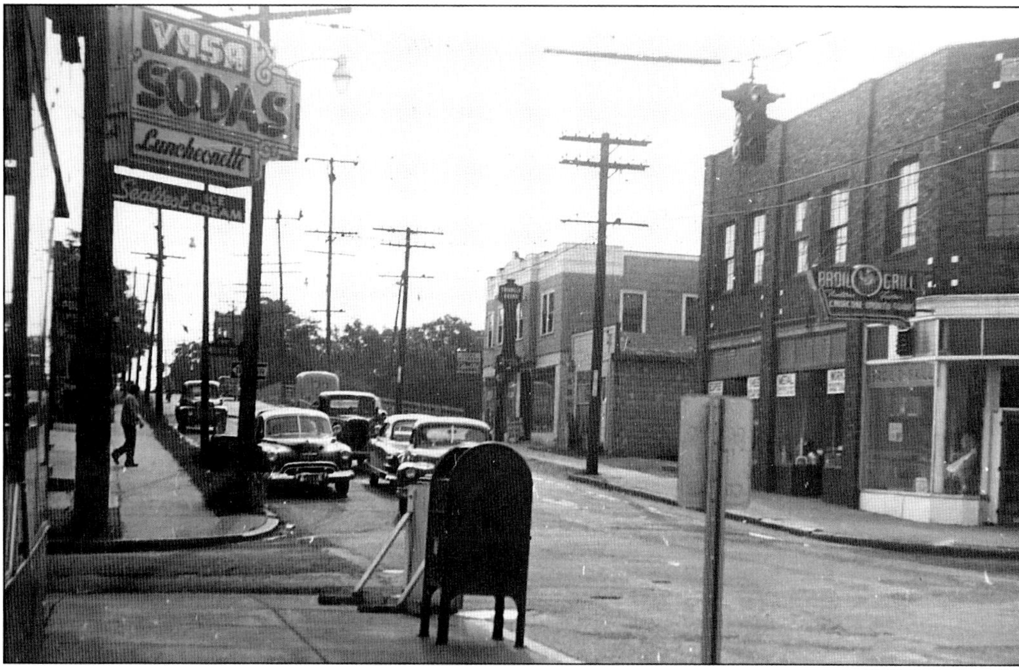

Park and Wellington Avenues, c. 1950. Auburn changed considerably in 50 years. By the time this photograph was taken, Slocum's ice cream sign had been replaced with a Sealtest Ice Cream sign, and the drugstore Slocum ran had become the Vasa Luncheonette.

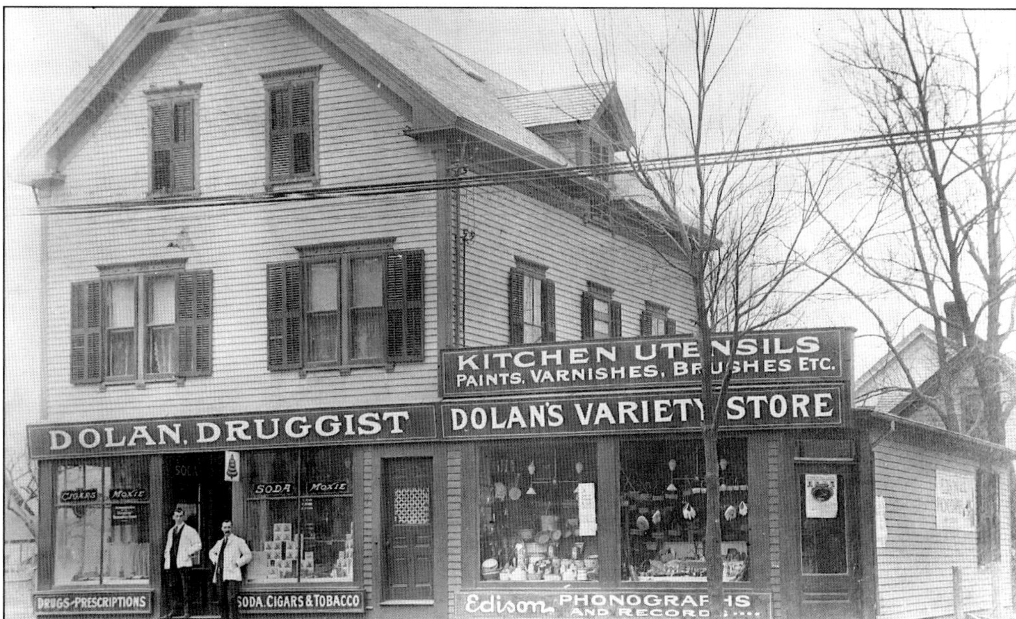

Dolan's Drug Store, 734 Park Avenue, c. 1930. John and Martin Dolan made coffee cabinets for 15¢ at their marble soda fountain. They also offered the finest collection of pipes for sale. The store served as a post office for a time. While getting the mail, customers could order a Moxie or a Coca-Cola, which was made on the spot with carbonated water and syrup.

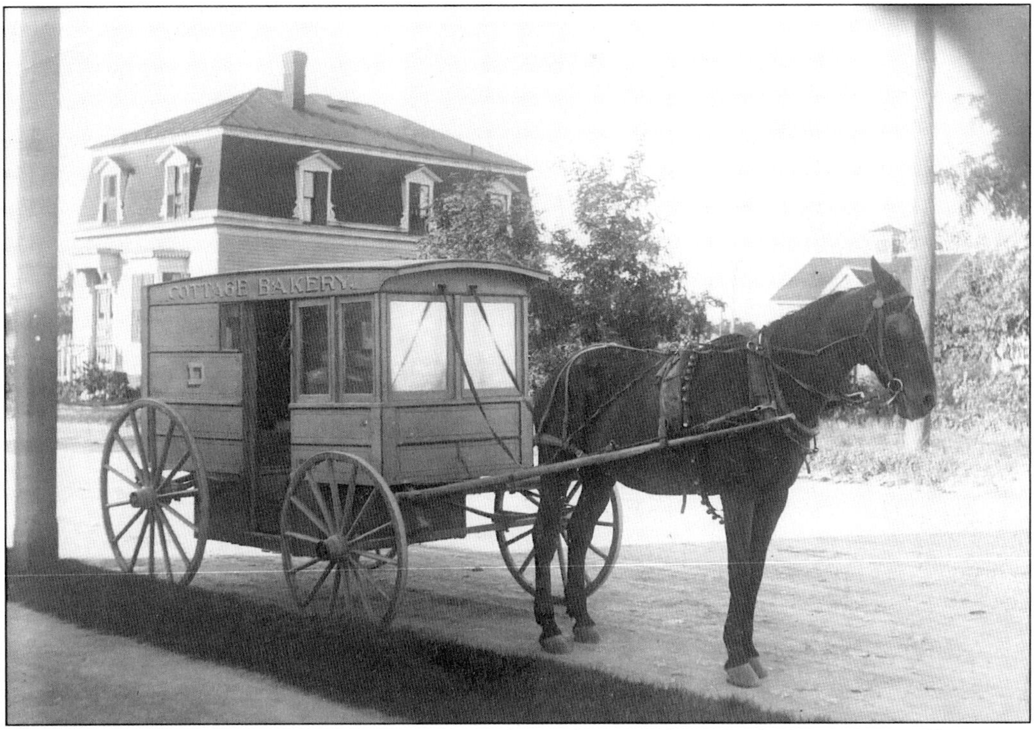

The Cottage Bakery Wagon, c. 1900. Making the rounds on Park Avenue near Reservoir Avenue, this mule patiently awaits its owner before moving on to the next stop on the daily route. This was just one of the many different kinds of delivery wagons to be seen on the streets of Cranston.

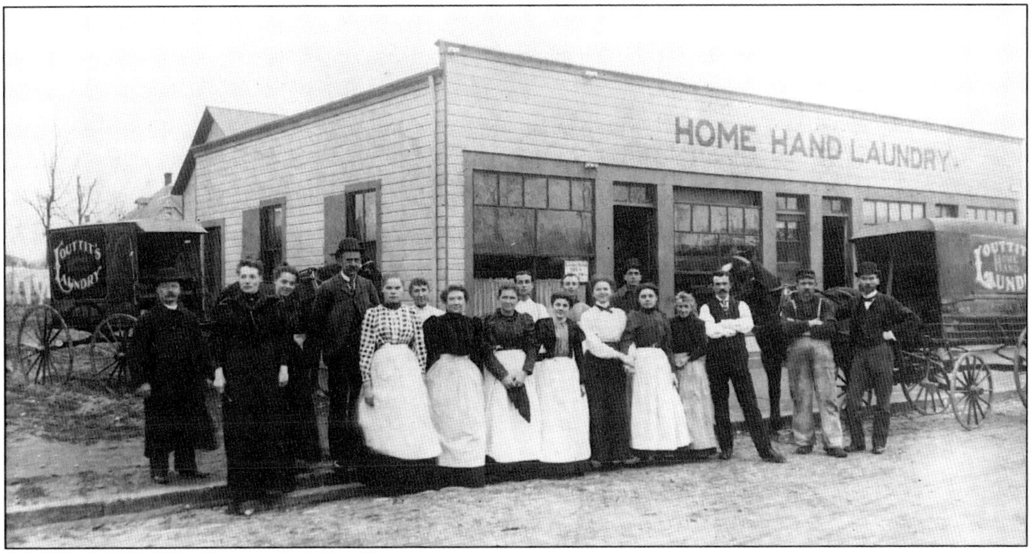

Louttit's Home Hand Laundry, Cross and Station Streets, c. 1898. Shown here, from left to right, are Benjamin Reading, Edith Slater, unknown, Joe Sanders, Hilda Johnson, unknown, Sadie Tate, May Fowler, Fred George, Mrs. C.H. Drummond, Charlie, Olive, David Grant, Clara Gardner, Mrs. Mullen, C.H. Drummond, Harvey Shaw, and W.E. Louttit. The Louttit Laundry building was destroyed by fire on January 17, 1907.

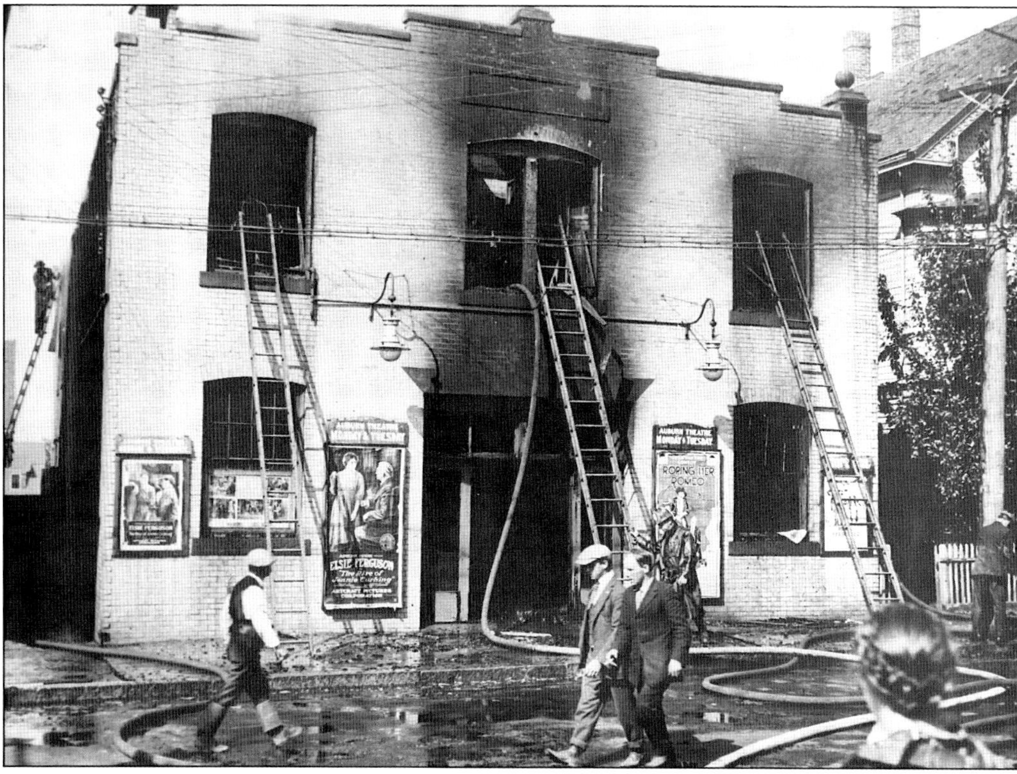

THE AUBURN THEATER FIRE, PARK AVENUE NEAR ELMWOOD AVENUE, 1918. The featured film was *The Rise of Jennie Cushing*, starring the famous silent film star Elsie Ferguson, the day the Auburn Theater was destroyed.

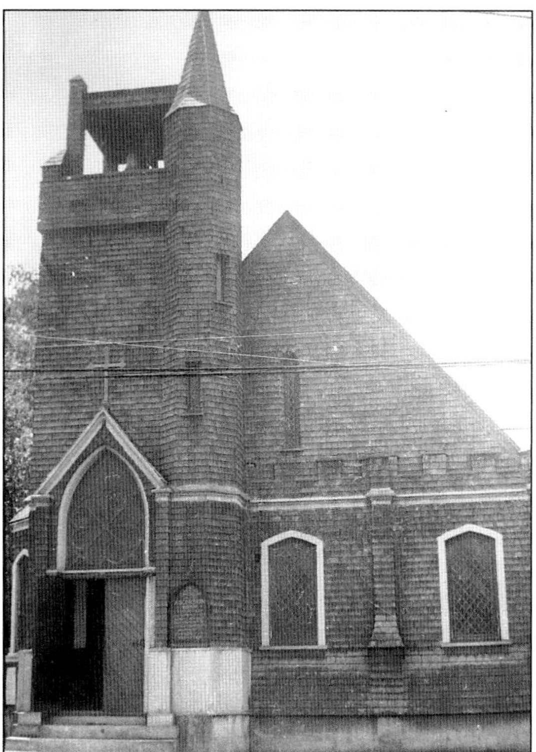

THE CHURCH OF THE ASCENSION, PARK AVENUE, C. 1889. When the Church of the Ascension opened its doors for the first time in 1889, the welcoming service was offered the Right Reverend Henry Potter of New York. The memorial windows honored the memory of three veterans of World War I. In 1956 the parish moved to a new home on Pontiac Avenue. A few years later this building was destroyed by fire.

The Phillips Memorial Church, Pontiac Avenue, c. 1948. Originally built in 1901 on land donated by James Budlong, the Phillips Memorial Church has undergone two other phases of construction. It is named in memory of Reverend James Phillips, a medical missionary in India. Phillips had served three years as interim pastor at the forerunner to this church, the People's Church.

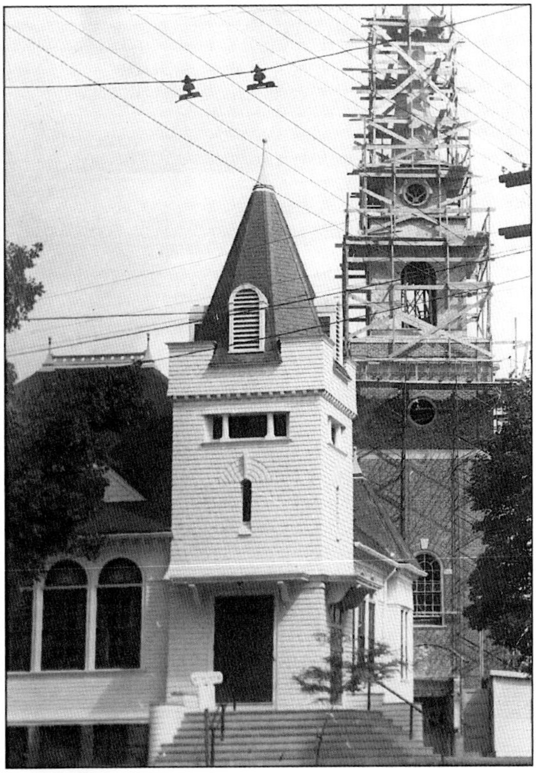

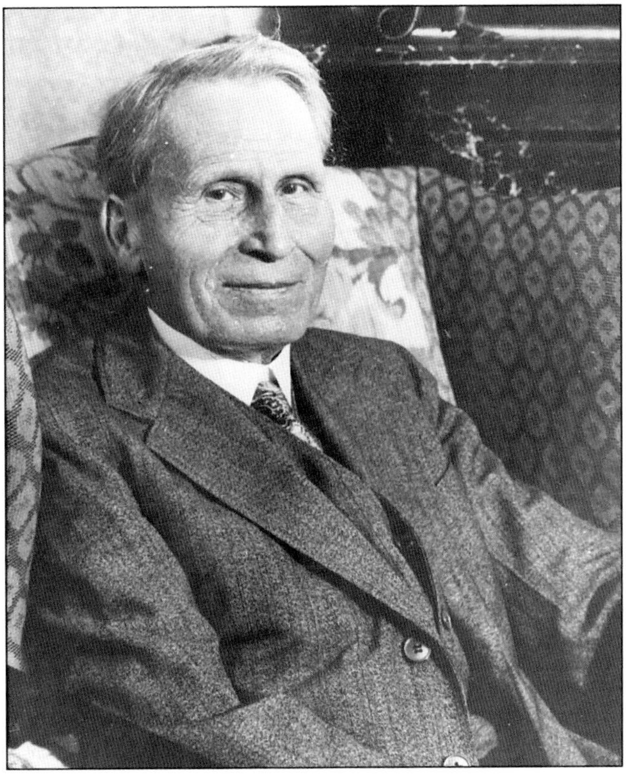

Professor Austin H. Keyes, the First Principal of Cranston High School in 1892. Professor Keyes was at the new high school at Wellington and Cross Streets for seven years, keeping a watchful eye on his students and faculty.

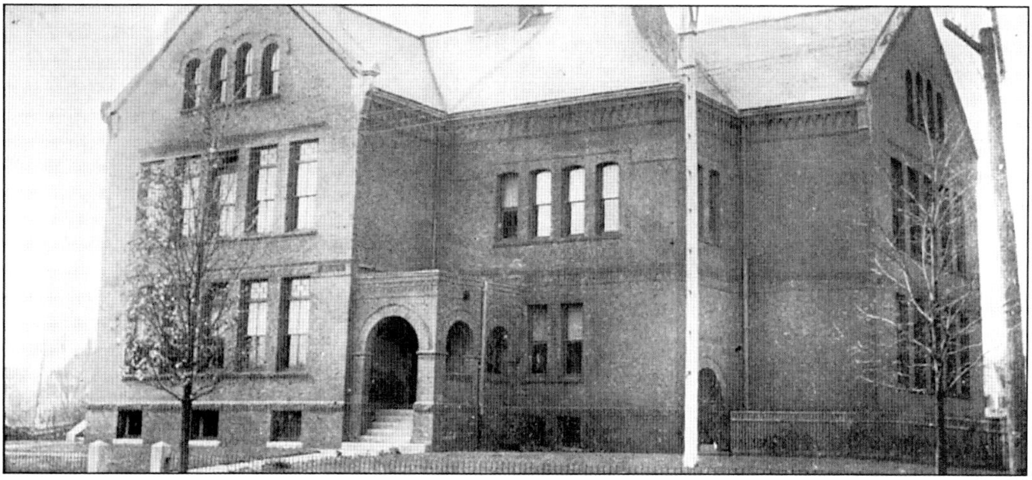

THE AUBURN GRAMMAR SCHOOL, c. 1907. Serving as the first high school in 1892, the Auburn School on Wellington Avenue was originally built to be a grammar school. A fire that started in the Louttit Home Hand Laundry building was driven by whipping winds and spread to the Auburn Grammar School on the night of January 17, 1907, destroying both buildings.

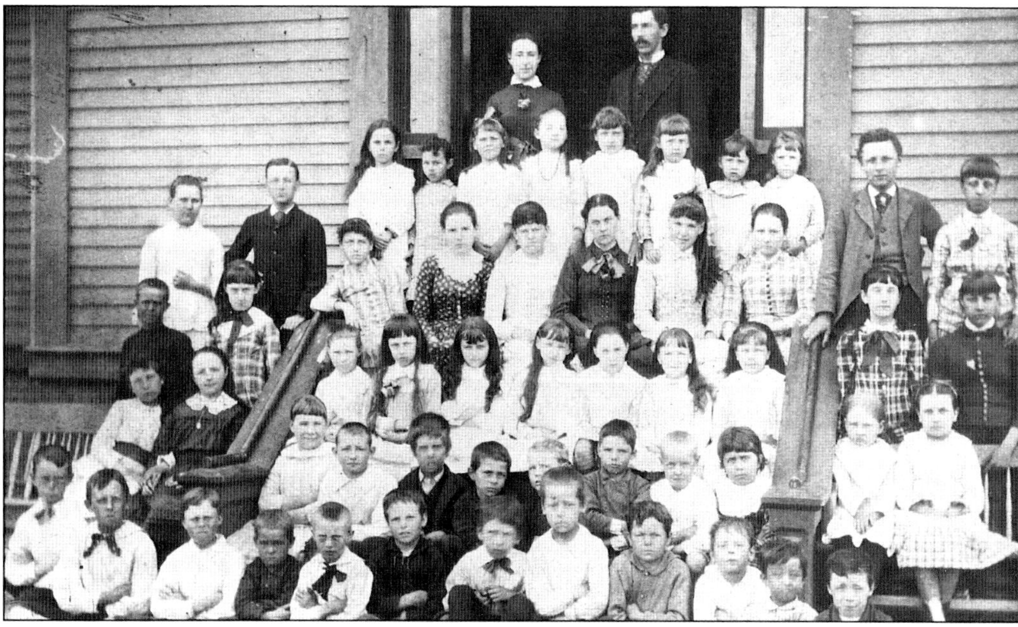

AN AUBURN GRAMMAR SCHOOL CLASS, c. 1890. Principal Charles Earle and his assistant, Miss King, are shown here with a group of students. From left to right are as follows: (front row, seated) Charles Greene, Robert P.Windsor, Arthur Streeter, Everette Potter, ? Greene, Arthur Smith, Fred Crawford, Howard Pierce, David Stone, Charles Potter, George Rundell, and John Chatwin; (second row) Lena Roundelle, Eva Pryor, Jennie Boyle, William Eddy, Walter Place, Raymond Chandler, Irvin Potter, Russell Franklin, unknown, unknown, Florie Williams, and Cora Nelson; (third row) unknown, Courtland Potter, Alice Pratt, Lizzie Streeter, Florence Budlong, ? Dunham, unknown, unknown, Carrie Franklin, Alice Greene, and unknown; (fourth row) Annie Boyle, Frank Streeter, Mary Knowles, Elizabeth Greene, Clara Reed, Clara Wood, Jennie Greene, Martha Waite, and Walter Pierce; (back row) Jennie Chandler, Julia Trescott, Jennie Eddy, Hattie Chambers, and four unidentified students.

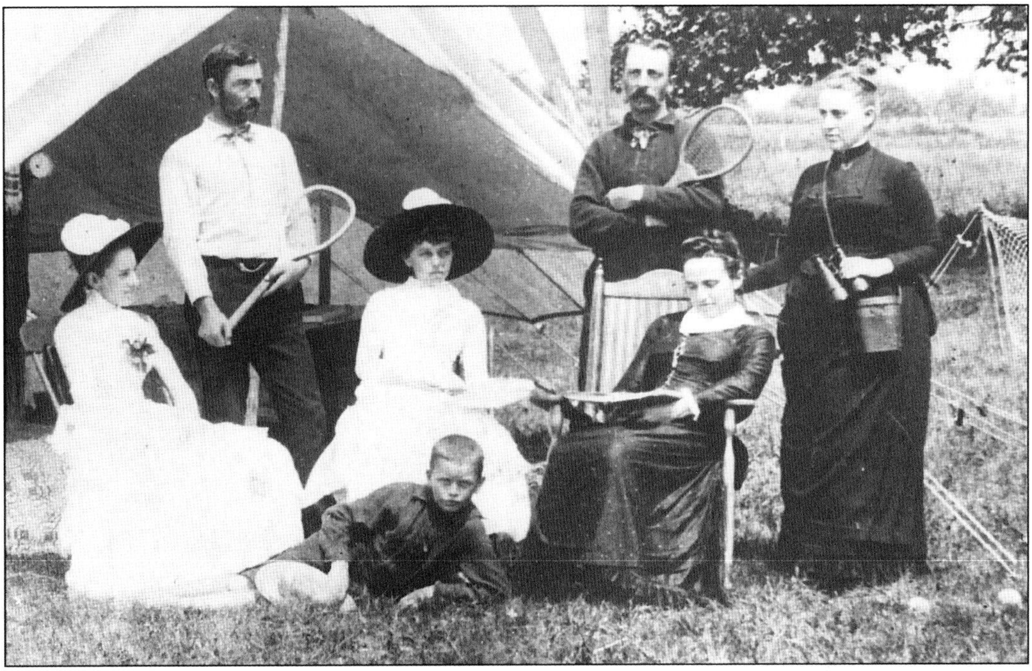

The Earle Family, c. 1890. In the 18th century the Earle family included five school teachers, two of which were school principals. They are, from left to right, as follows: (front row) Anne, an unidentified woman and child, and Mrs. James H. Earle; (back row) Charles (principal of the Auburn Grammar School), James H. (principal of the Arlington Grammar School), and Alice.

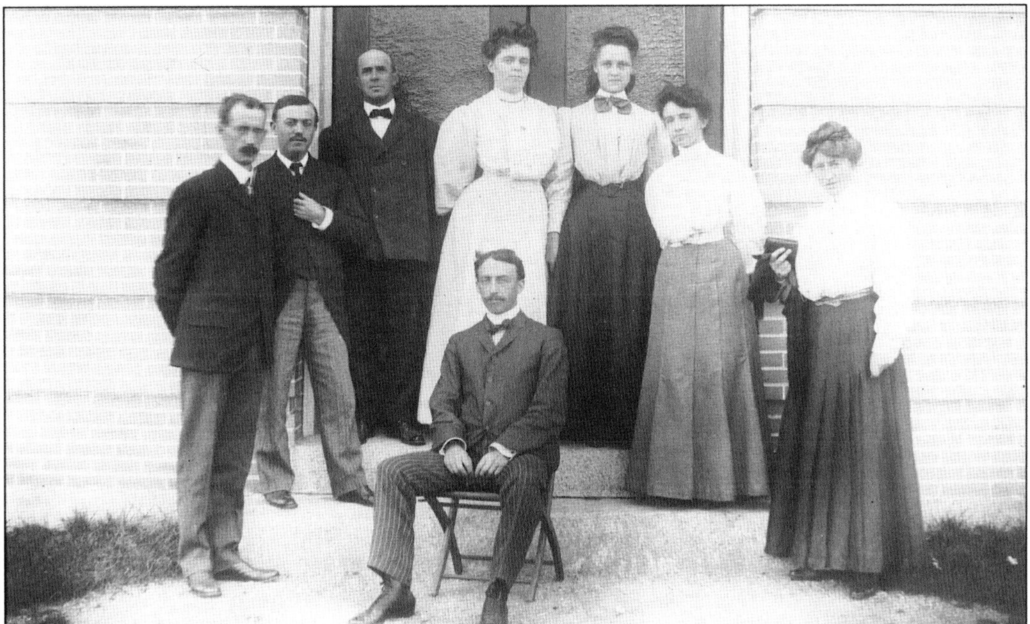

Teachers at the Cranston High School (Briggs School), c. 1907. From left to right are John K. Fenner, John C. Hayward, Willard J. Reynolds, Eulalia Towne, Mary Brennan, Ethel Tower, and Sara L. McCormack. Seated is Dr. Charles M. Poor, principal.

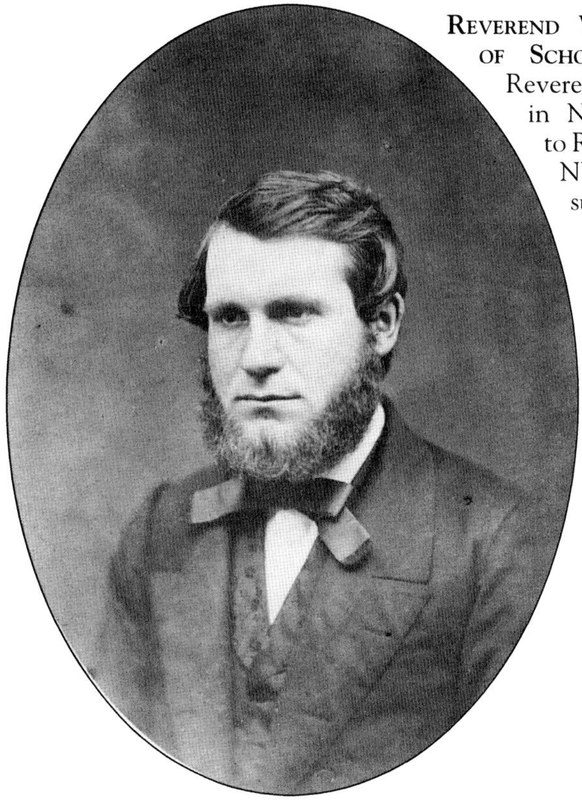

REVEREND WILLIAM A. BRIGGS, SUPERINTENDENT OF SCHOOLS, C. 1891. A Baptist minister, Reverend William Briggs served at churches in Natick and Oak Lawn. Before coming to Rhode Island, he was the mayor of Homer, NY. Reverend Briggs served Cranston as its superintendent of schools for nine years.

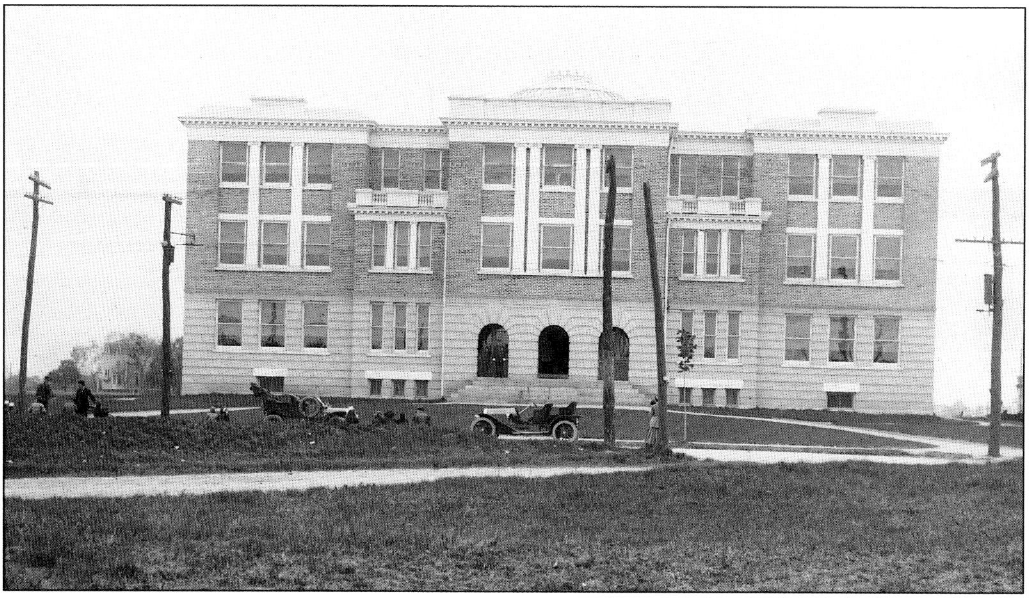

BRIGGS SCHOOL, ON THE CORNER OF PONTIAC AND PARK AVENUES. This school opened as a high school in 1904, but enrollment soon forced the building of the new high school. The old school then became the junior high school. One former student recalled the fire slides at the school and the fact that the boys all hoped they would be on the top floor for the fire drills while the girls dreaded the thought they might have to use the slides in their long dresses.

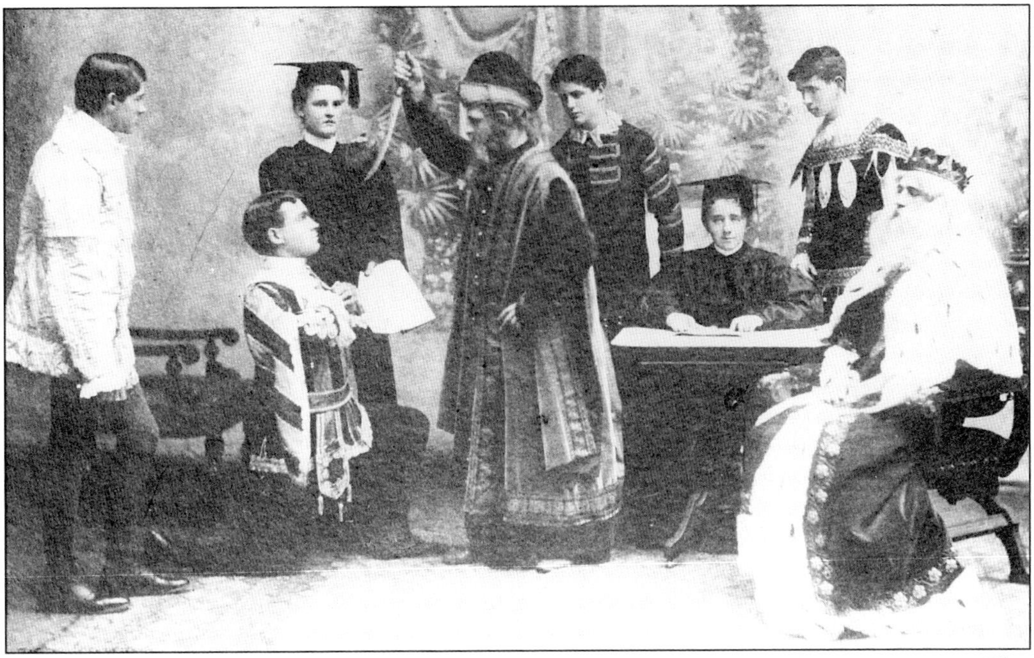

MERCHANT OF VENICE, PERFORMED BY THE CRANSTON HIGH SCHOOL CLASS OF 1898. This graduation play was given in the spring of 1898 and held at the Talma Theater, South Main Street, Providence. From left to right are Ernest Baker as Bassanio, Everette C. Potter as Antonio, Anna Perry as Portia, William Bottomley as Shylock, Charles Tanner as Salerino, Alice Hopkins as Nerossa, Niles Westcott as Solenio, and Wilfred Stone as the Duke of Venice.

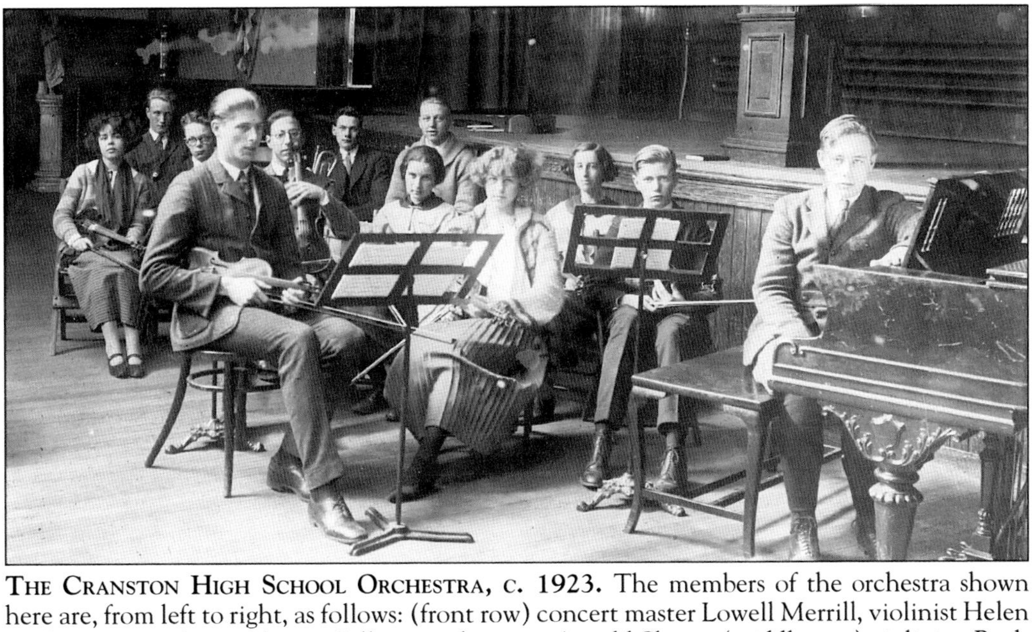

THE CRANSTON HIGH SCHOOL ORCHESTRA, C. 1923. The members of the orchestra shown here are, from left to right, as follows: (front row) concert master Lowell Merrill, violinist Helen Williamson, violinist Clinton Billson, and pianist Arnold Skoog; (middle row) violinists Ruth Grant, Hugo Norden, Haig Baligian, Gwendolyn Pettis, and Emily Millard; (back row) flutist Carl Malmborg, cornetist Gerald Bean, and violinist Spencer Worrall.

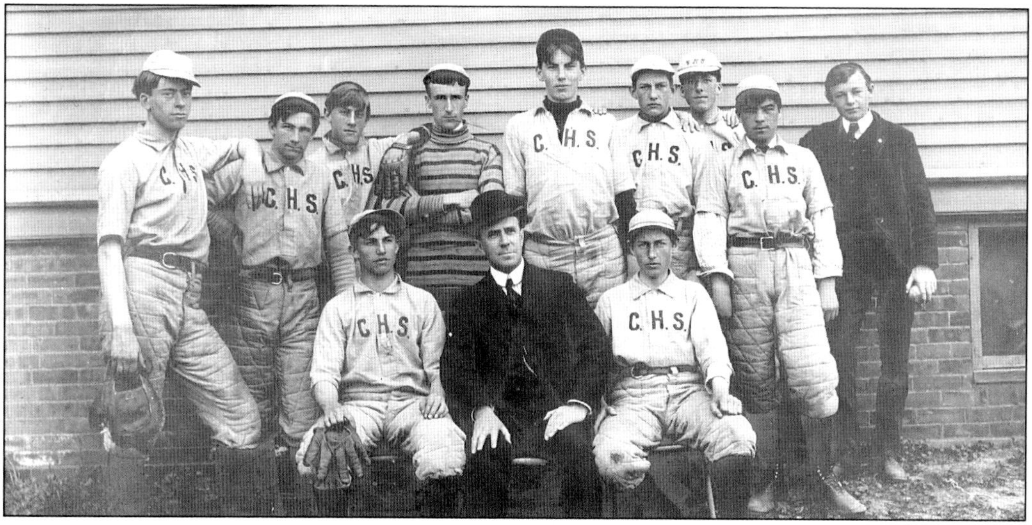

The Cranston High Baseball Team, c. 1903. Members of the team included manager Harry Sandager, captain Earl Bates (pitcher), mascot W.J. Reynolds, Leslie E. Bushnell (first base), Robert Lee (right field), Ben Johnson (second base), Henry Conyers (center field), Ralph Griffith (right field), James Tabb (catcher), Roger Withey (shortstop), Edger Walker (third base), and Frank Webb (left field).

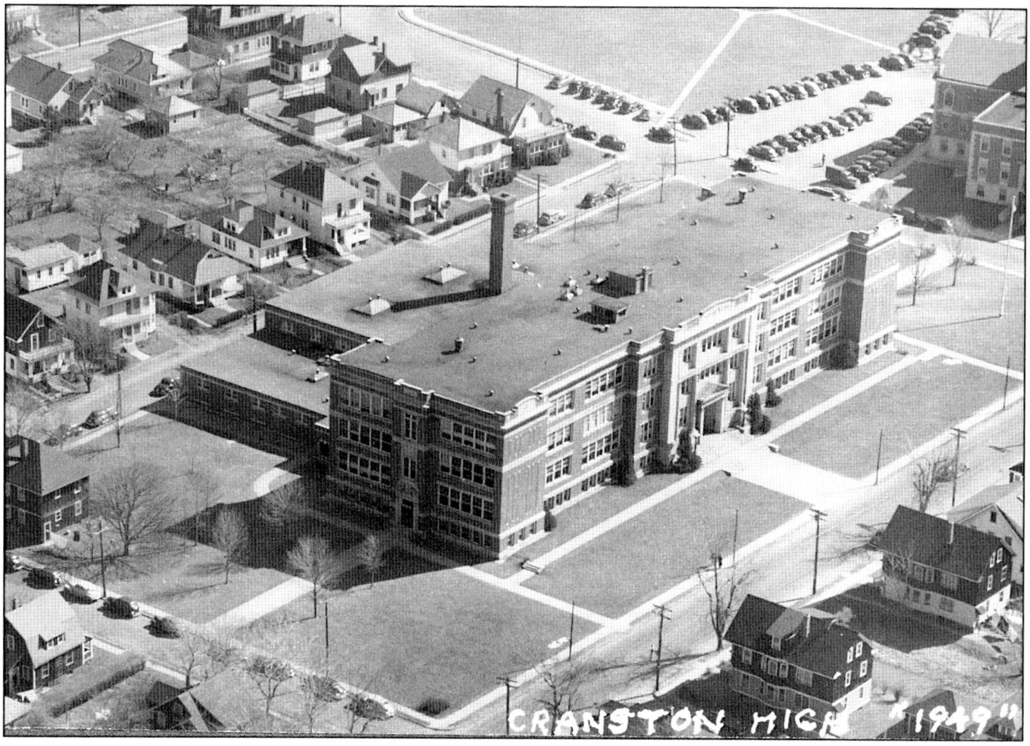

Cranston High School, Park Avenue, in 1949. Built in 1927, Cranston High School was designed by William Walker and Sons. A large four-story addition was constructed in 1956. The building remained Cranston's only high school until 1960, when the doors opened to Cranston West on Metropolitan Avenue. This high school was then re-named Cranston East.

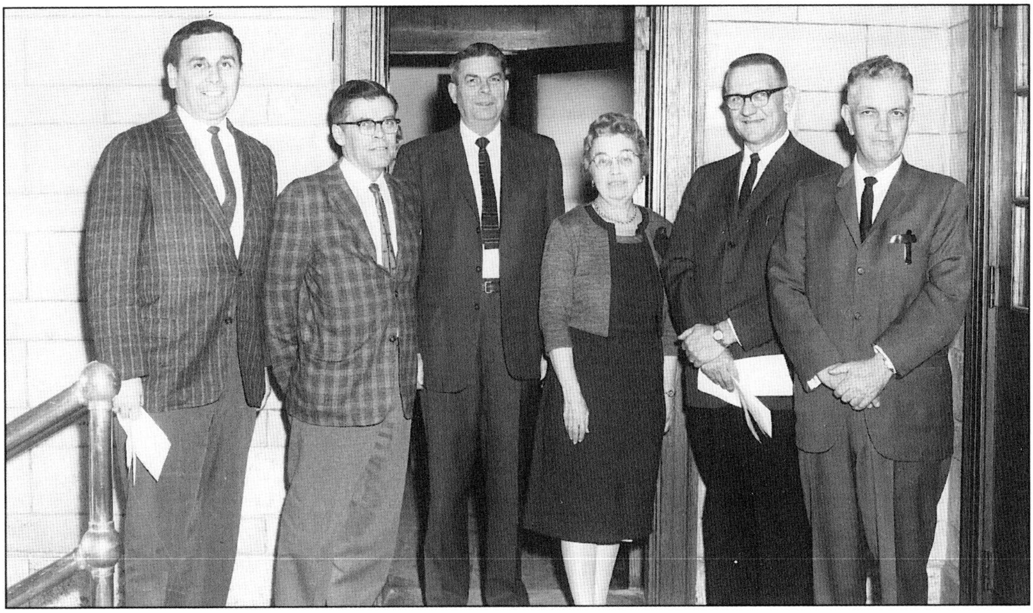

Cranston East High School Administration, 1963. From left to right are Dean of Boys Joseph Ventetuolo, Director of Athletics Frederic "Fritz" Etter, Director of Guidance John B. Thayer, Dean of Girls Vera L. Milliken, Principal Bill Kutneski, and Administrative Assistant George N. Linnane.

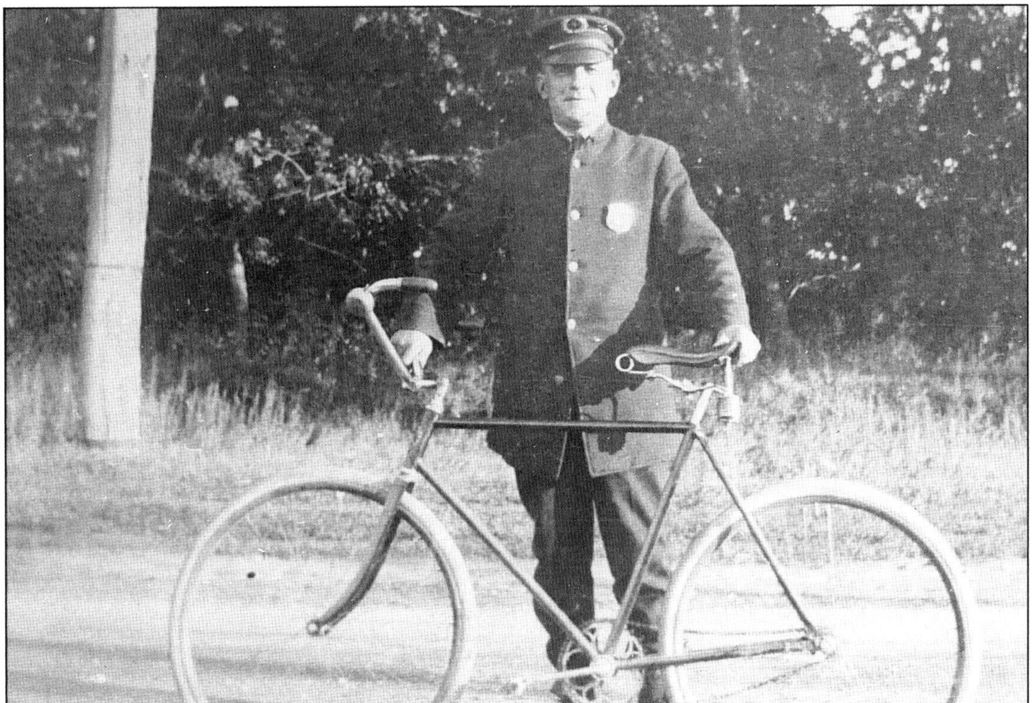

John McGee, Appointed a Police Officer in 1909. Police officers of the early 1900s rode through neighborhoods on their bicycles or, in some cases, on horses. Bicycle officers were quite effective in snaring runaway horses and livestock in a hurry.

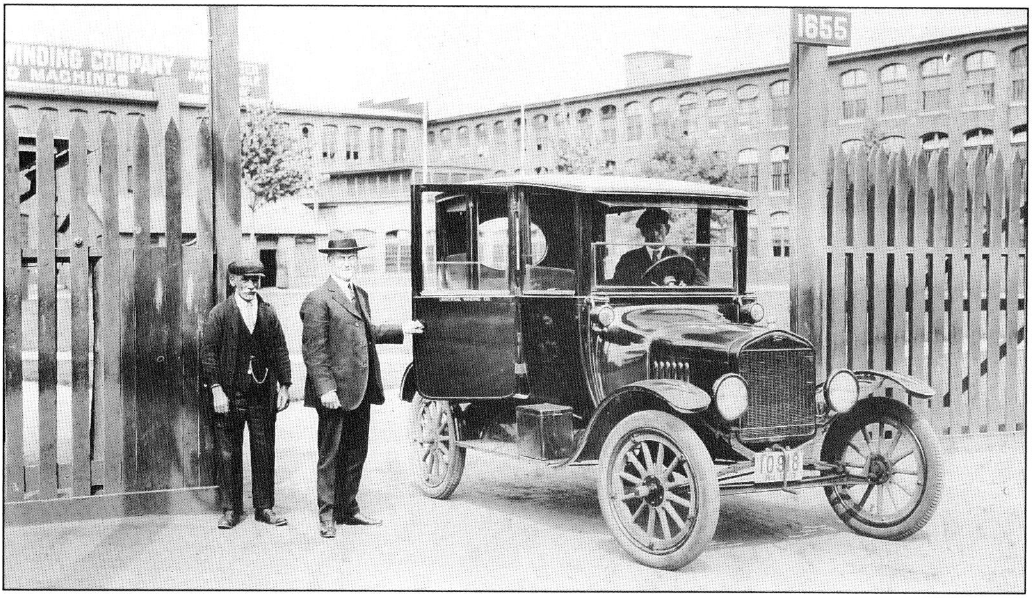

The Universal Winding Company, 1655 Elmwood Avenue, c. 1915. Robert Leesona, chairman of the board of directors of the Universal Winding Company, prepares to go for a ride in his Ford. The buildings of the Universal Winding Company were the home of the Maxwell Motor Car Company in 1908.

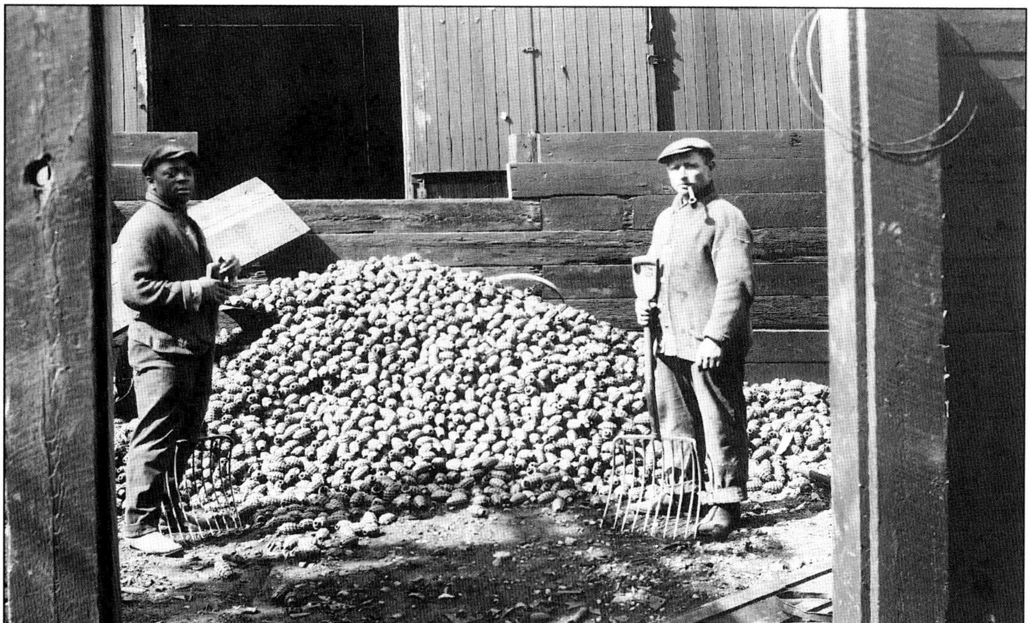

The Universal Winding Company, c. 1915. During World War I, the Universal Winding Company made hand grenades and other supplies for the allies. During World War II they made everything from parachutes to small machinery parts for the war effort. The Universal Winding Company foundry building was home to the Cranston Arms Company, which manufactured the Johnson Automatic Machine Gun (later rejected by the military in favor of the Garand rifle).

Cranston's Draft Board. June 5, 1917, was "registration day" for male citizens of the United States between the ages of 21 and 30. This registration was for future drafting into military service. Seated on the left is Benjamin S. Lee; standing on the right is Deputy Sheriff George E. Rhodes.

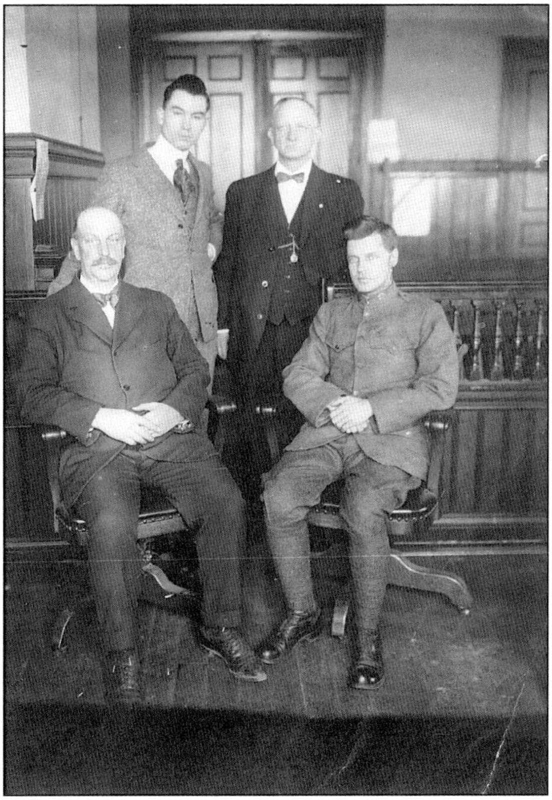

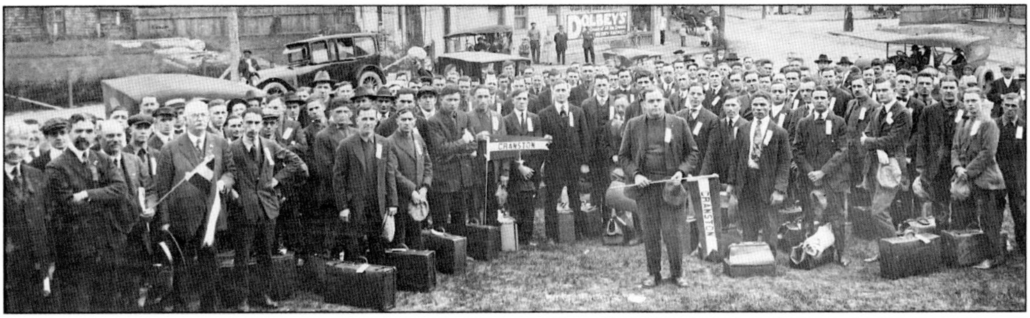

Cranston's Largest Group of Draftees, 1918. One hundred and eighteen draftees gathered in front of the city hall on May 30, 1918, and posed for this photograph before they boarded special cars that took them to Union Station in Providence, and from there to Camp Upton, Long Island, NY.

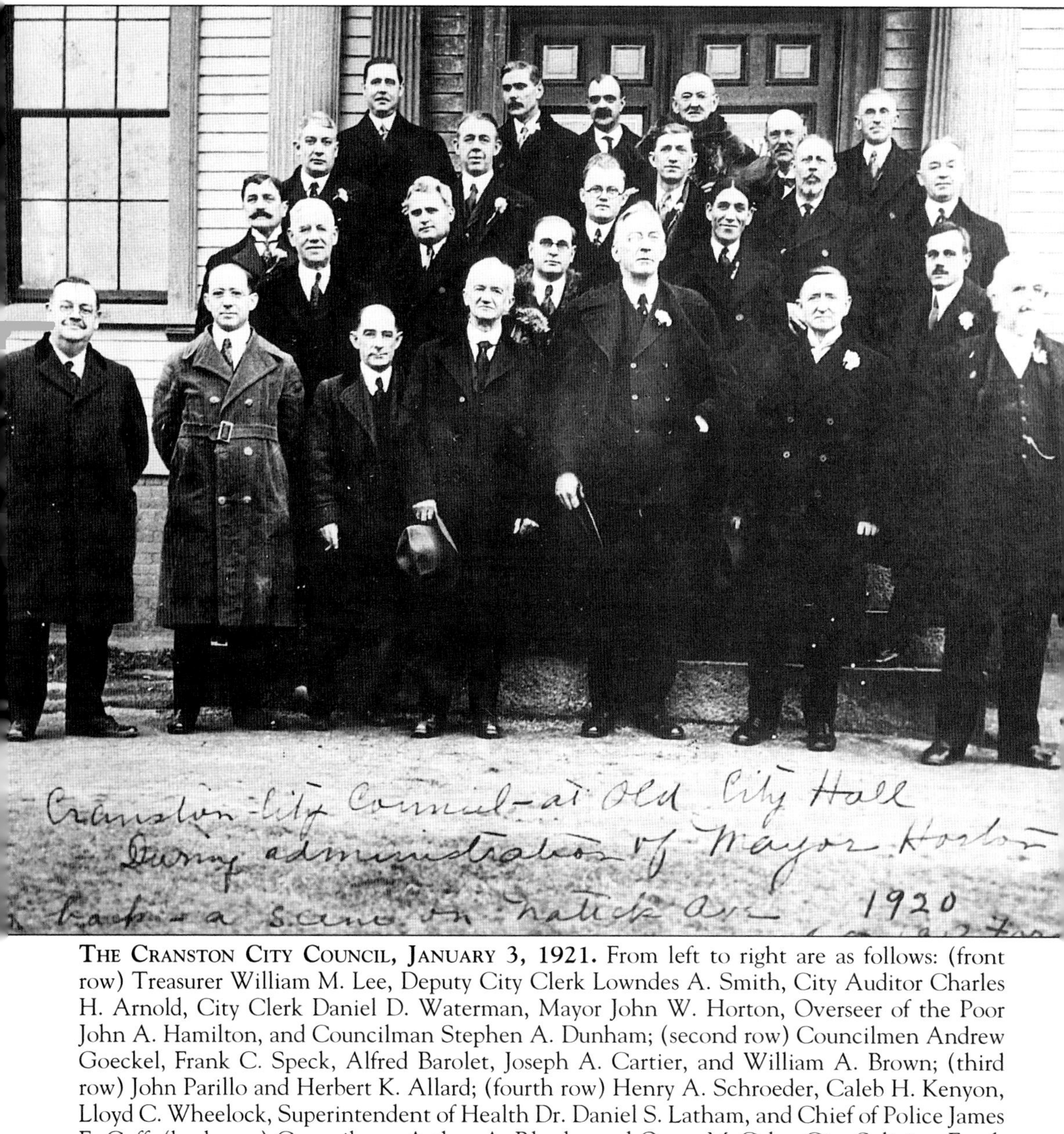

THE CRANSTON CITY COUNCIL, JANUARY 3, 1921. From left to right are as follows: (front row) Treasurer William M. Lee, Deputy City Clerk Lowndes A. Smith, City Auditor Charles H. Arnold, City Clerk Daniel D. Waterman, Mayor John W. Horton, Overseer of the Poor John A. Hamilton, and Councilman Stephen A. Dunham; (second row) Councilmen Andrew Goeckel, Frank C. Speck, Alfred Barolet, Joseph A. Cartier, and William A. Brown; (third row) John Parillo and Herbert K. Allard; (fourth row) Henry A. Schroeder, Caleb H. Kenyon, Lloyd C. Wheelock, Superintendent of Health Dr. Daniel S. Latham, and Chief of Police James E. Cuff; (back row) Councilmen Arthur A. Rhodes and Owen McCabe, City Solicitor Frank H. Wilder, Councilman Eugene F. Bennett, Truant Officer Benjamin S. Lee, and Councilman Albertus M. Colvin.

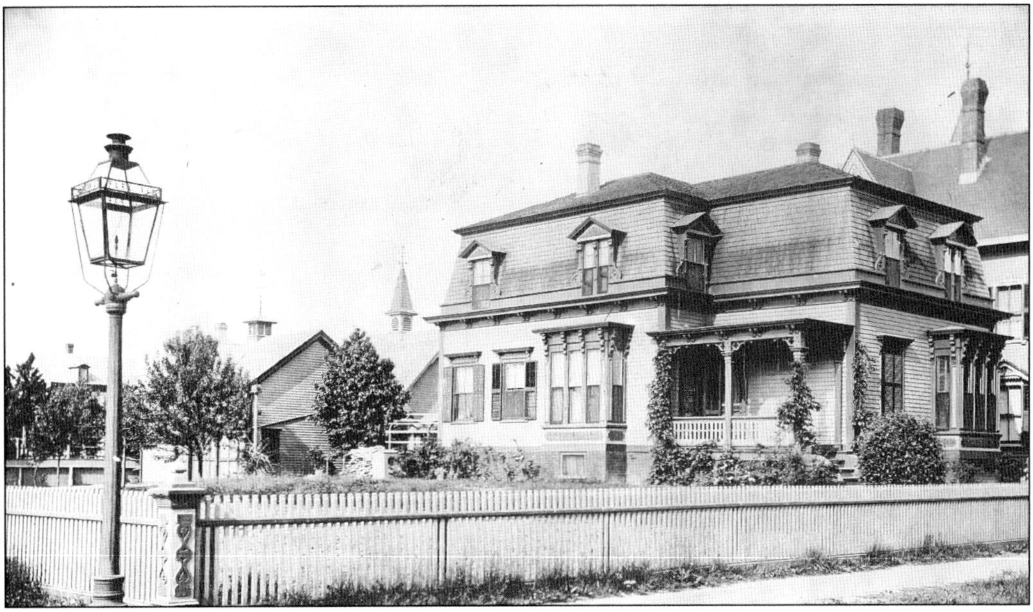

The Home of Dr. Daniel Latham, 678 Park Avenue, c. 1920. This house at the corner of Clarendon and Park Avenues was built about 1882 and was the home of Superintendent of Public Health Dr. Daniel Latham. Dr. Latham died here on September 21 during the Hurricane of 1938. The death of the 76-year-old doctor was due to shock brought on by the intensity of the hurricane.

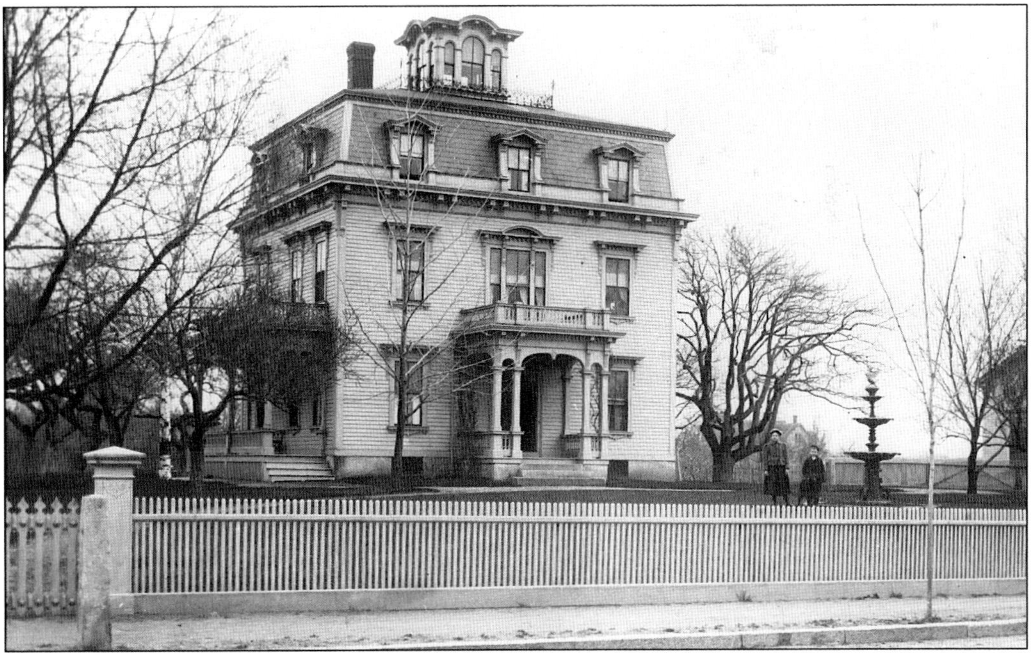

Ladd Mansion, The Banker Estate, c. 1865. This estate at 813 Park Avenue included 3 acres of land. The three-story house had 16 rooms and a staircase made of black walnut. It was torn down in 1948 to make way for stores and parking lots.

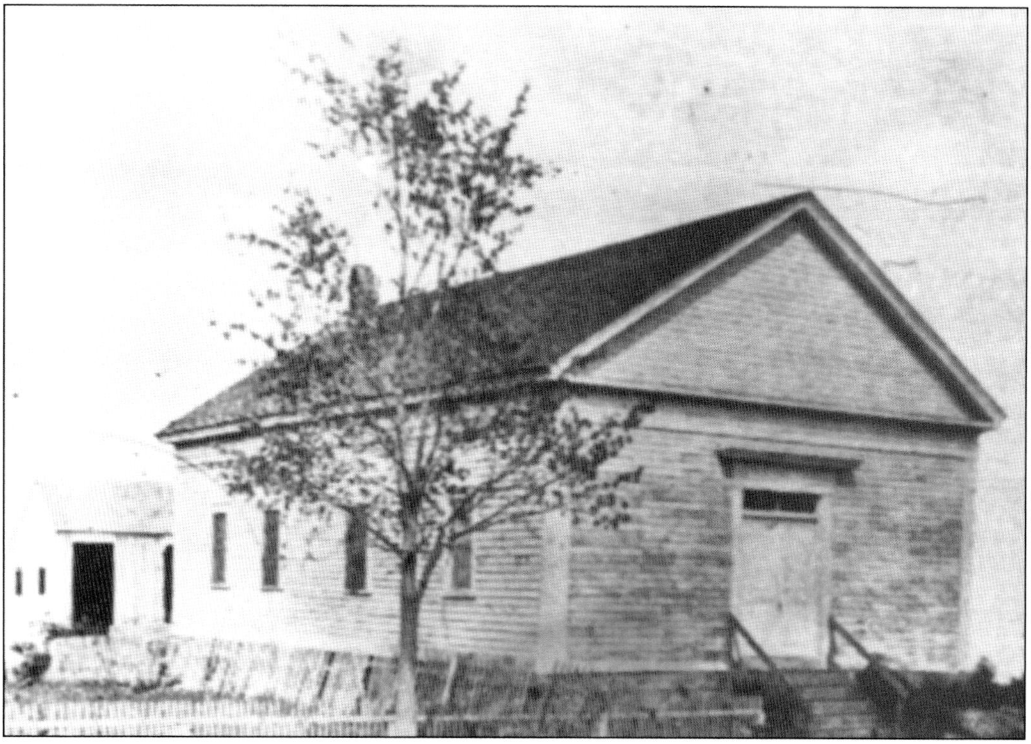

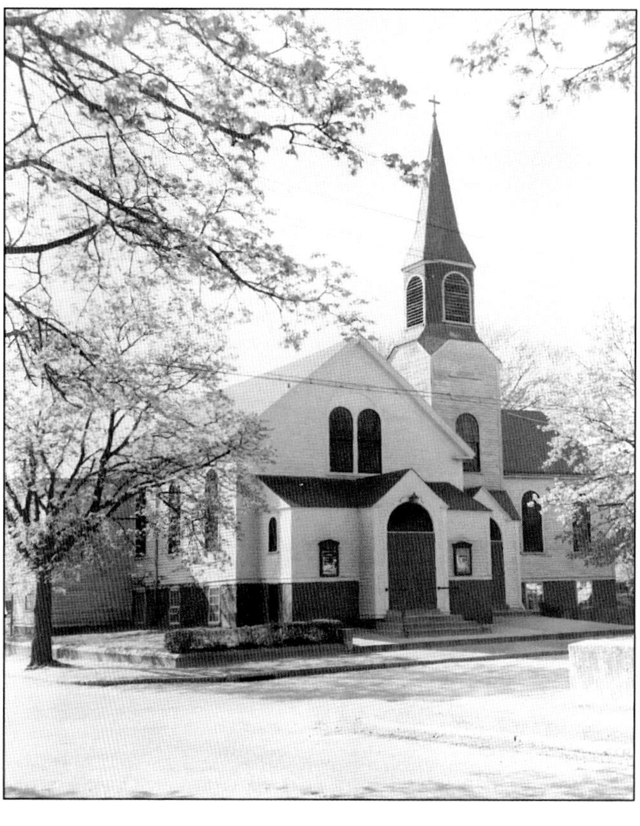

MASHPAUG CHURCH PARK AND ELMWOOD AVENUE, C. 1900. This one-story structure was built in 1851 and began its service as the Mashpaug Free Will Baptist Church. In 1882 the small membership moved to a new building east of this structure and became the People's Baptist Church. Reverend Arthur Given mortgaged his own home to provide funds for building the new church.

THE BETHANY LUTHERAN CHURCH, C. 1954. Located at Lauren and Magnolia Streets, this church was built in 1894 and officially closed on September 12, 1954, when the membership celebrated services in their new church on Rolfe Street.

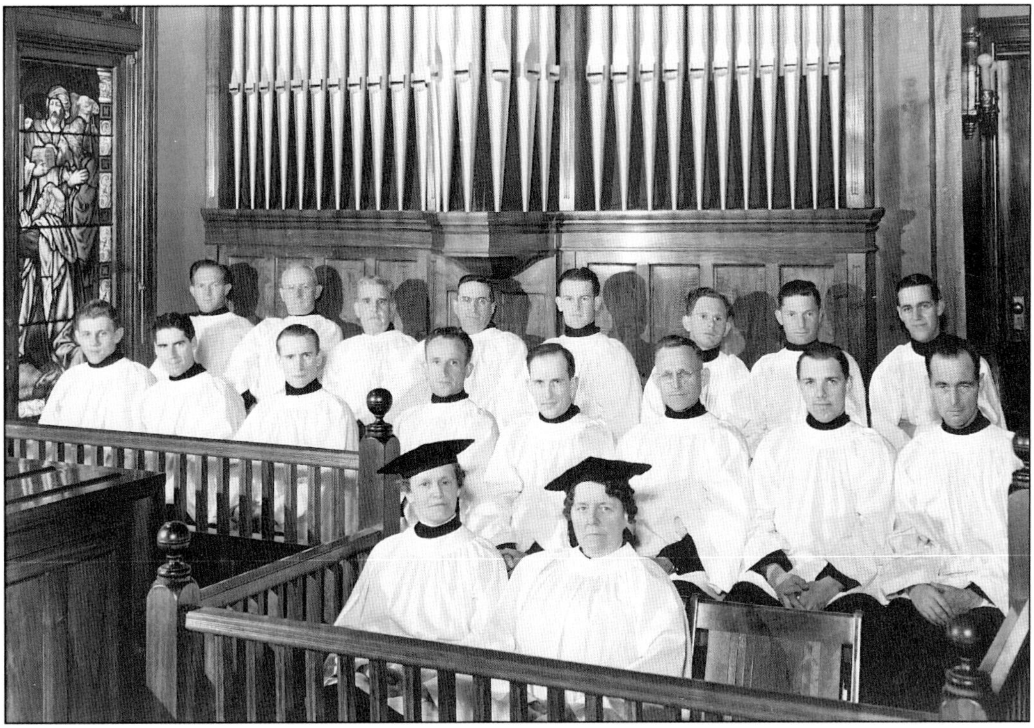

THE PEOPLE'S BAPTIST CHURCH CHOIR AND ORGANISTS, C. 1940. From left to right are as follows: (front row) organists Edna Matthewson and Florence MacKenzie; (middle row) Albert Spratt Jr., Robert Cotton Jr., Junior Miller, Jack Carroll, Elmer Douglas, Ray Finley, Edward Marsh, and George Davis; (back row) Gardner Anthony, Bert Allebaugh, Ralph Miller Sr., Allan Farrar, Richard Possner, Walter Nelson, Bill McLeod, and William Cotton.

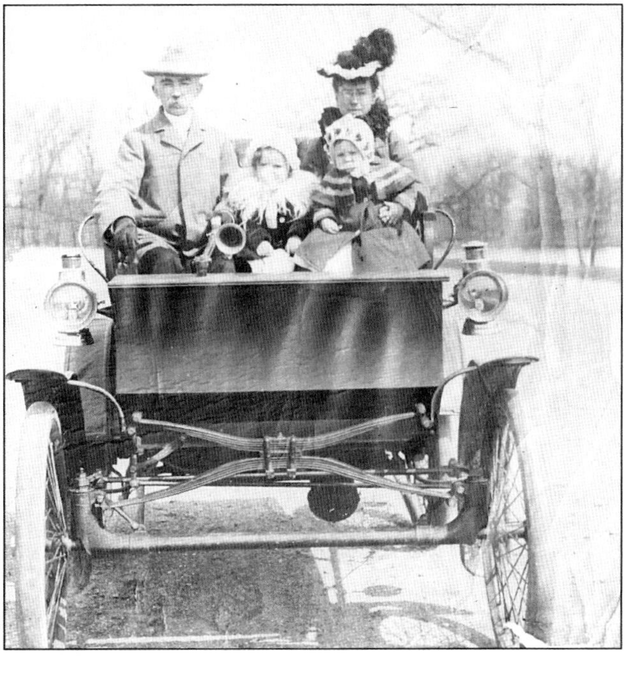

THE SLOCUMS, OWNERS OF SLOCUM'S DRUG STORE, C. 1898. Mr. and Mrs. Harold Slocum and their children, Everett and Minnie, are bundled up to go for a ride in their car. This was certainly a fair weather vehicle, as were most models in the late 1890s and early 1900s. The lack of a registration plate shows that "horseless carriages" were still few and far between.

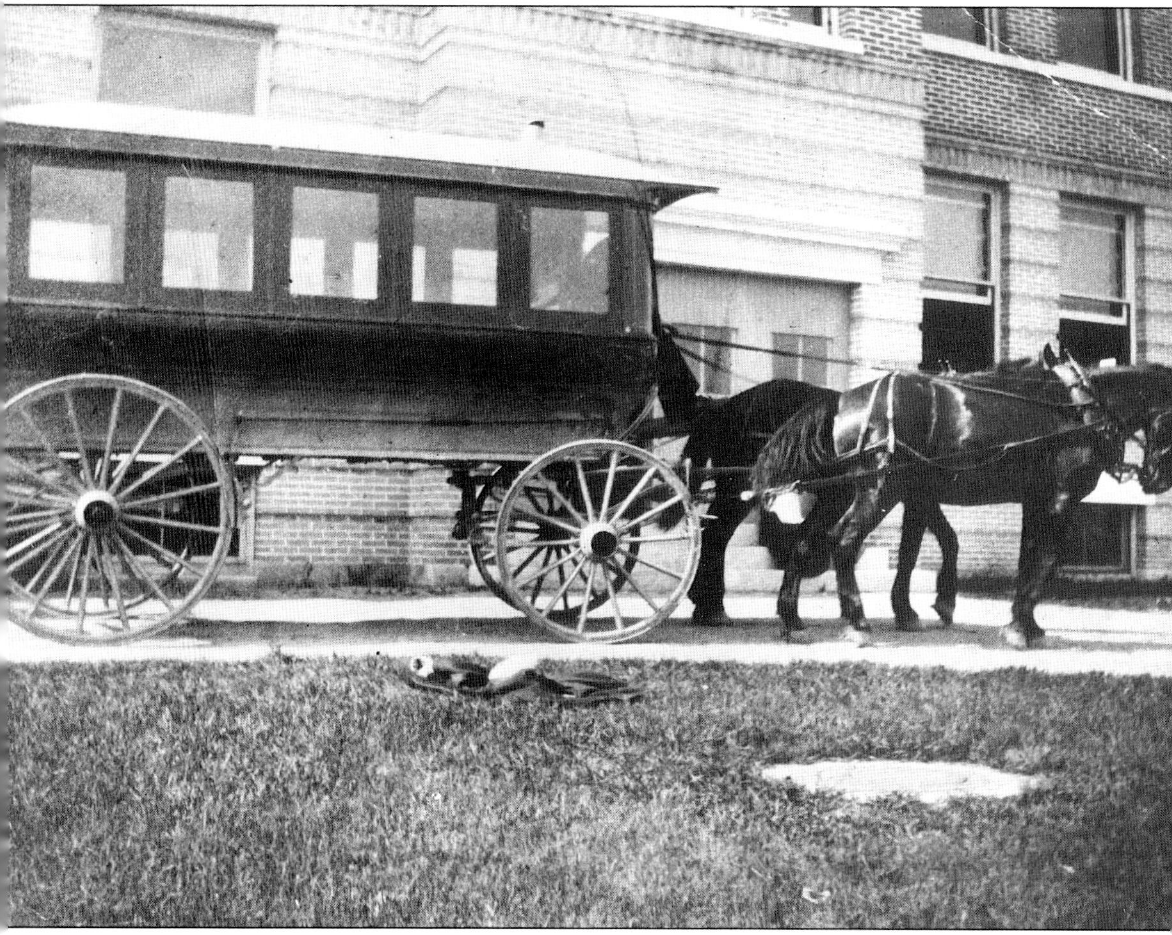

A Crosstown Bus in back of Briggs High School, c. 1904. For those who didn't own a horseless carriage, the crosstown bus was still available. It was the means of transportation from Knightsville to Pawtuxet; the trip took approximately one hour.

Three

Eden Park and Meshanticut

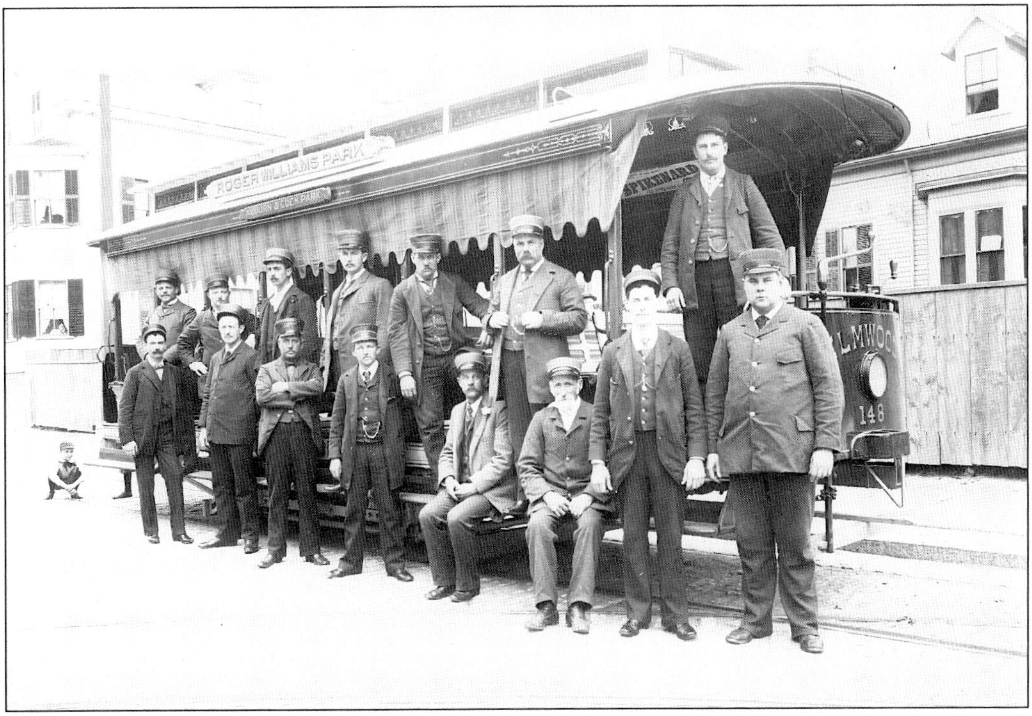

The Auburn & Eden Park Trolley, c. 1900. This trolley car was known as a "bloomer" because it was open during the months of pleasant weather. Notice the boy who took the opportunity to make some personal history. The Elmwood trolley traveled to Roger Williams Park, a pleasant place to hear a band concert or just enjoy a quiet stroll about the park on a Sunday.

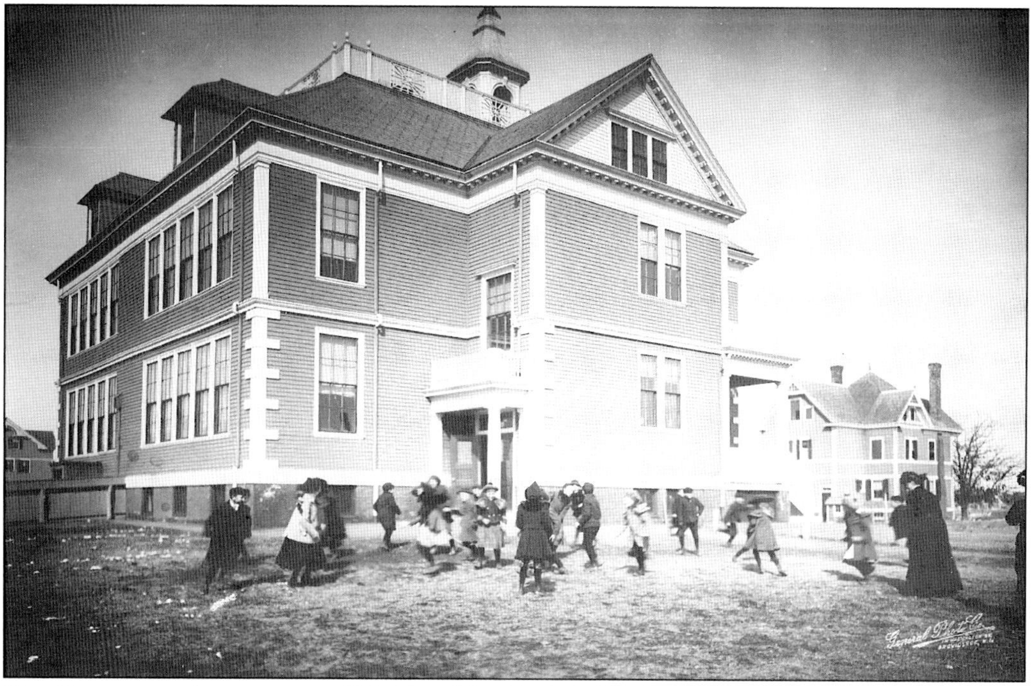

THE EDEN PARK SCHOOL, c. 1897. The Eden Park School opened for the September term in 1897 and served the needs of Cranston students for the next 55 years. The school on Pontiac Avenue was enlarged to 20 rooms in 1920. In 1952 the new Eden Park School on Oakland Avenue opened.

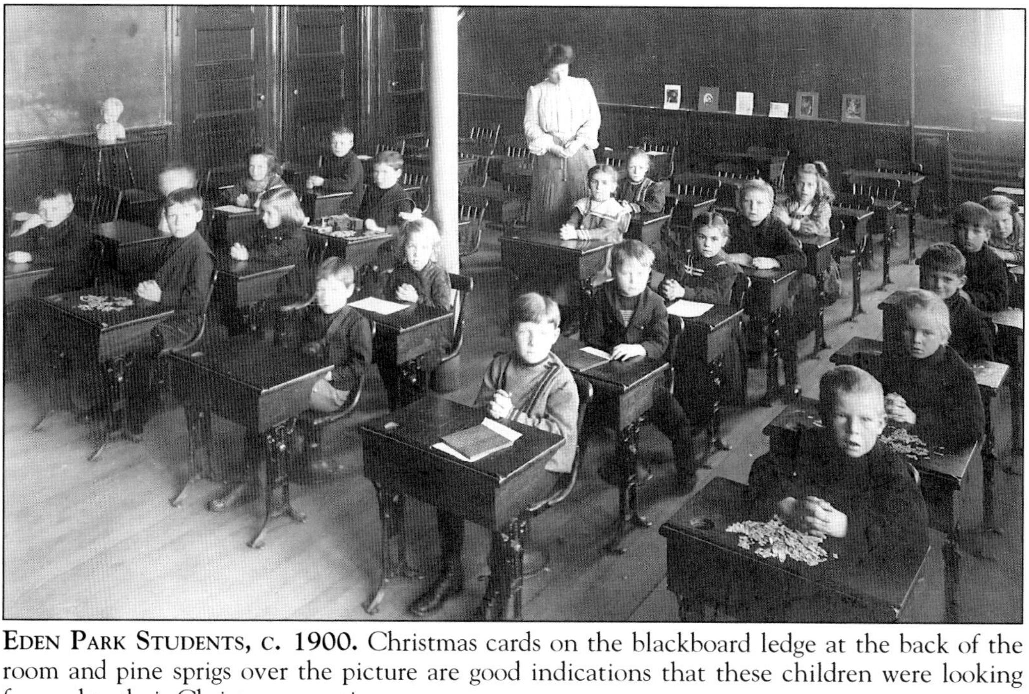

EDEN PARK STUDENTS, c. 1900. Christmas cards on the blackboard ledge at the back of the room and pine sprigs over the picture are good indications that these children were looking forward to their Christmas vacation.

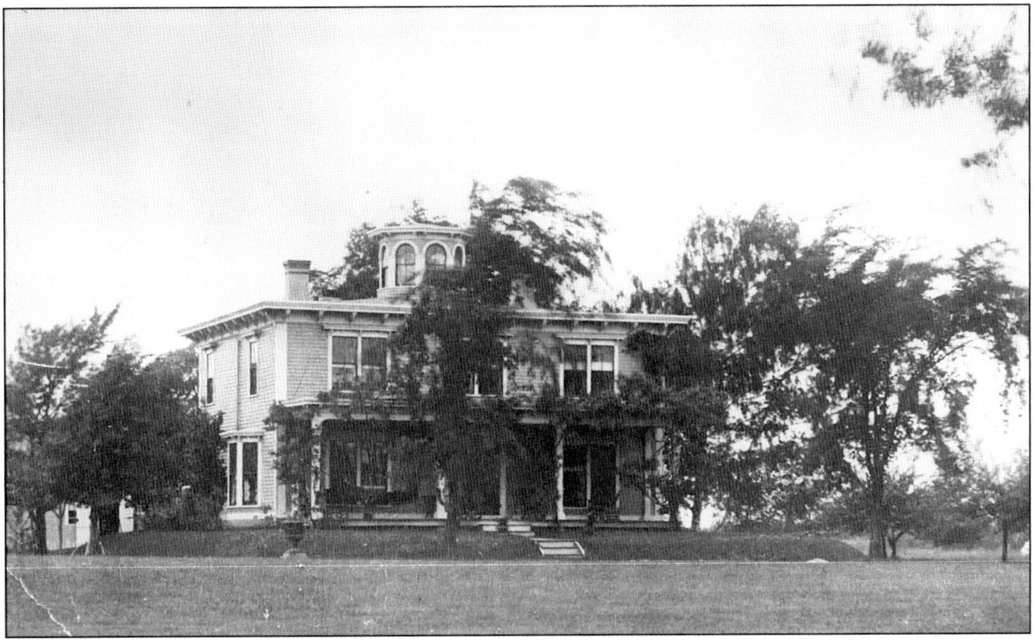

The Tallman Estate, 685 Pontiac Avenue, c. 1900. Cranston in the 19th century was a time of big houses topped with cupolas. The home of Henry Church Tallman was known as Abbott Place, and had a cupola as well as typical old-fashioned furnishings. Mr. Tallman was the grandson of Colonel Benjamin Tallman, a ship builder in the 18th century. Colonel Tallman's most famous ship was the *Ann & Hope*. Mr. Tallman died in this house on December 20, 1907, at the age of 97.

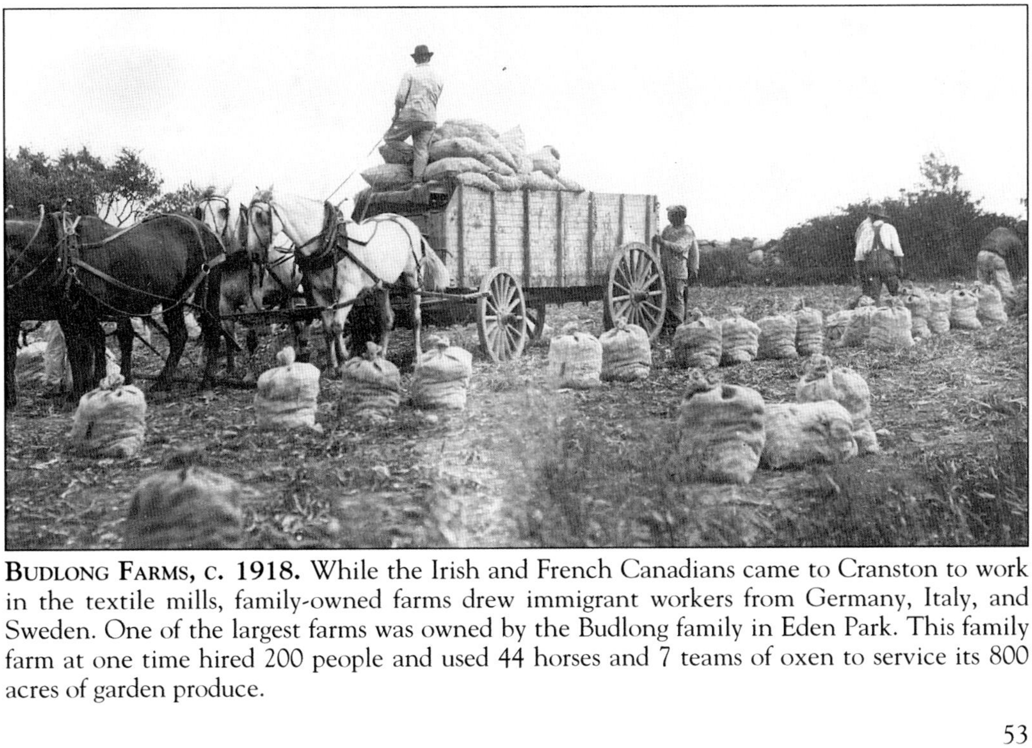

Budlong Farms, c. 1918. While the Irish and French Canadians came to Cranston to work in the textile mills, family-owned farms drew immigrant workers from Germany, Italy, and Sweden. One of the largest farms was owned by the Budlong family in Eden Park. This family farm at one time hired 200 people and used 44 horses and 7 teams of oxen to service its 800 acres of garden produce.

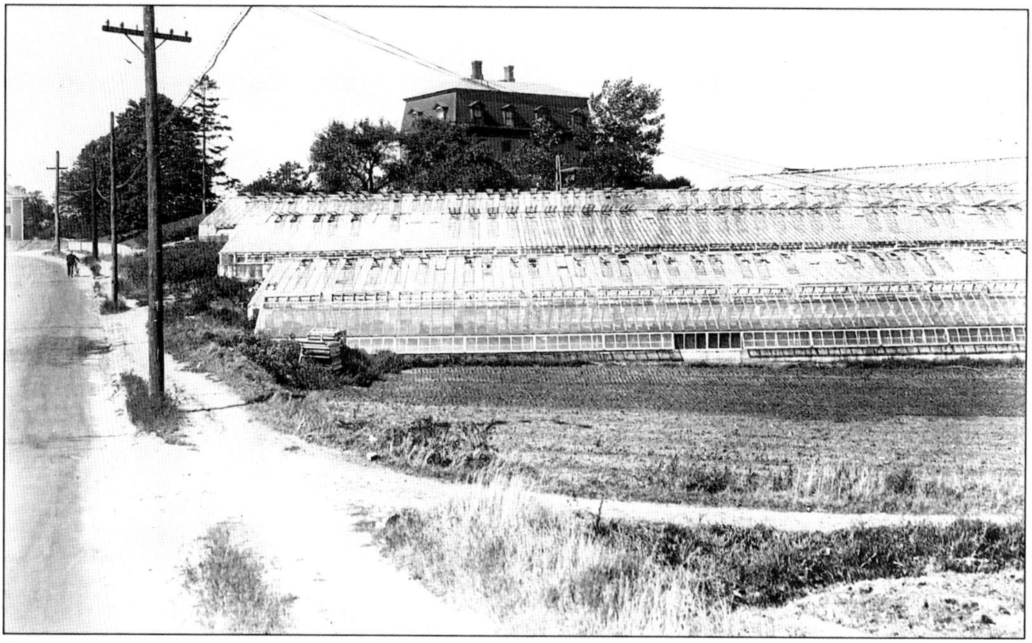

Budlong Farms, c. 1920. In 1902, the Budlongs could boast of having 25 greenhouses, one of which they claimed was 500 feet long and stretched from Rolfe Street to Wellington Avenue. The 1938 Hurricane destroyed the greenhouses and the Budlong's rose-growing business.

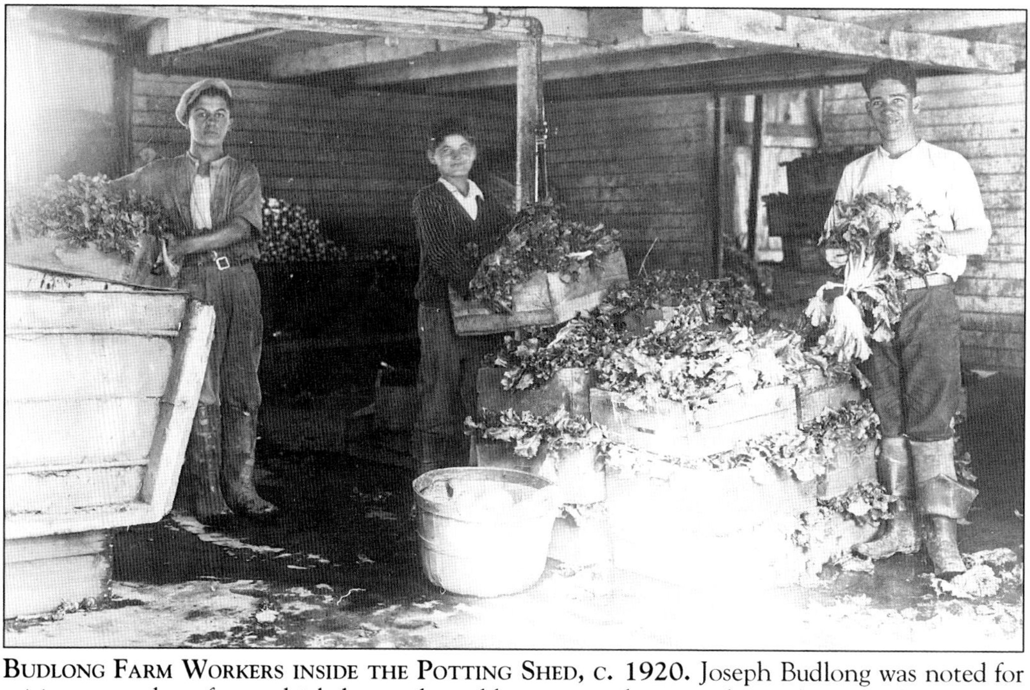

Budlong Farm Workers inside the Potting Shed, c. 1920. Joseph Budlong was noted for raising cucumbers from which he made pickles, giving the area the nickname of Cucumber Town or Pickleville. In 1895 a ketchup factory and pickle factory were established to take advantage of the bountiful produce grown on the farm.

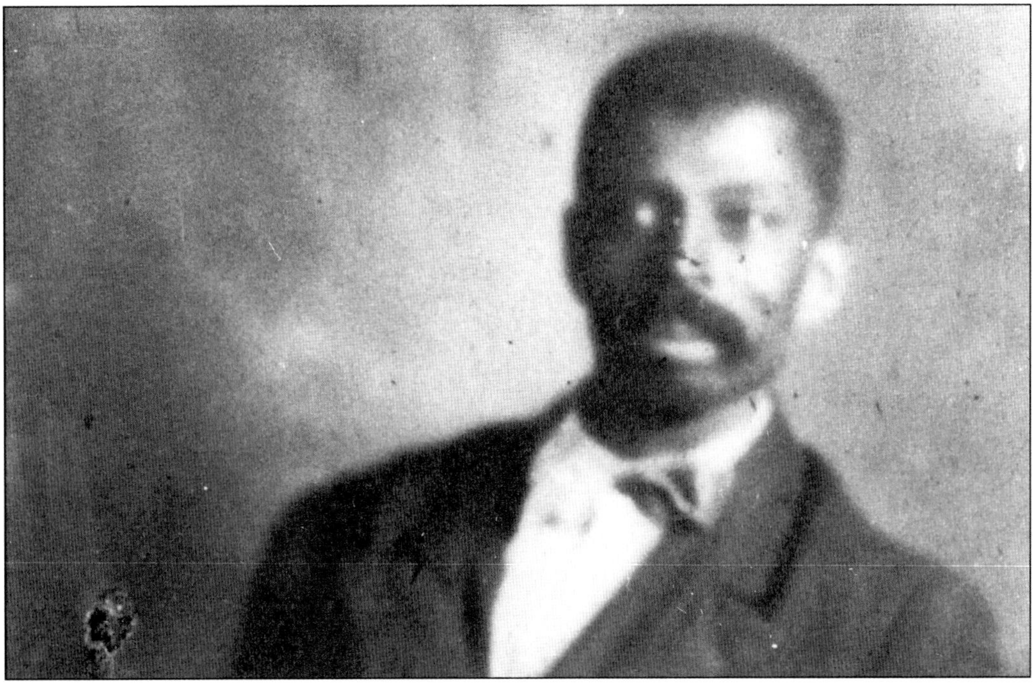

James William White. White was foreman of the C.S. Mann and Son Horse Team and a shipping clerk for the Sand, Taylor and Weed Company during the late years of the 19th century.

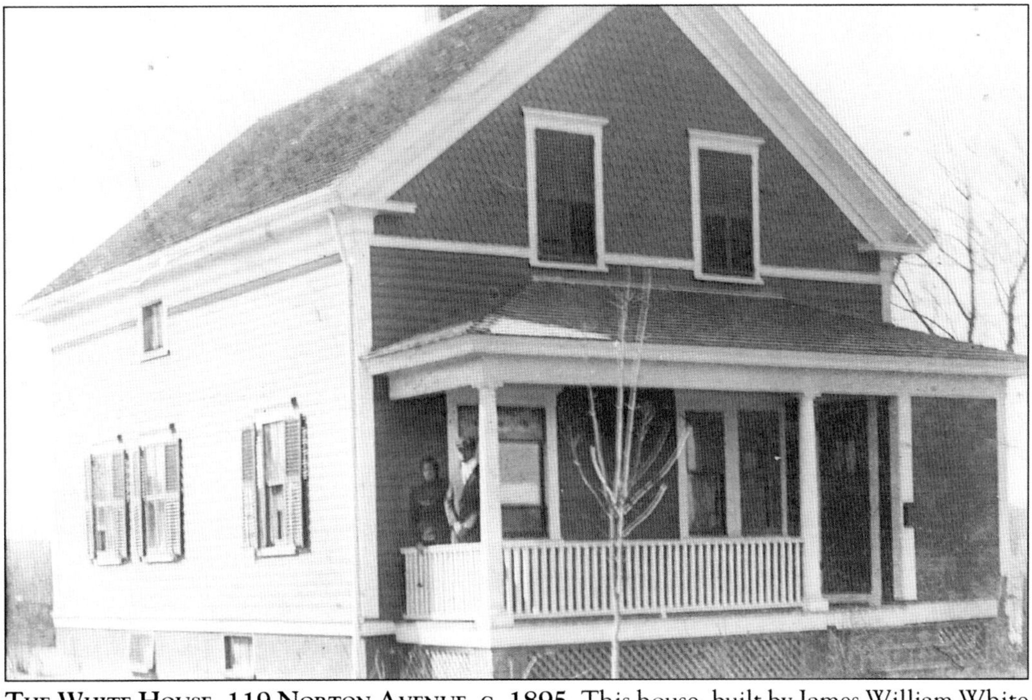

The White House, 119 Norton Avenue, c. 1895. This house, built by James William White and Eliza Ann White, remained in their family until 1962, when it was sold by their eldest son, William T. White Sr.

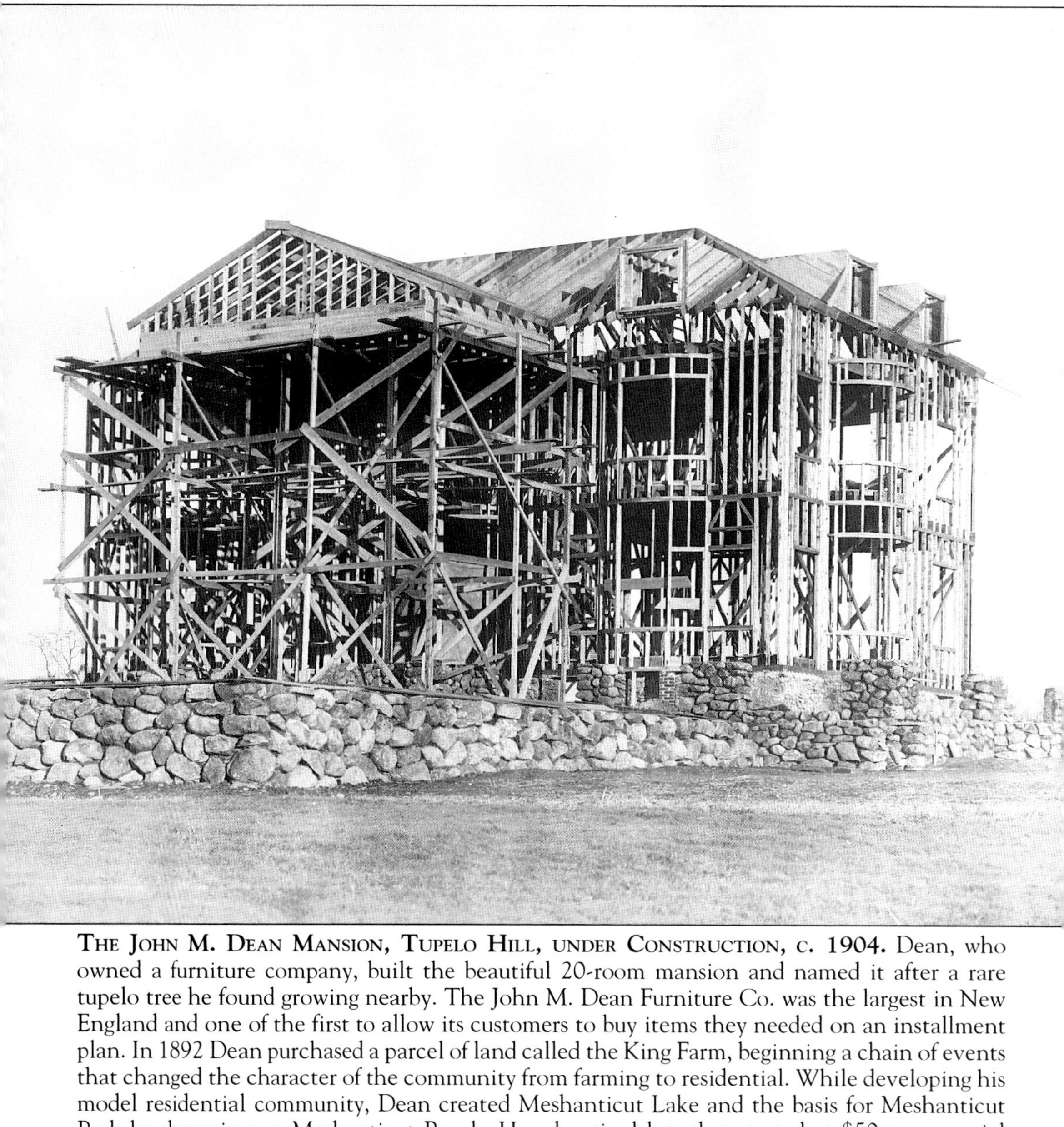

THE JOHN M. DEAN MANSION, TUPELO HILL, UNDER CONSTRUCTION, C. 1904. Dean, who owned a furniture company, built the beautiful 20-room mansion and named it after a rare tupelo tree he found growing nearby. The John M. Dean Furniture Co. was the largest in New England and one of the first to allow its customers to buy items they needed on an installment plan. In 1892 Dean purchased a parcel of land called the King Farm, beginning a chain of events that changed the character of the community from farming to residential. While developing his model residential community, Dean created Meshanticut Lake and the basis for Meshanticut Park by damming up Meshanticut Brook. He advertised lots that started at $50 to potential homeowners on property that is known today as Dean Estates.

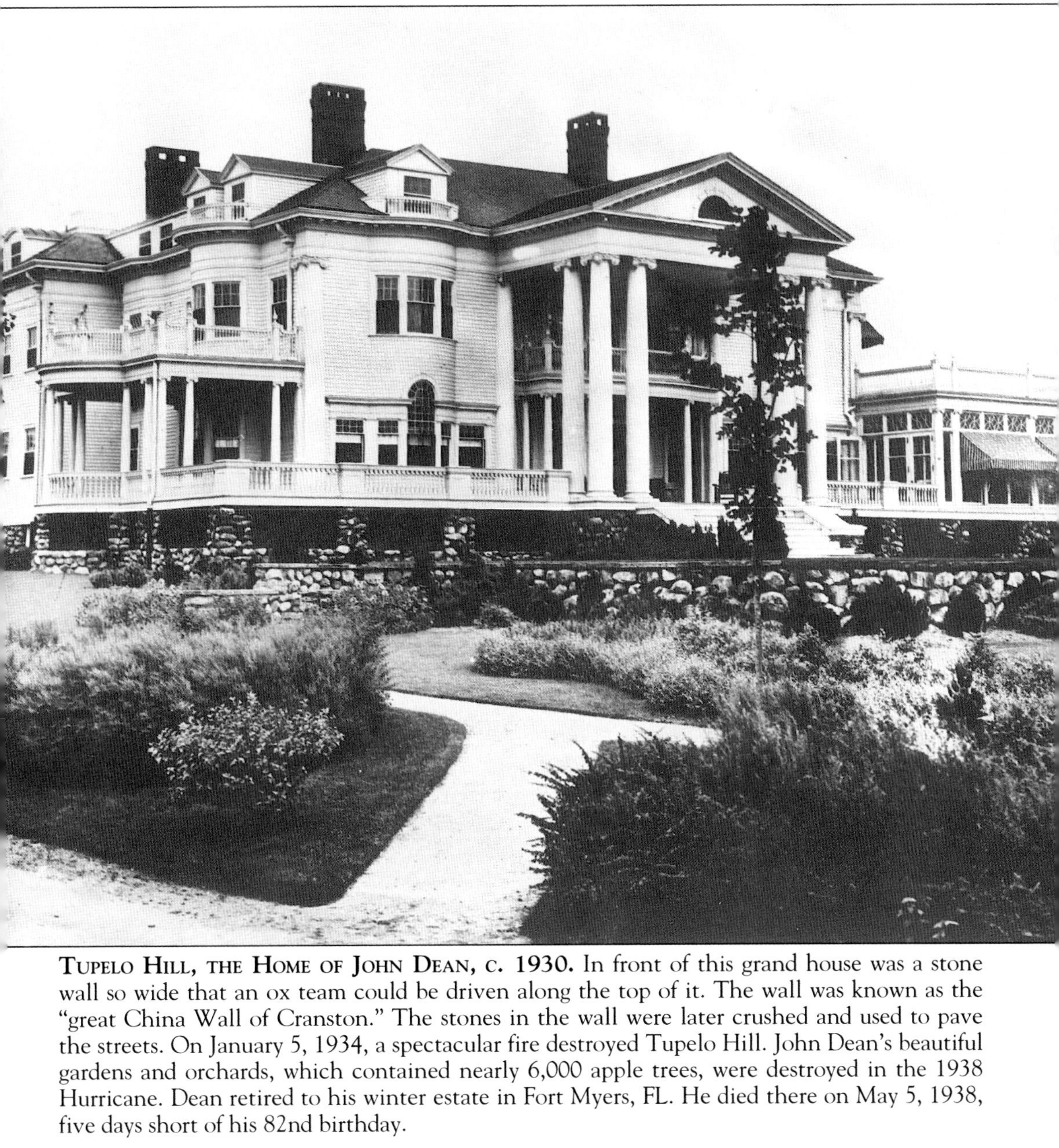

TUPELO HILL, THE HOME OF JOHN DEAN, C. 1930. In front of this grand house was a stone wall so wide that an ox team could be driven along the top of it. The wall was known as the "great China Wall of Cranston." The stones in the wall were later crushed and used to pave the streets. On January 5, 1934, a spectacular fire destroyed Tupelo Hill. John Dean's beautiful gardens and orchards, which contained nearly 6,000 apple trees, were destroyed in the 1938 Hurricane. Dean retired to his winter estate in Fort Myers, FL. He died there on May 5, 1938, five days short of his 82nd birthday.

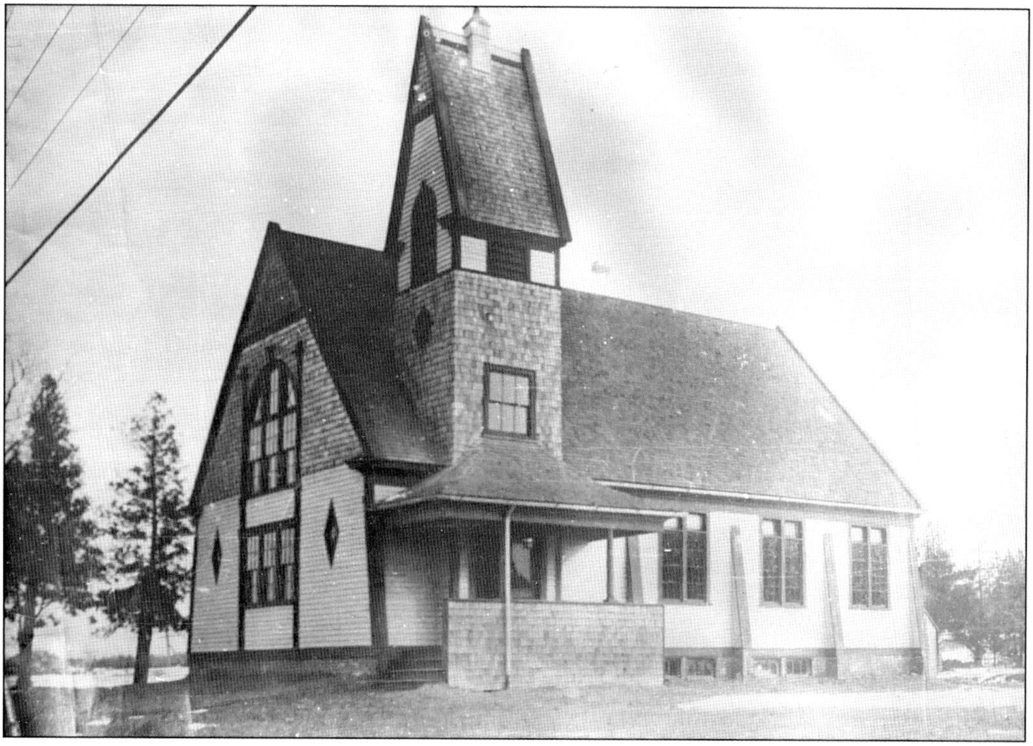

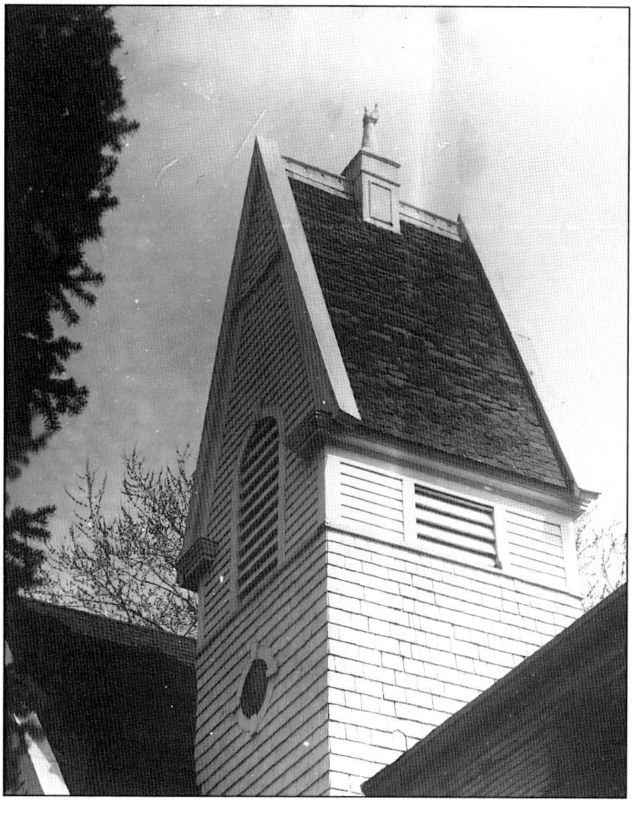

The Meshanticut Baptist Church, Cranston Street, c. 1901. This church was the Little Community Chapel in Meshanticut. Reverend Cyrus Hart, a Congregational minister from Oberlin, OH, advanced his own money to build the structure and became the minister of the non-sectarian community church. In 1909, since a good many of the members were Baptists, the church became an independent Baptist church.

The Meshanticut Baptist Church, c. 1950. The church was mentioned in Ripley's *Believe It or Not* for the symbolic "Hand of God" that adorned its steeple. It was one of only three churches in the United States to have a "Hand of God"—the others were in Oberlin, OH, and in Gibson, MS, at the First Presbyterian Church.

REVEREND JOHN C. ZUBER WITH THE SYMBOLIC "HAND OF GOD" IN 1957. The Meshanticut Baptist Church erected a new building in 1957 at 180 Oak Lawn Avenue. The "Hand of God" was out of proportion on the 8-sided, 30-foot-high steeple that tapers into a point, so the painted metal hand is in the vestry of the new church. Reverend John Zuber served the church for 23 years.

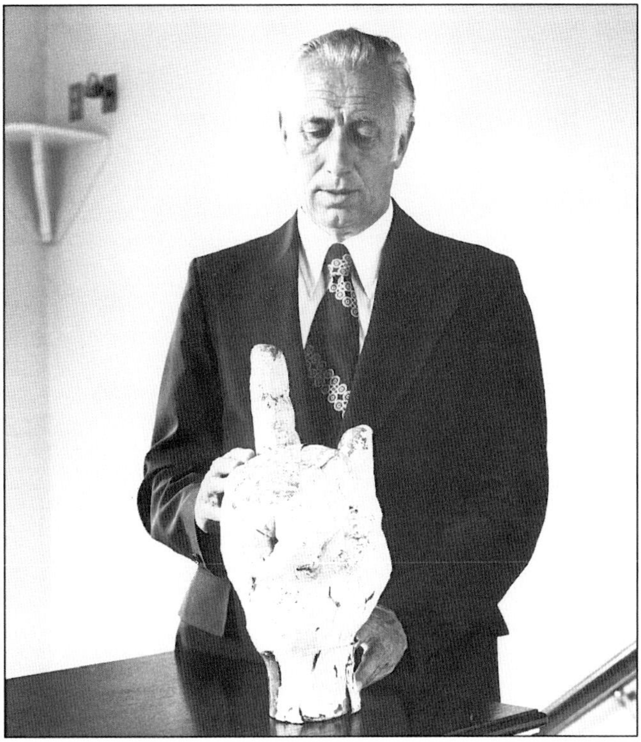

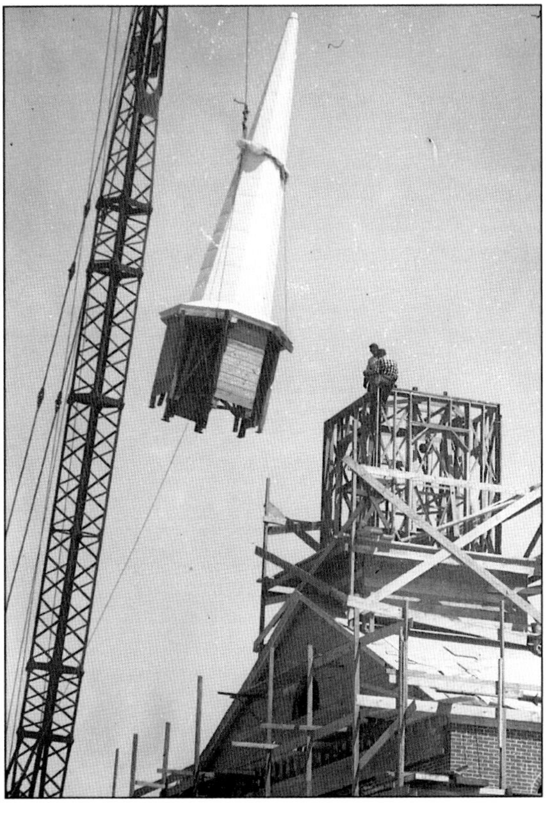

THE MESHANTICUT BAPTIST CHURCH, 180 OAK LAWN AVENUE, 1957. The new church is shown here getting part of its 30-foot-high steeple in March of 1957. When it was placed atop the church, the completed steeple measured about 84 feet. The new church opened for the first time on December 8, 1957.

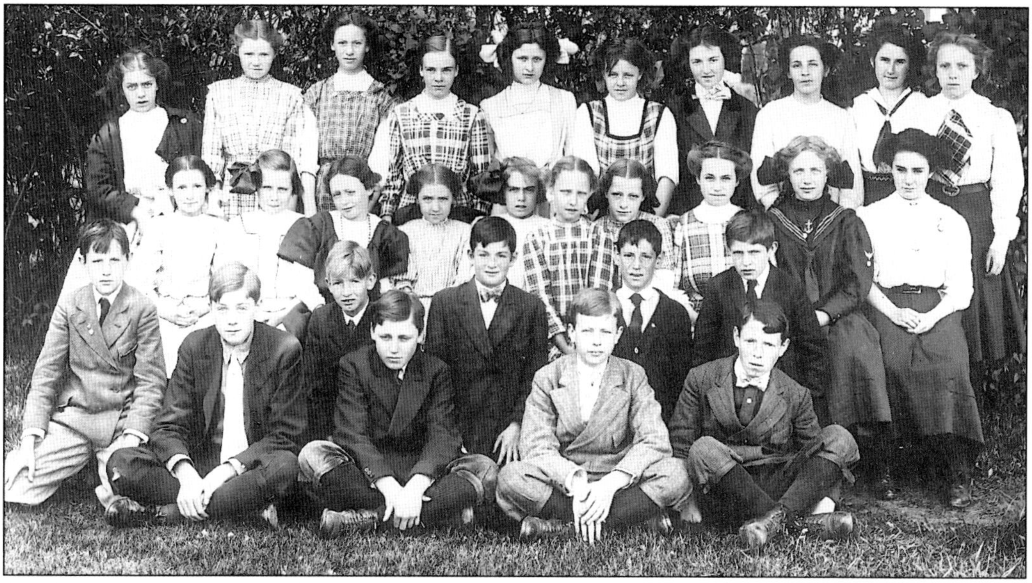

The Meshanticut Park Grammar School Class of 1910. From left to right are as follows: (front row) Charles McMahon, Jack Kendrick, Raymond Miller, and Norman Crooker; (second row) Edgar Flanders, Herbert Knight, Arthur Stone, and Elton Rider; (third row) Marion Brown, Gladys Day, Edith Brown, Gertrude Redding, Lillian Redding, Alice Stone, Edith Potter, Edith Earle, Isabel Taylor, and Ruth Booth; (back row) Anna Redding, Bertha Brown, Marion White, Marion Walker, Ruth Holiday, Mollie Per Lee, Annie Marshall, Emily Stone, Ruth Aldrich, and Vera Hopkins.

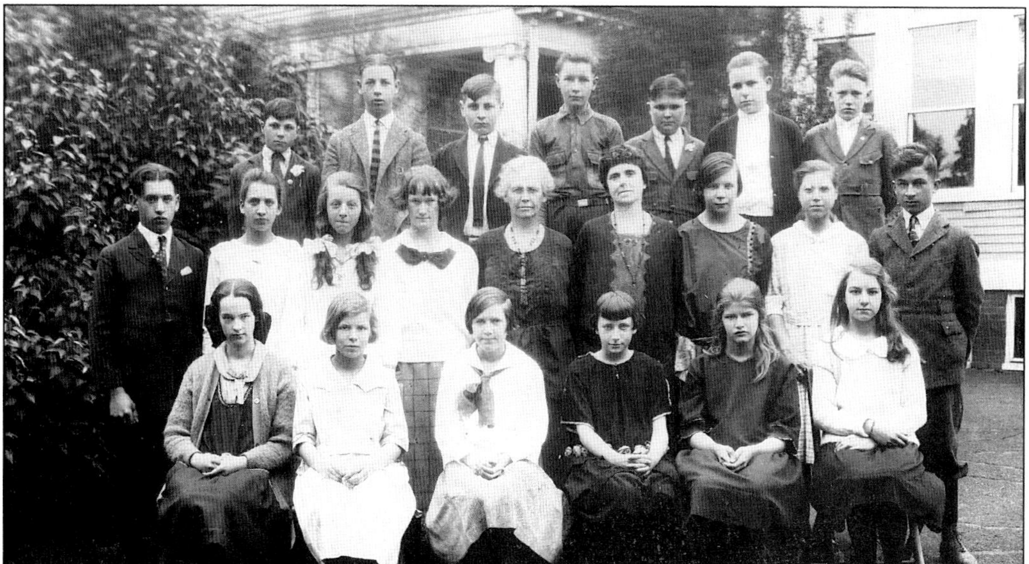

The Meshanticut Park Grammar School Class of 1923. From left to right are as follows: (front row) Ruth Nickerson, Marion Marshall, Pearl Phelan, Doris Burke Lois Leathers, and Dorothy Shippie; (middle row) Manuel Bettencourt, Marion Bettencourt, Isabel Asbury, Virginia Townsend, Mrs. Campbell, Miss Carpenter, Mildred McCarron, Mary Souza, and Philip Judge; (back row) George Raymond, Harley Trice, Rocco Del Bonis, Phil Chace, William Hines, Edward Cull, and Victor Wakely.

Four

Edgewood and Pawtuxet

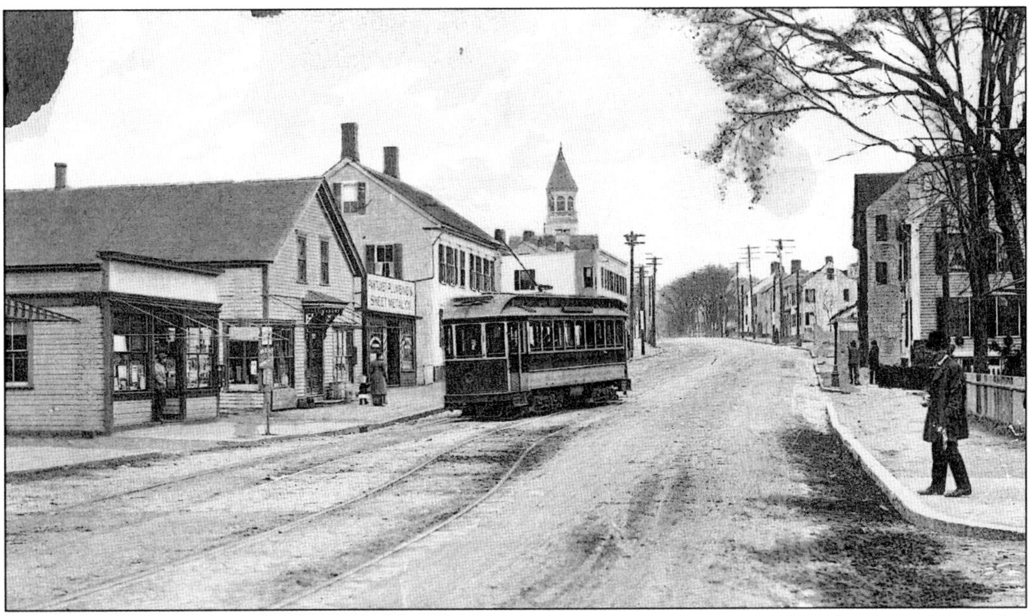

A Trolley on Broad Street, c. 1908. Once the vacation spot of only the well-to-do, Edgewood and Pawtuxet were changed by the invention of the trolley. The trolley brought working people from Providence and other cities and towns to the shoreline of Narragansett Bay to enjoy a day at the beach and a dinner at the shore dinner hall.

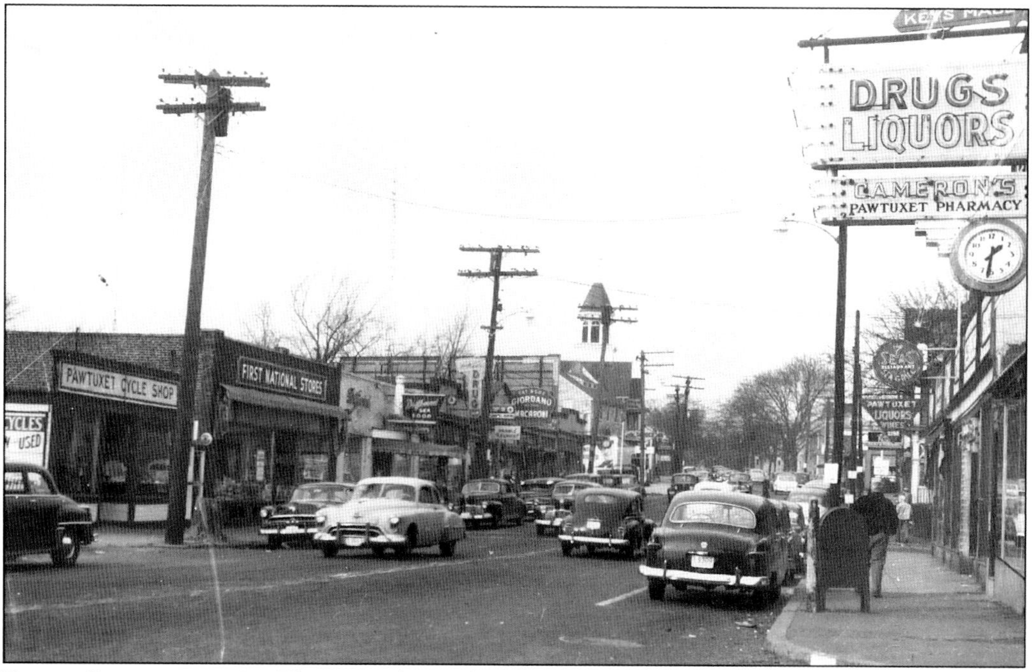

BROAD STREET, C. 1953. This view shows the same corner as in the previous picture, only over 50 years later. The trolley has been replaced with automobiles and a First National Store has moved in, but the view is nearly the same as it was in 1908.

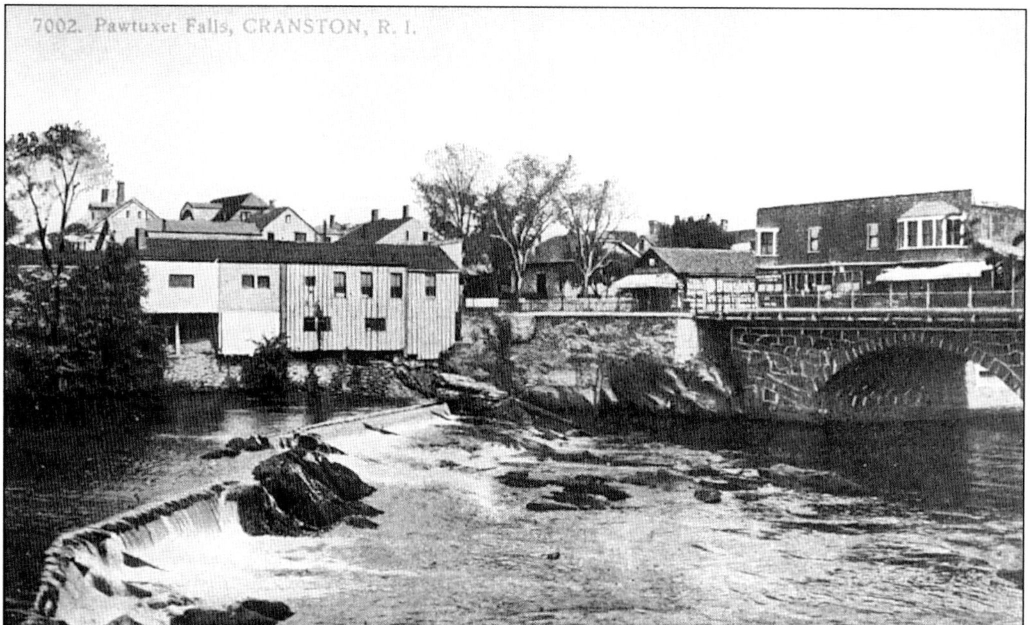

THE PAWTUXET FALLS AND BRIDGE, C. 1908. Before a bridge was constructed, the only way to cross the Pawtuxet River at this point was by ferry. The bridge in this photo was constructed of stone and completed in 1810. The center building is Frank Johnson's fruit store; it also housed a poolroom, a barbershop, a variety store, and, later in the era, a hay and grain store.

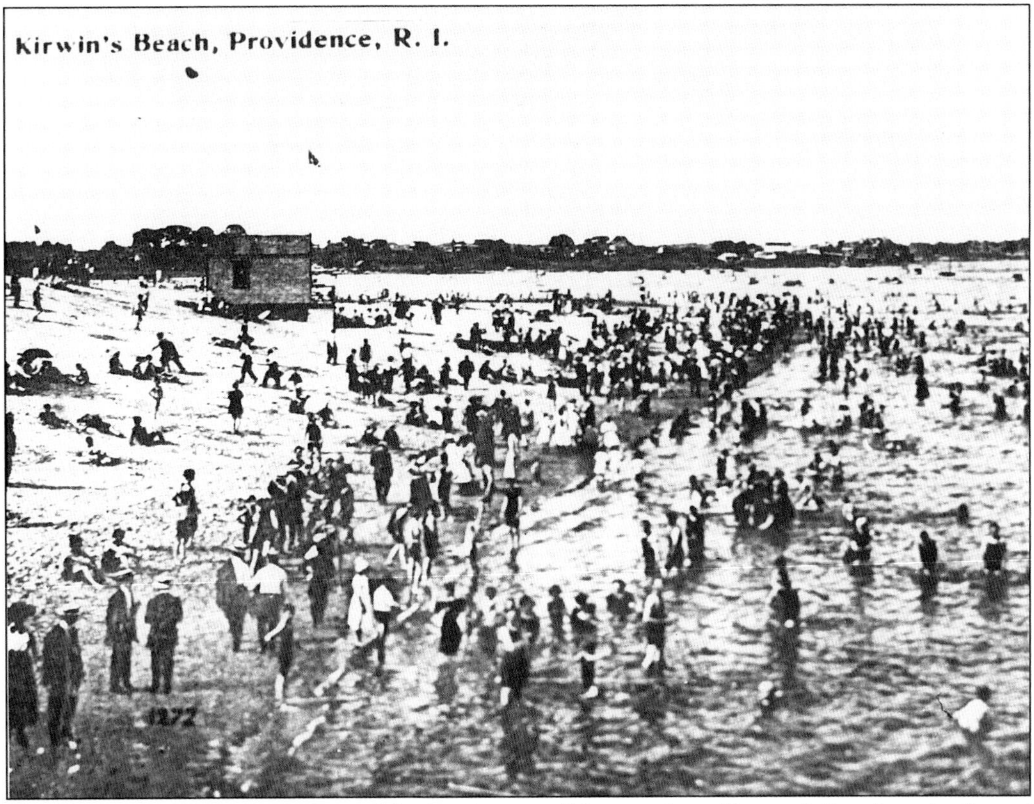

Kerwin's Beach, c. 1904. One of the big draws to Edgewood was Kerwin's Beach at the foot of Smith Avenue. For a nickel, bathers could use a bathhouse to change into their bathing suits.

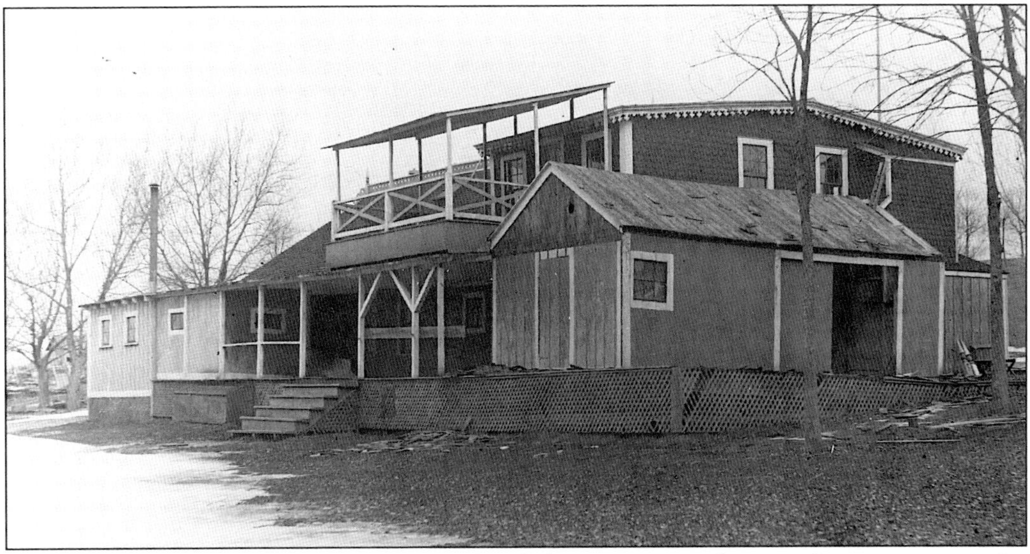

A Clam Pavilion at Rhodes, c. 1920. Clam bakes, picnics, and carnivals were very popular with beach-goers. Thomas Rhodes was the bake master until he bought this clam pavilion (or one similar) and had it moved to his property on the Pawtuxet River. Later he developed it into Rhodes-on-the-Pawtuxet.

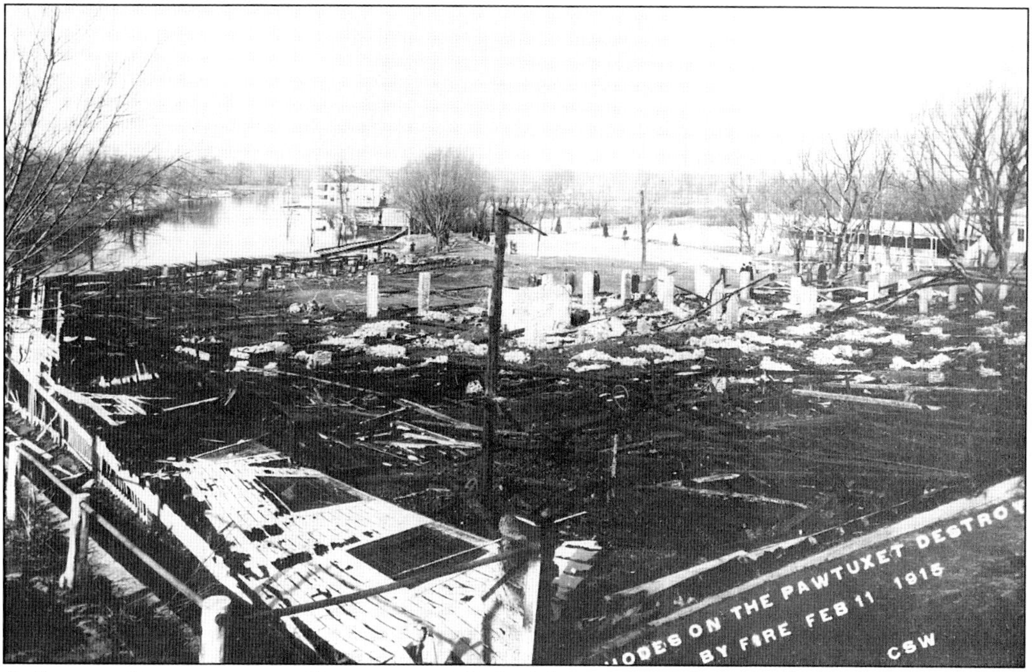

A Fire at Rhodes-on-the-Pawtuxet, 1915. After moving the clam house to his property in 1898, Thomas Rhodes added another story to the building. He offered music and dancing for his customers' pleasure. His sons inherited the dance hall after his death and made many improvements. On February 11, 1915, a fire consumed most of the Rhodes casino.

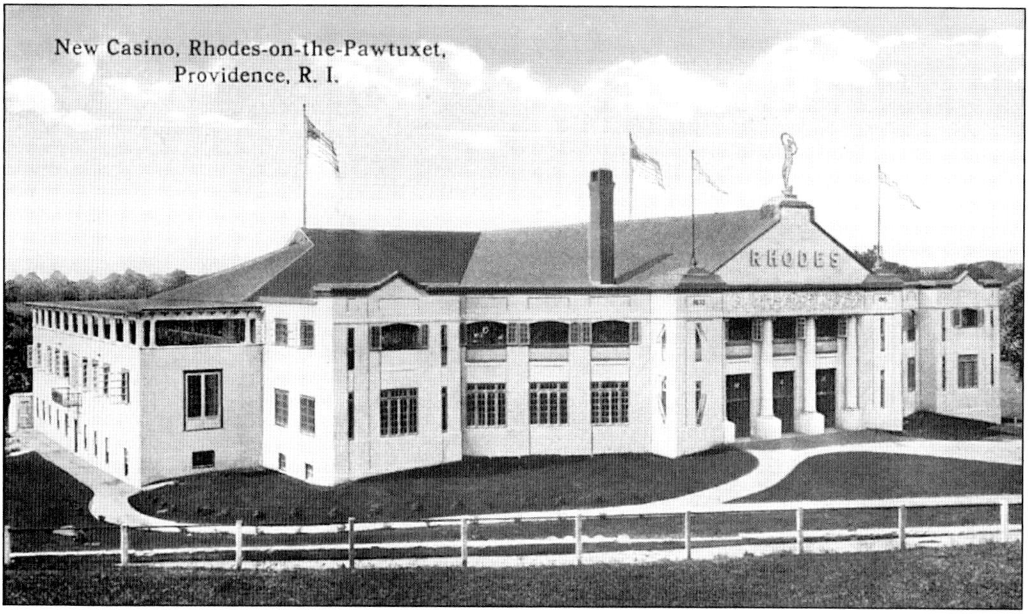

Rhodes-on-the-Pawtuxet, the New Casino, c. 1915. It took the Rhodes brothers four months to construct the present casino on the site of the old building. The new casino opened in August 1915 as "Palais du Dance" with 10,000 in attendance. (Lydia Rapoza Collection.)

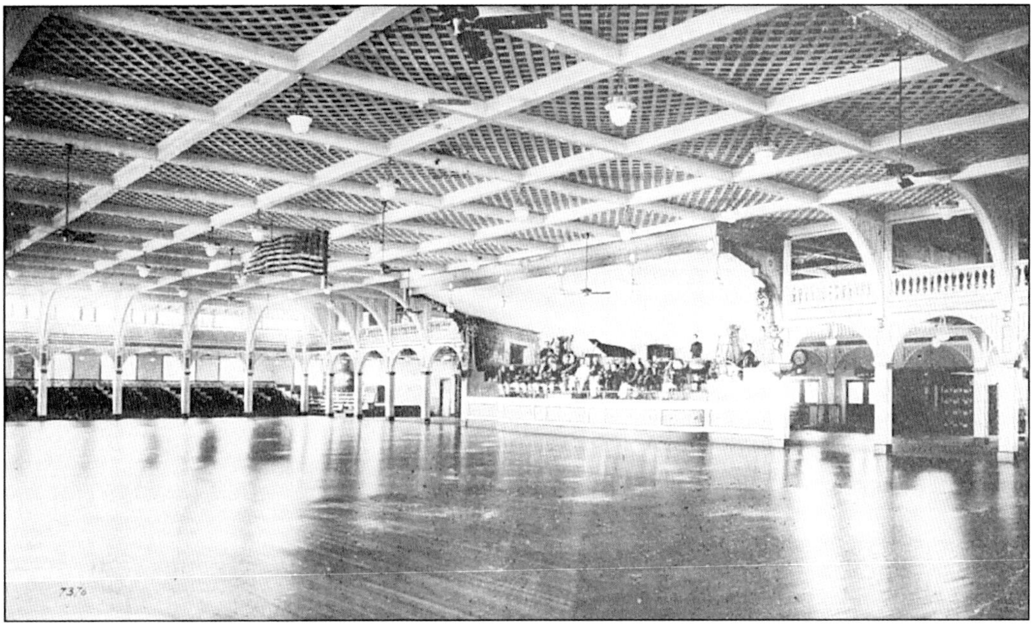

The Grand Ballroom at Rhodes-on the-Pawtuxet, c. 1920. Many young women have felt like queens at their proms as they glided across the dance floor at Rhodes. It is the oldest dance hall in the state and such performers as Glenn Miller and Guy Lombardo appeared here in its glory days. Today the ballroom retains much of its charm.

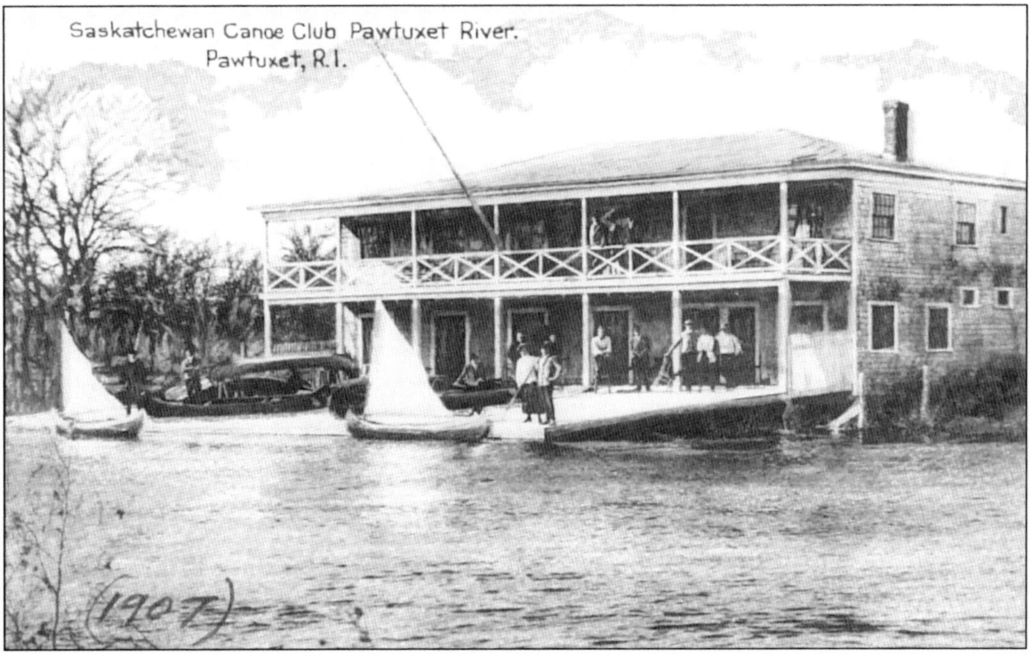

The Saskatchewan Canoe Club, c. 1907. Canoe clubs, like the Saskatchewan, Swastika, and Cayugus, had their hey-days in the early 1900s, meeting their peak in 1929. The clubs had friendly competitions. Long before Providence's popular Water Fire, red fire was set off from boats on the Pawtuxet. Firework displays lit up the sky over Cranston and Warwick in 1903 to celebrate a canoe carnival on the Pawtuxet.

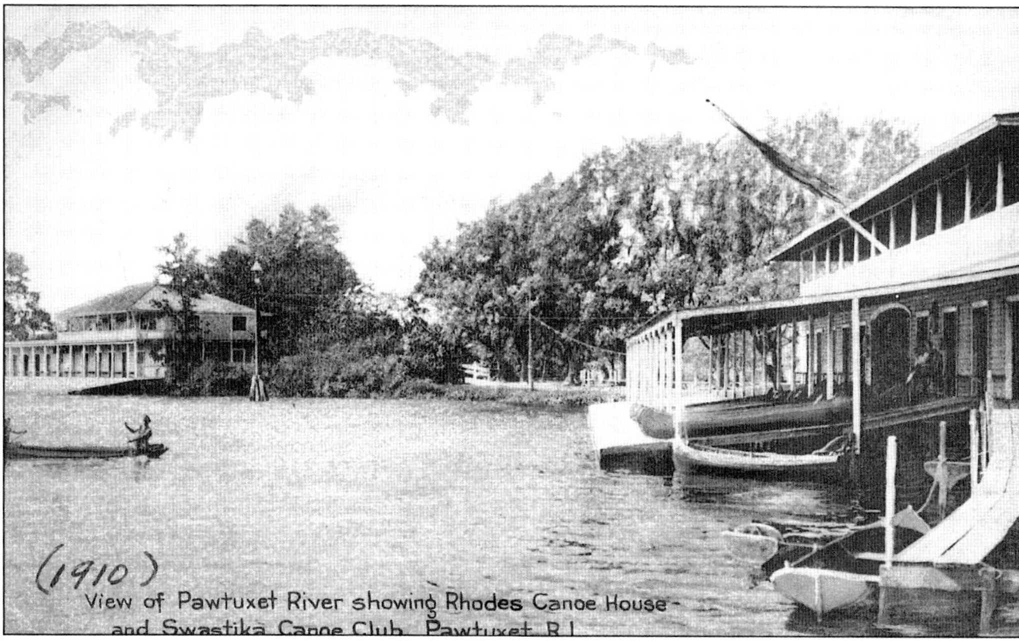

THE RHODES CANOE HOUSE AND THE SWASTIKA CANOE HOUSE, C. 1910. The heat of the Christmas Day fire of 1913 at the Swastika Club was so intense that it melted ice in the river. The Pawtuxet Volunteer Fire Company and the Edgewood Volunteer Fire Company did what they could, battling the blaze for more than two hours, but to no avail.

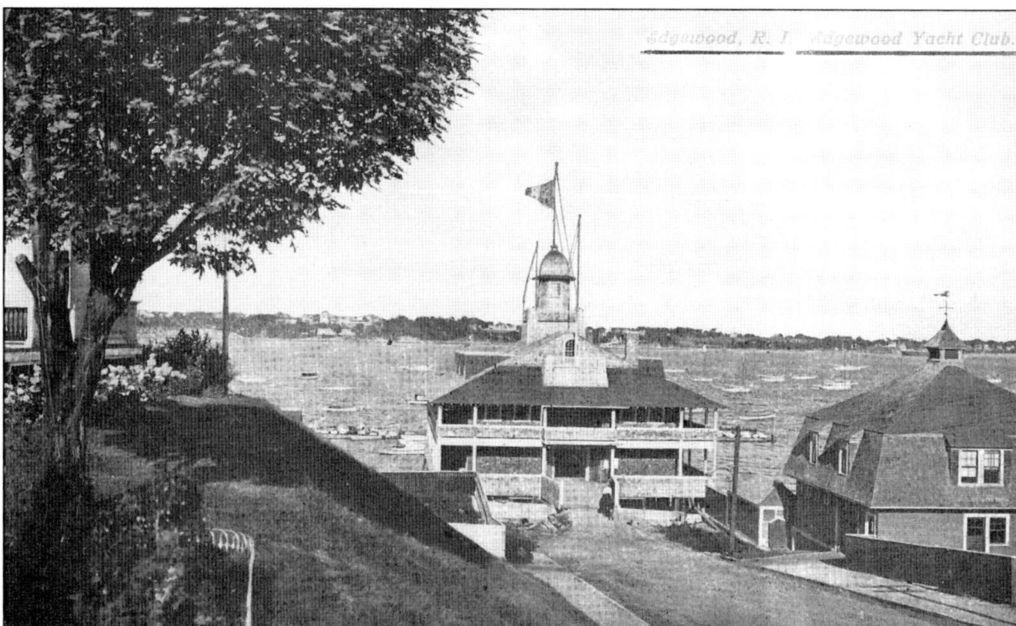

THE EDGEWOOD YACHT CLUB, C. 1940. The Edgewood Boat Club, as it was originally known, was founded in 1885 by 12 local families. Three yacht clubs lined the banks of the Narragansett Bay. Only the Edgewood and Rhode Island clubs survive today, and they have had to rebuild and improve their buildings due to fires and hurricanes.

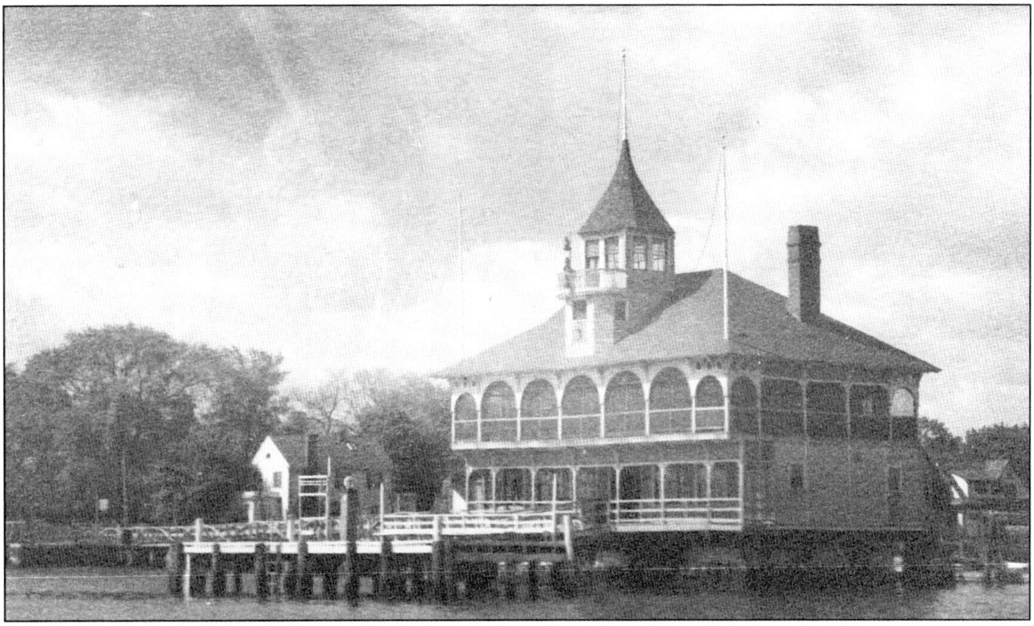

The Rhode Island Yacht Club, c. 1920. The club was incorporated in 1877 as the Providence Boat Club. Ten years later they changed its name to the Rhode Island Yacht Club and began to build a boathouse just north of Sassafras Point. Some time later they built another clubhouse at Stillhouse Cove on Great Rock.

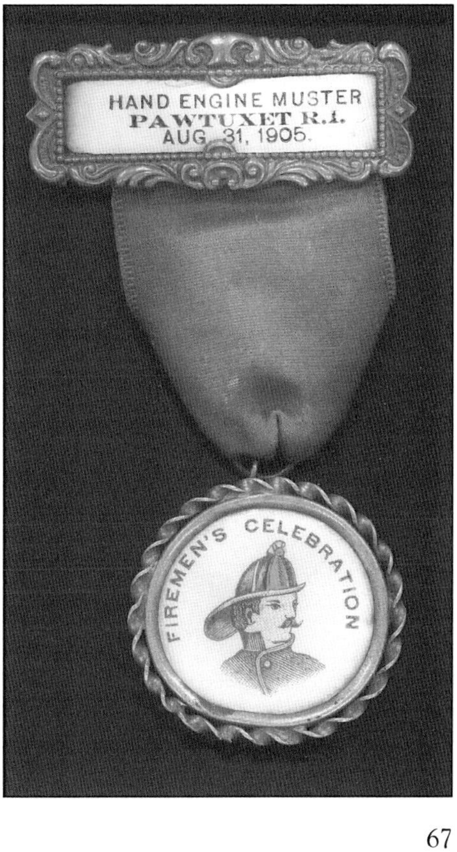

Firemen's Day at Pawtuxet, August 31, 1905. As part of the "Old Home Week" celebration, a Firemen's Day was held. A big crowd turned out for the parade. Firemen's Day was the best attended event of the week-long celebration. The Knightsville Fire Company won the "Squirt" competition, with a squirt of 165 feet and 5 inches! (Lydia Rapoza Collection.)

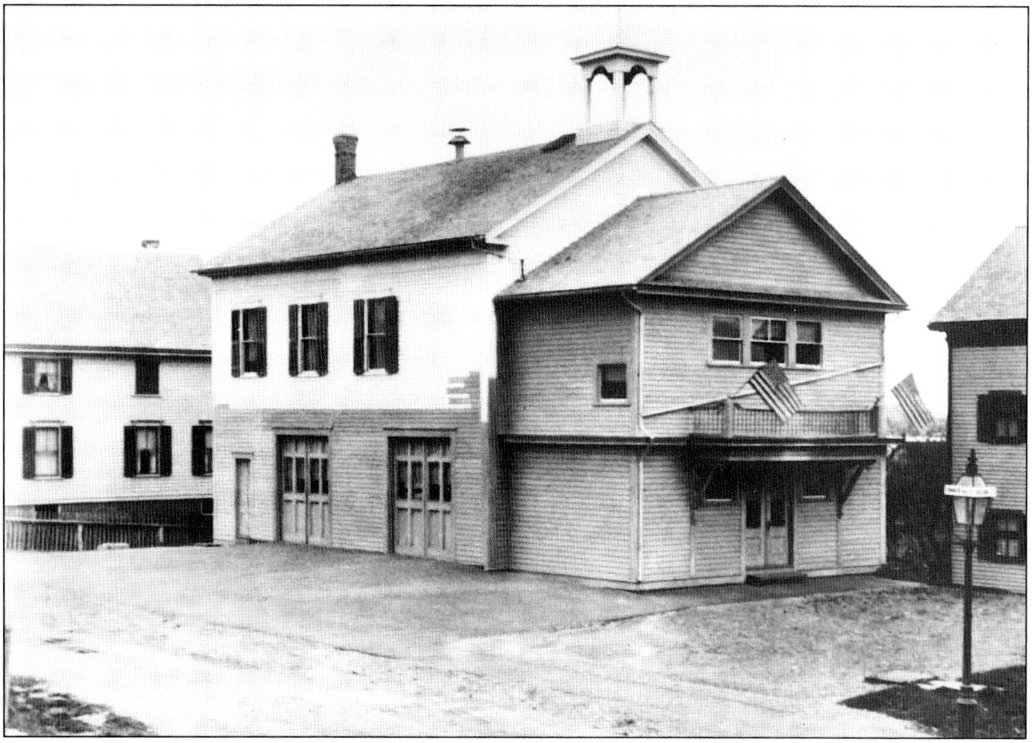

The Pawtuxet Volunteer Fire Company Headquarters, c. 1897. The Pawtuxet Volunteer Fire Company purchased the Commercial Street School for $50 and moved it to the corner of Commercial and Sheldon Streets. The firemen bought the school to house their new engine, the Fire King. Many fund-raisers were held to pay for improvements to the station and to the school building. In order to build a garage for the Fire King the school was raised and a garage was built underneath.

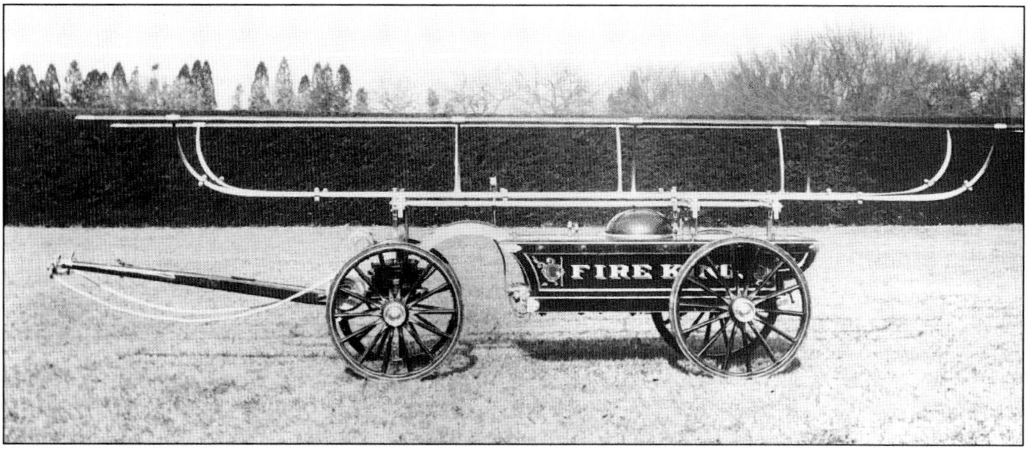

The Fire King, c. 1892. The Pawtuxet Volunteer Company purchased the Fire King hand engine from a fire company in Connecticut. Soon after, they bought the Commercial Street School building to house the Fire King. When they were not busy fighting fires, working on the fire station, or having fund-raisers, the volunteers were training with the Fire King. They won state championship musters three times and in 1906 won the New England championship. In 1916 they won over $4,000 in prize money.

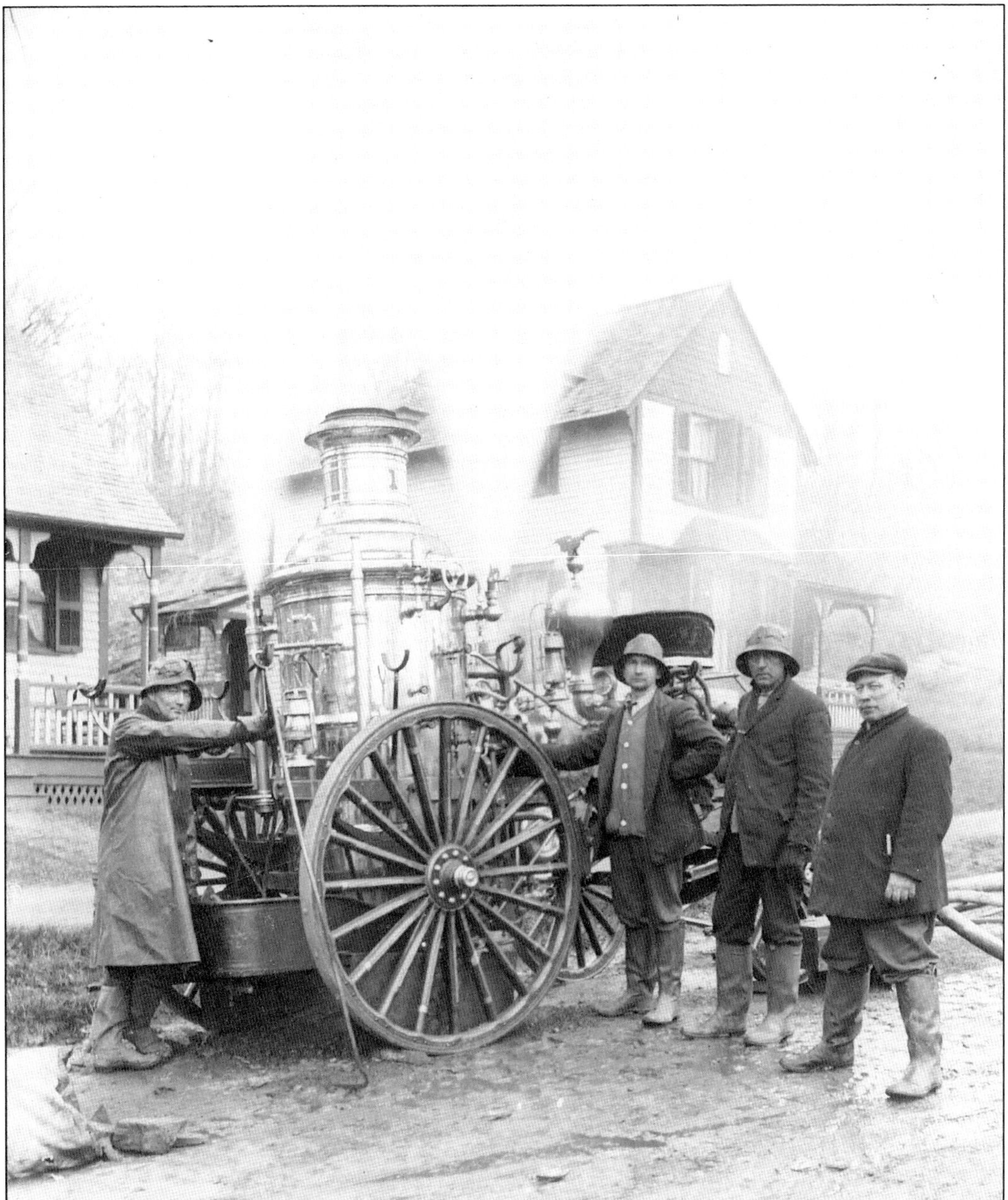

The Pawtuxet Volunteer Fire Company with a Horse-drawn Steam-powered Fire Engine, c. 1880. Steam-powered fire engines were first made about 1859 and were widely used until the advent of gasoline-powered apparatuses in the early 1900s. The disastrous fire at the C.G. Bloomer and Company jewelry shop in the winter of 1891 caused the Pawtuxet Volunteer Fire Company to be formed. The company had 32 members and was the predecessor of all fire departments in Cranston. Their apparatus was a hose reel that they pushed in shifts. Albert Potter, president of the Rhode Island Company (the trolley car company), issued orders to the motormen to hitch the fire apparatus to the back of trolley cars. The trolley would then rush the apparatus to the area of the fire. In 1910 this fire company was the first motorized company in the state thanks to the trolley cars.

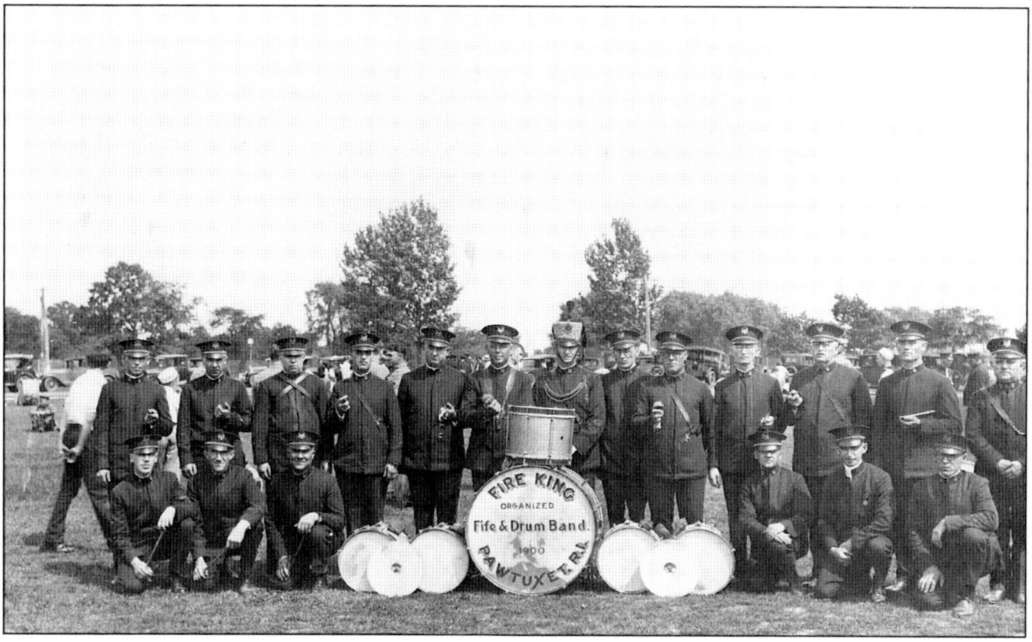

THE FIRE KING FIFE AND DRUM BAND, 1900. This band was organized on February 24, 1900, to provide music for the Pawtuxet Volunteer Fire King muster team when they paraded at musters. It had the distinction of being the only fife and drum band to march and play on the field at the West Point Military Academy. The last meeting of the band was held in North Kingston in 1958.

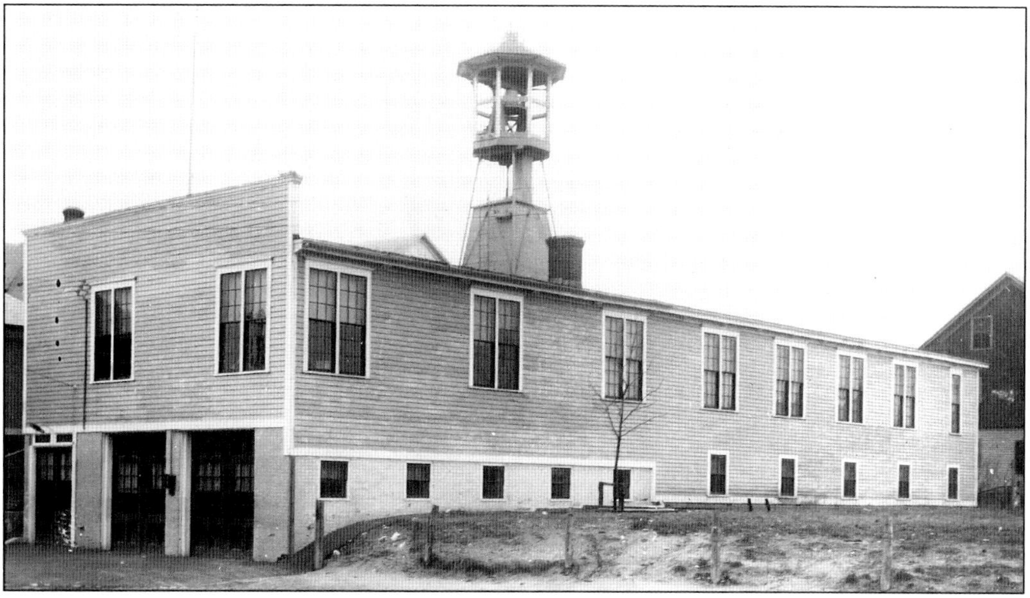

THE EDGEWOOD VOLUNTEER FIRE COMPANY STATION, C. 1920. Prior to 1920, all fire protection in Cranston was provided by volunteer fire companies that were situated in various areas and villages of the city. The Pawtuxet Volunteer Fire Company and the Edgewood Volunteer Fire Company on Pawtuxet were two of the 11 fire companies that were operating in the 1920s.

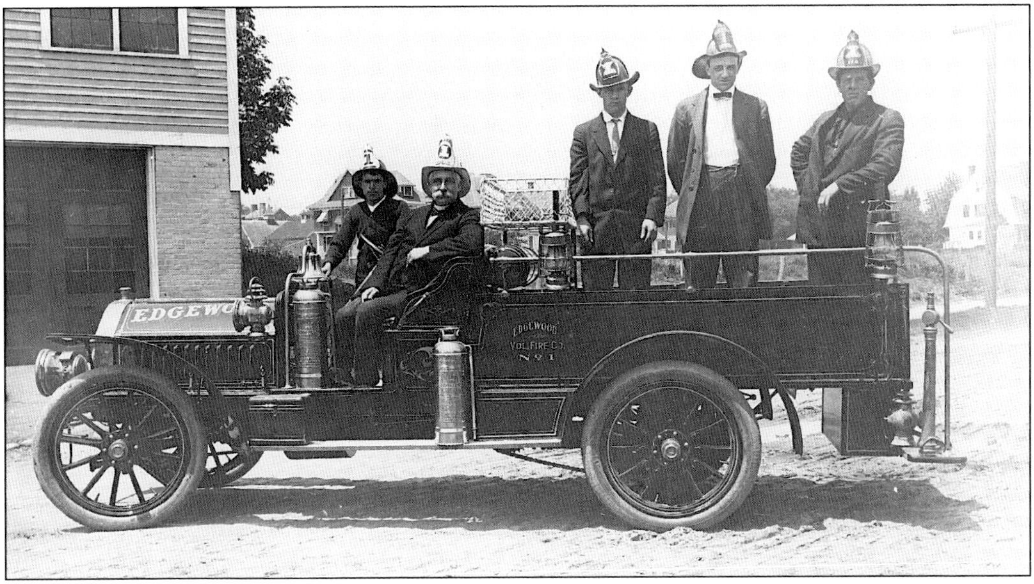

The Edgewood Volunteer Fire Company, c. 1920. The proud crew of Engine No. 1 consisted of driver Archie Hebb, Captain Charles Vanstone, an unknown fireman, Albert Wilson, and James Gilbert.

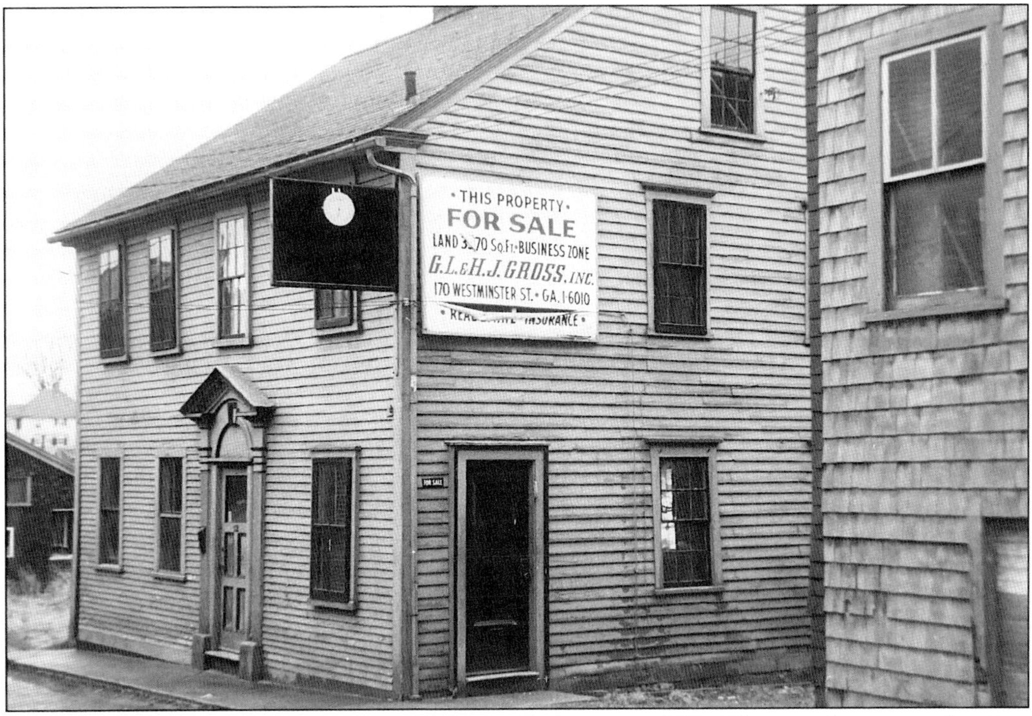

The Remington Arnold House, 12 Bridge Street, c. 1950. This is a fine example of an early 18th-century, two-and-one-half-story house. It was the home of Remington Arnold, a prominent trader in the days when Pawtuxet was an active seaport. Built about 1730, it has a large central chimney and a very handsome doorway.

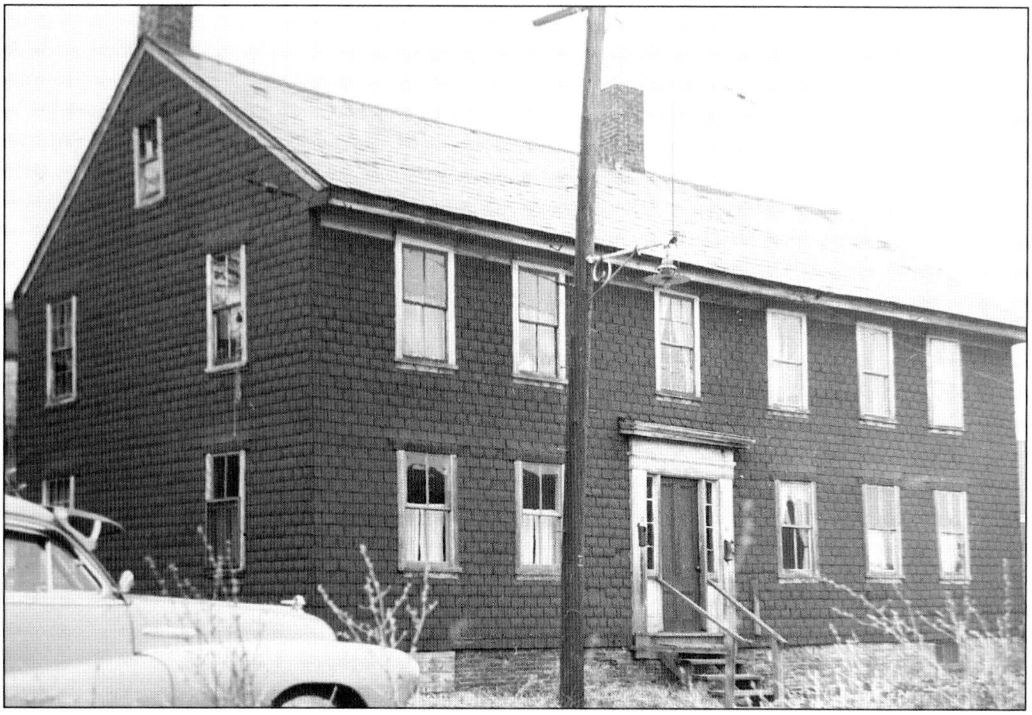

THE ABORN TAVERN, BRIDGE STREET, C. 1952. The Anthony Aborn Tavern was a stagecoach stop on the route to Providence. Harmony Lodge No. 9 F&AM of Pawtuxet was organized here on April 12, 1805, and the Pawtuxet Artillery frequently met here. Anthony and Lydia Aborn served "big dinners with plenty of punch," according to Horatio Nelson Slocum, a member of the artillery. The tavern was torn down in 1954.

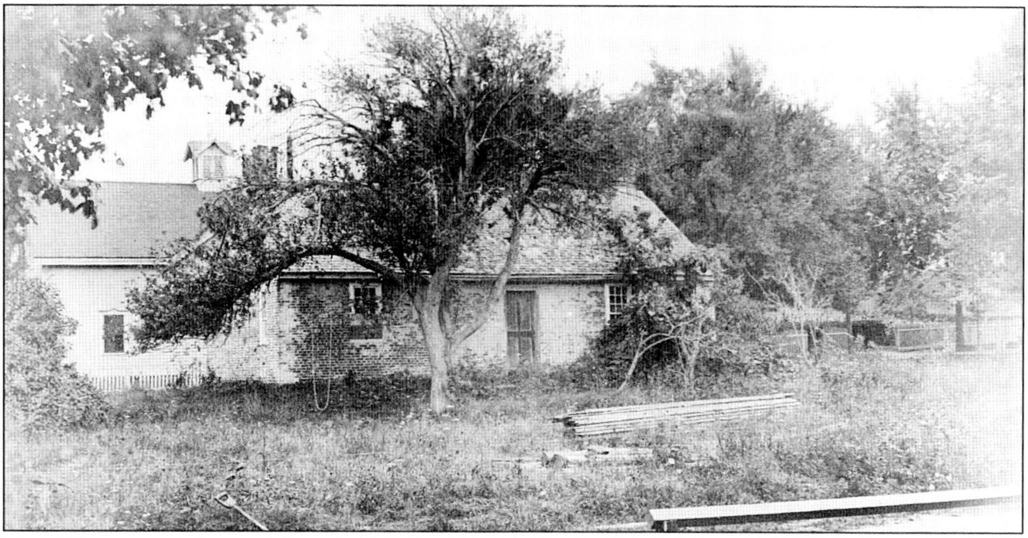

THE WATERMAN SMITH HOUSE, C. 1896. Located on the corner of Ocean and Fort Avenues in Pawtuxet, this house was built sometime previous to 1815 and was torn down in 1896. Fort Avenue was named when a fort was built nearby in 1775, before the American War of Independence. It was manned by the Pawtuxet Rangers in December 1776 and again during the War of 1812, but was gone by 1896.

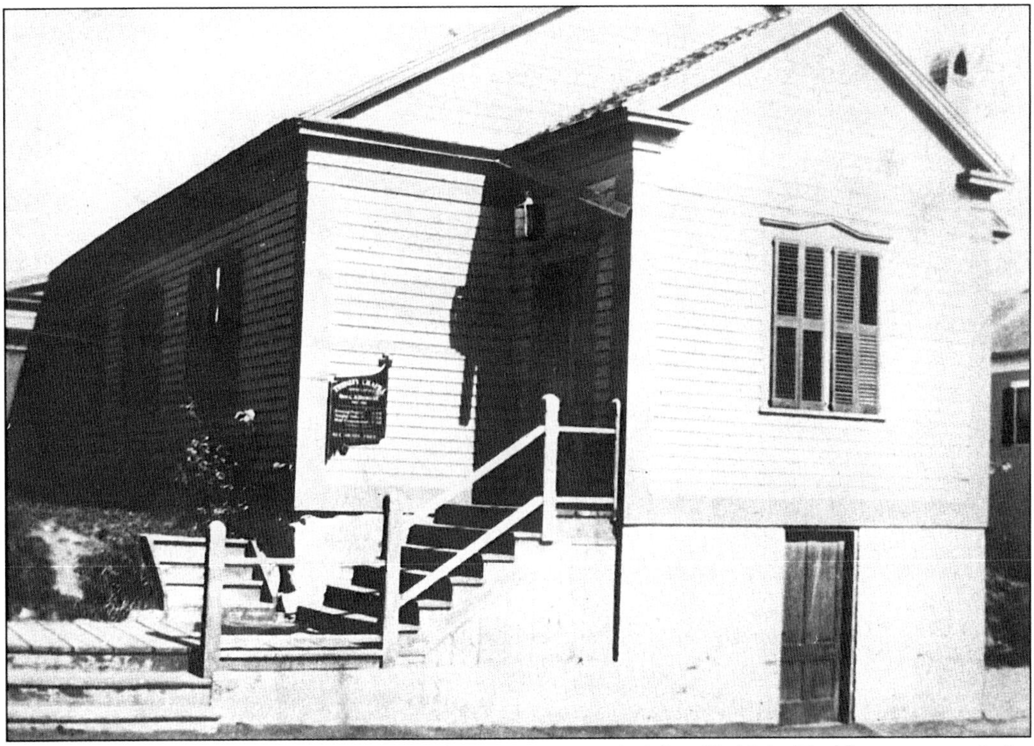

Old Trinity Chapel at 12 Sheldon Street, c. 1900. Miss Huldah Sheldon proposed the name "Trinity Chapel" and it was unanimously adopted. This was a mission church of the Grace Church in Providence. The first service was held here August 12, 1883.

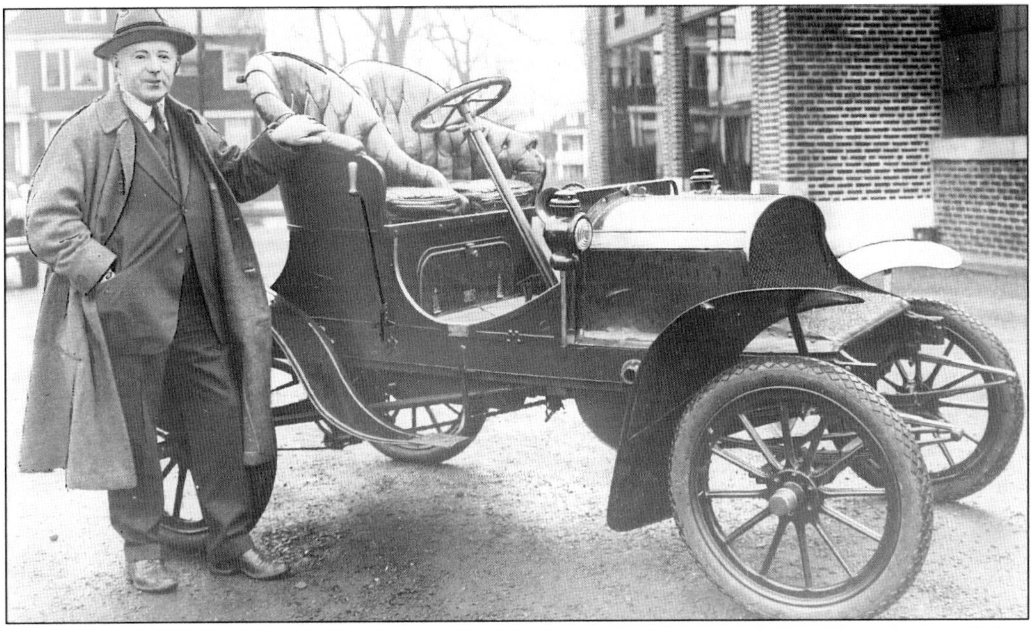

Wallace L. Wilcox, 1904. Mr. Wilcox was a distributor of Franklin Automobiles. He is shown here standing in front of his dealership at 320 Broad Street with a 1904 Franklin Runabout.

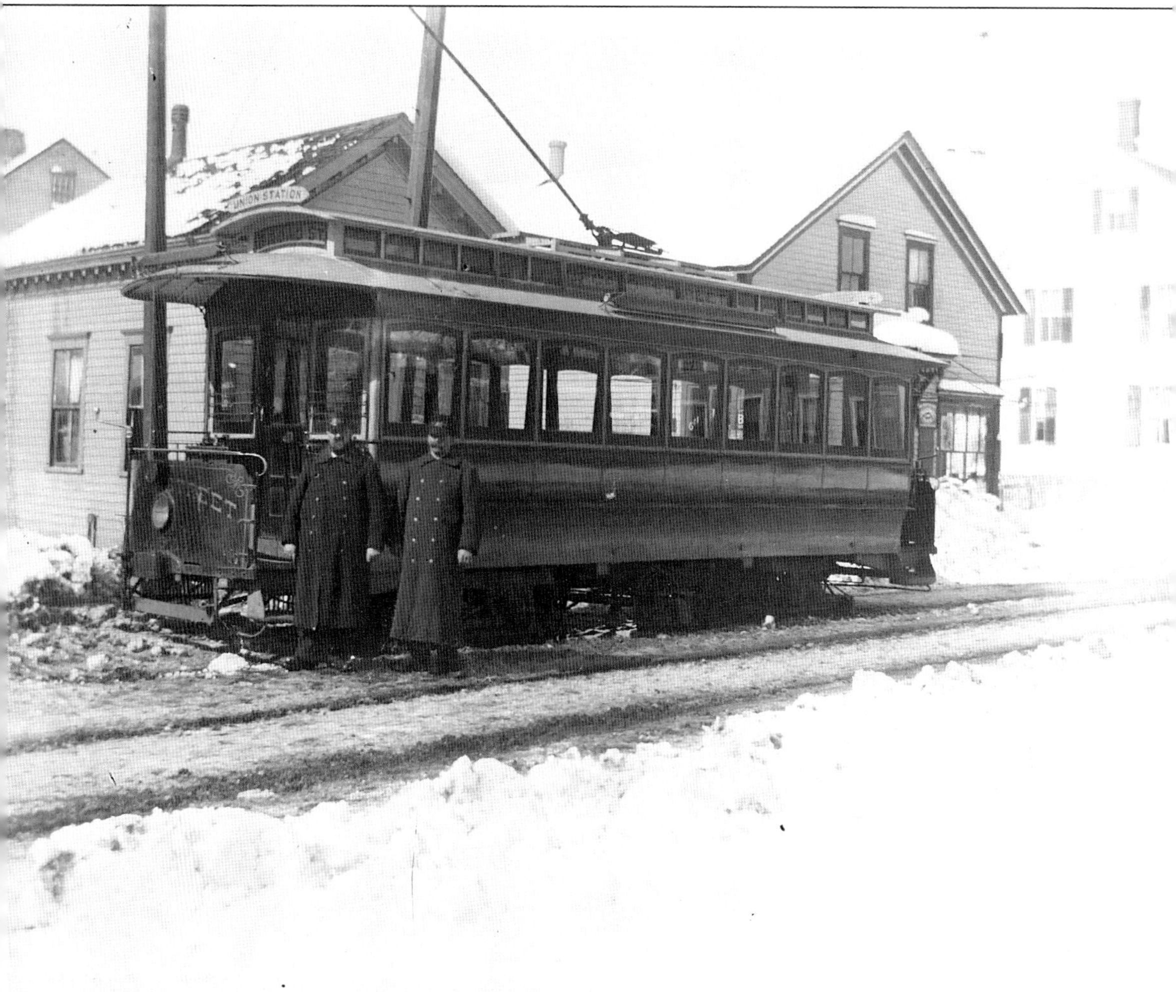

The Broad Street Trolley, c. 1900. These men are waiting for passengers to board a "winterized" trolley for a ride to Union Station in Providence. There are few people left who can claim to have experienced riding one of these "rolling gems."

Five

HOWARD AND PETTACONSETT

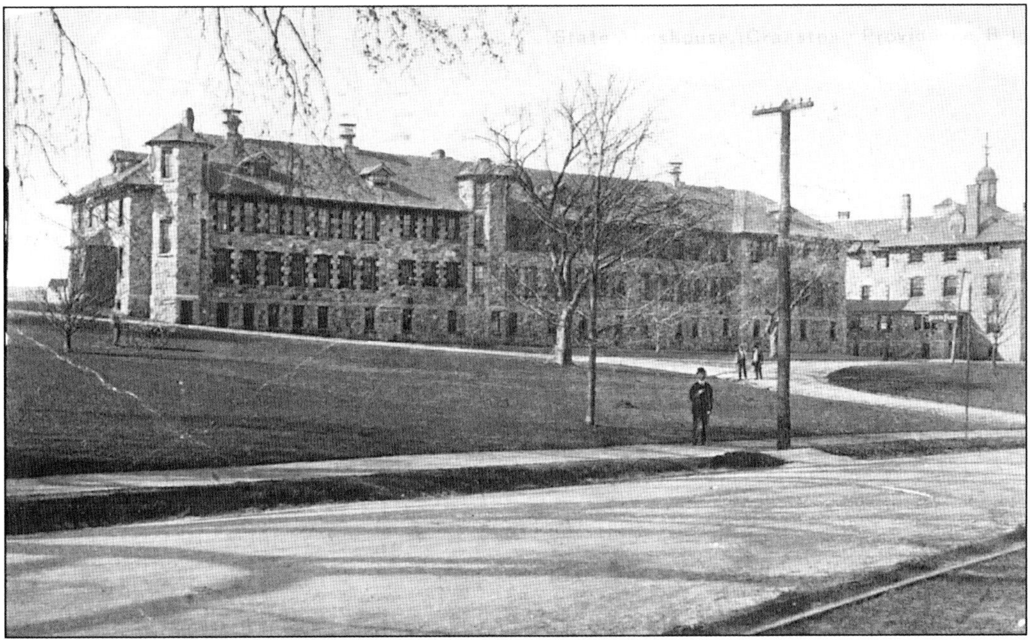

THE STATE ALMSHOUSE, C. 1911. This is the Howard Complex overlooking Pontiac Avenue. In 1888 the Rhode Island General Assembly appropriated funds for this building when it became apparent a new one was needed to replace the wooden framed building that had, up to that time, housed the mentally handicapped. This stone, three-and-one-half-story building opened for patients in 1890. The Almshouse was designed by Stone, Carpenter and Wilson.

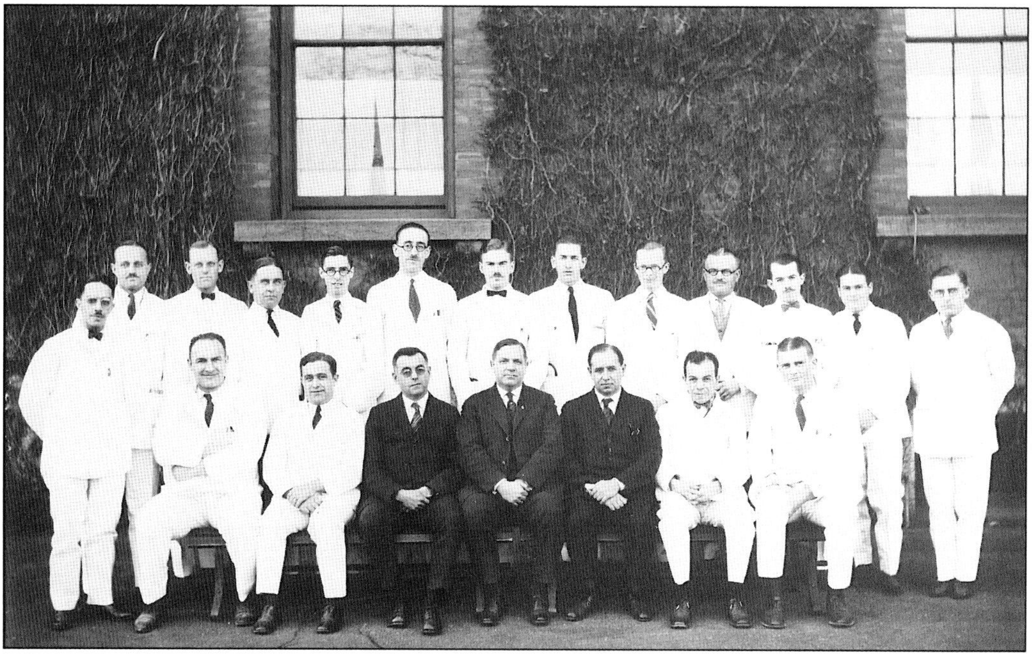

Dr. Niles Westcott (fifth from the left in the front row) and Attendants at the State Institution, c. 1930. In the 1860s, the State of Rhode Island purchased 417 acres of land in Cranston for use as a state farm. Later on more land was obtained to build the state prison, the general hospital, and the Howard Complex.

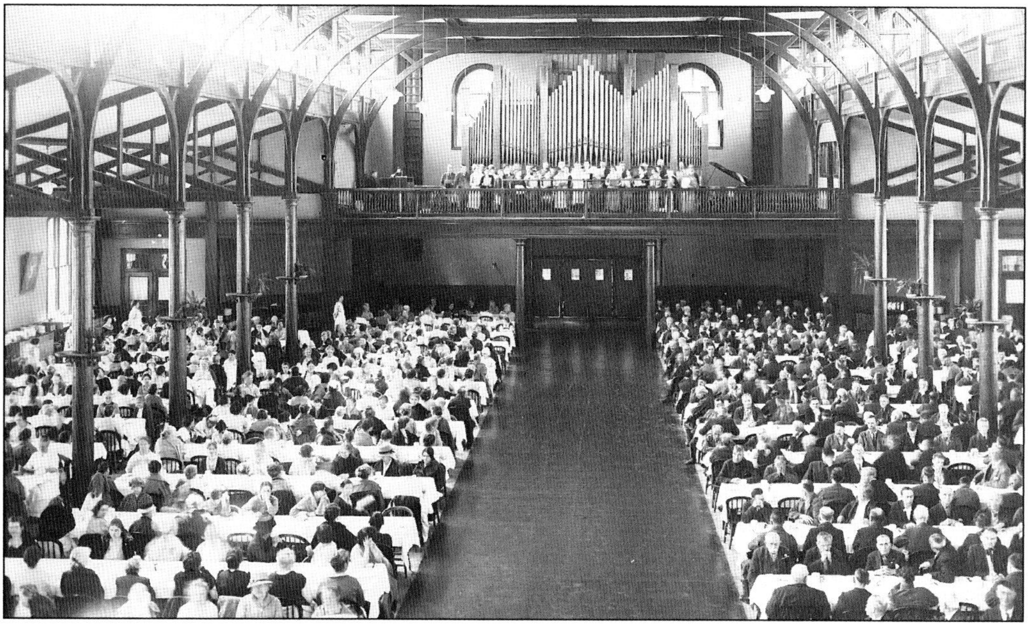

The Dining Hall at the State Hospital, 1926. Nearly 2,000 visitors attended the dedication of a new pipe organ on May 26, 1926, at the Congregate Dining Hall. The money used to pay for the organ was raised by voluntary subscriptions. On another occasion, the choir, under the direction of Dr. Arthur Harrington, traveled to the Outlet Company Building in Providence to perform on WJAR radio.

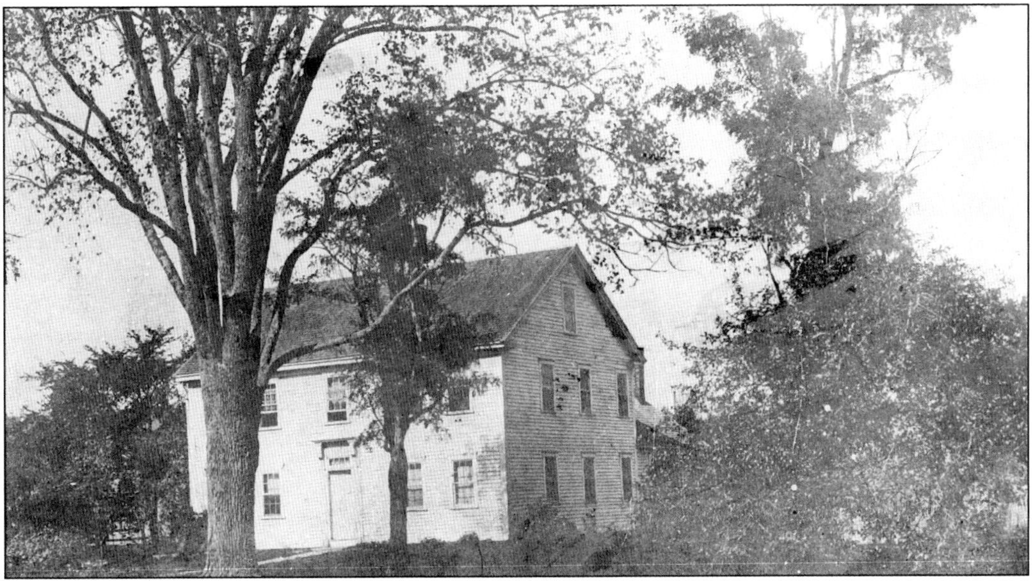

The Budlong Homestead, Pontiac Avenue, and Sockanosett Crossroads, c. 1930. This was the ancestral home of the Budlong family. At one time an upper room of this house served as a school. One of the Budlong daughters, Kate, married Daniel Burlingame and lived here. The house was taken down in 1986 to make room for a Burger King, but each piece was numbered and re-assembled in the Buttonwoods section of Warwick.

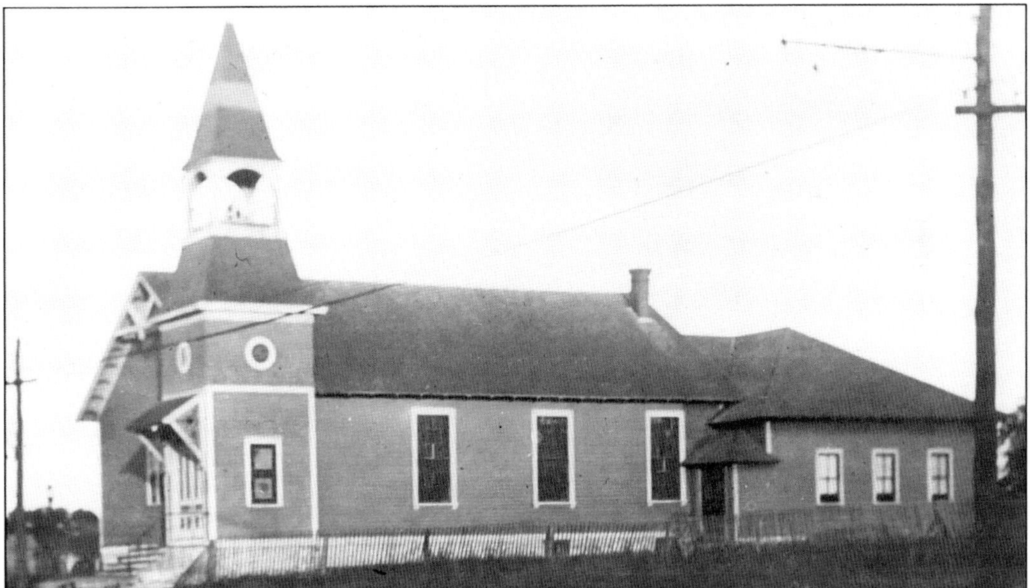

The Franklin Congregational Church, 1078 Pontiac Avenue, c. 1950. In 1922 the congregation of this church observed their 50th anniversary, and the Reverend Mr. Richard K. Wickett, who had been pastor from 1892 to 1911, was presented with the Bible from which he had preached. Herbert Durfee, the only surviving originator of the church, was also a speaker. In 1967 the congregation merged with the Knightsville Church. This church building is now an art gallery.

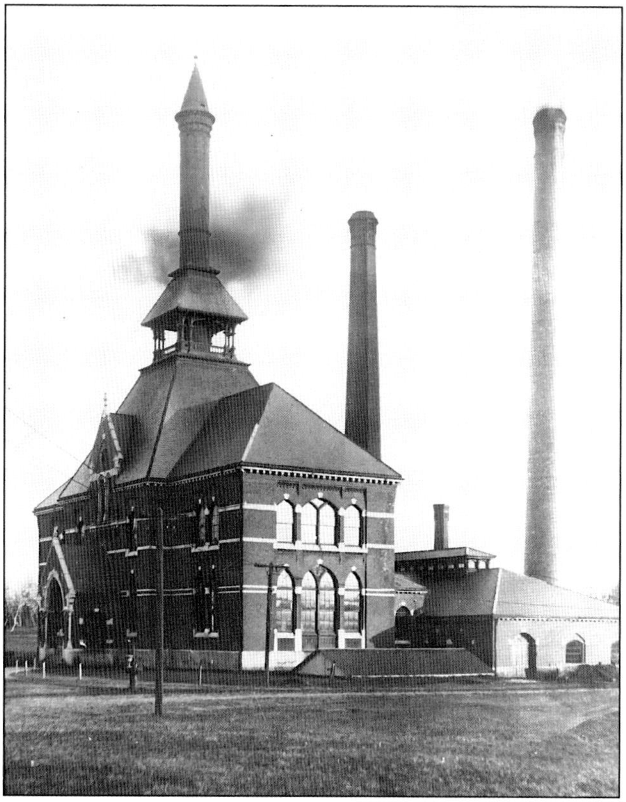

The Pettaconsett Pumping Station, c. 1920. In 1868 a central pumping station was built to utilize the water of the Pawtuxet River for the city of Providence. The capital city invested $500,000 in Cranston to complete the project. The station, which was capable of pumping 5 million gallons of water in 24 hours, went into service Thanksgiving Day 1871, and a great number of spectators turned out to witness the event.

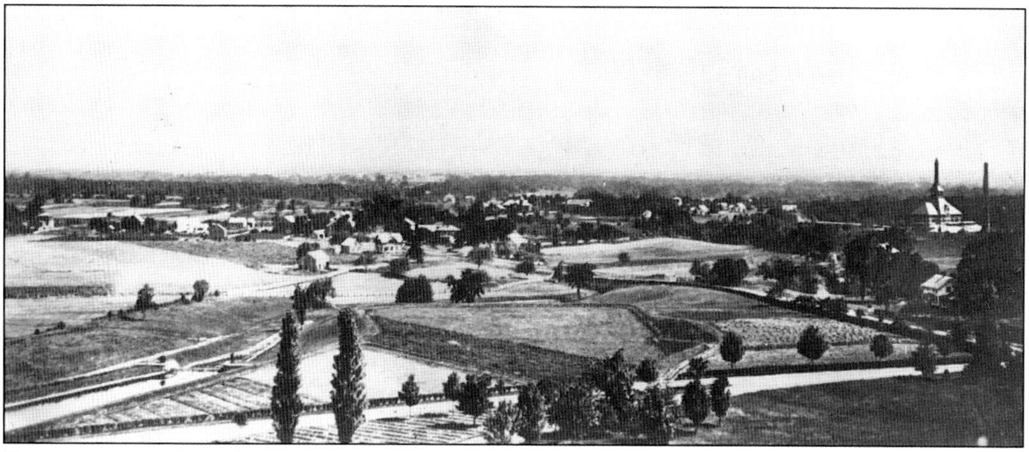

Sockanosett Hill, Site of the Pettaconsett Pumping Station, c. 1900. The opening of the Scituate Reservoir in the 1920s ended the need for the Pettaconsett Pumping Station and the Sockanosett Reservoir. A dynamite blast in 1933 razed the station. The reservoir was located across the street from Garden City. Reservoir Avenue was named after this project.

Six

KNIGHTSVILLE

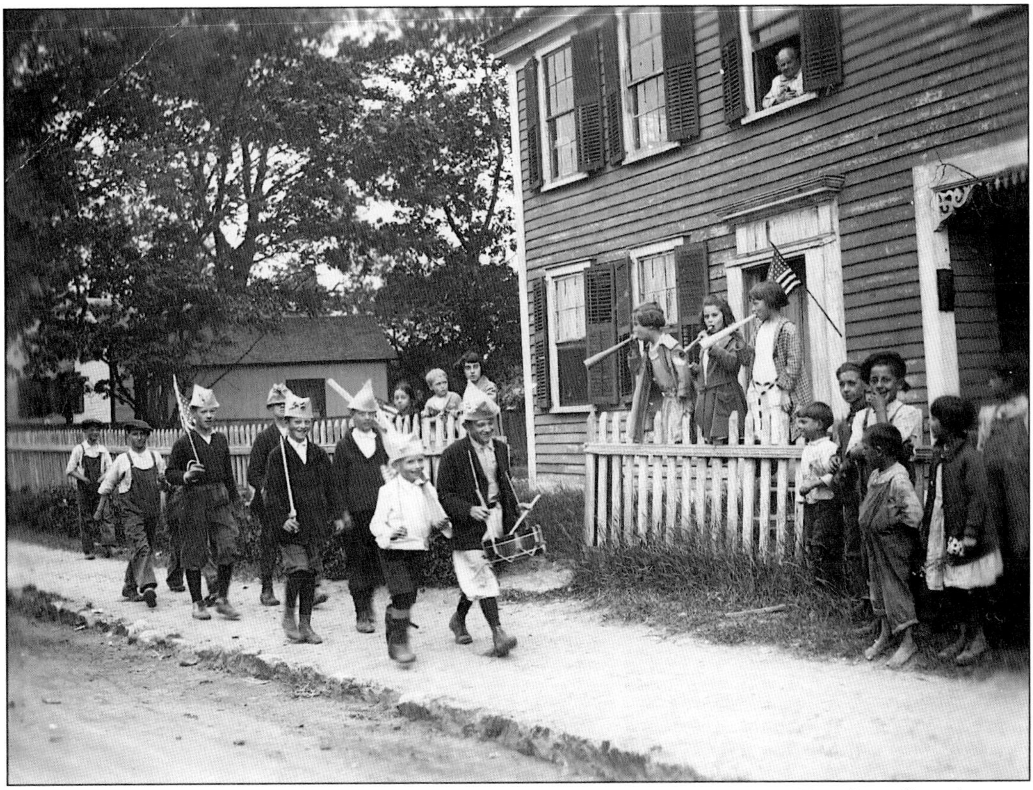

THE ALFRED BRIGGS HOUSE ON PHENIX AVENUE, FOURTH OF JULY, 1920. Knightsville is known to some residents as Monkeytown, and Cranston Street leading to Knightsville is sometimes referred to as Monkeytown Road. One legend has it that a local lad joined a seafaring voyage, and when he returned he brought back a most unusual creature with him—a monkey in a cage. People traveled from all over to see the animal. Monkeytown is hardly a respectable name for the community named after the Knight family, who owned much of the land and was dominant in state and local government.

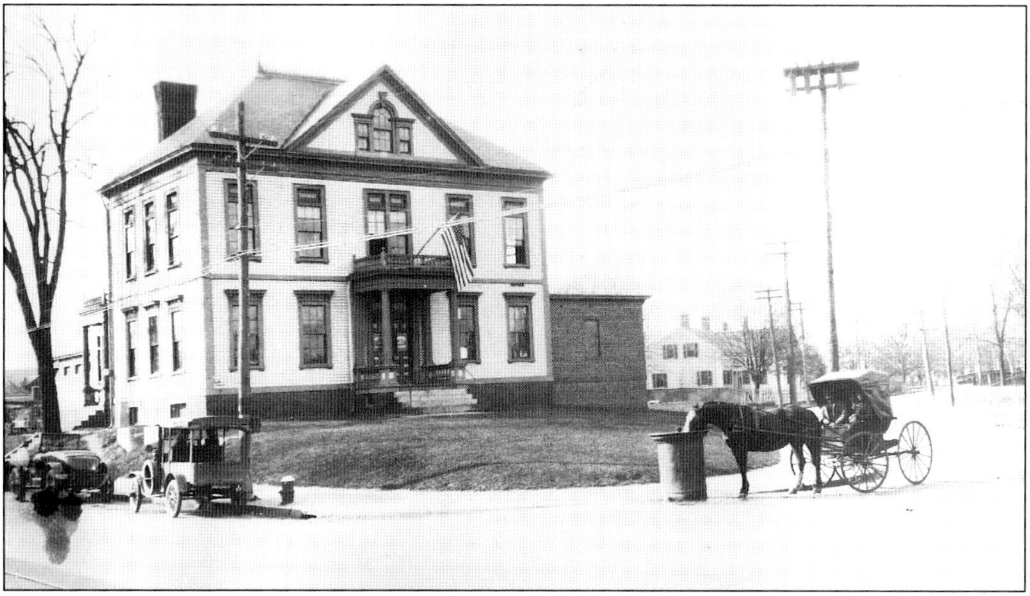

The Town Hall in Knightsville, Located at the Intersection of Cranston Street, Park Avenue, and Phenix Avenue, c. 1905. Town officials squabbled during much of the 18th century over where the center of government should be located. The A&W Sprague Company offered the use of the Brick Store on Cranston Street in Sprague's Village to serve as the town hall until they could decide. This building was built in 1886.

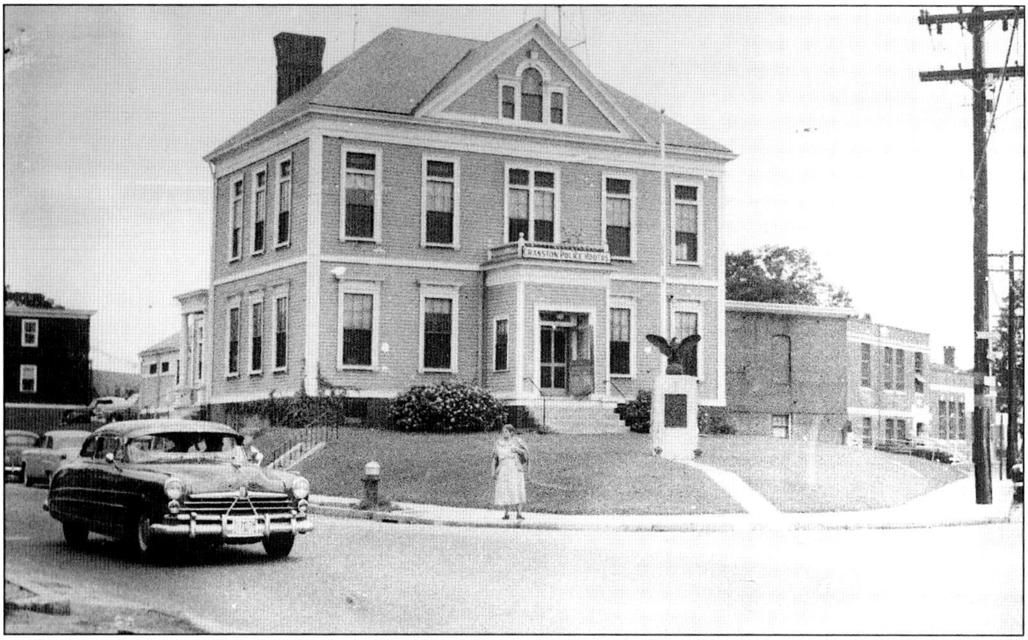

The City Hall in Knightsville, Formerly the Town Hall, August 10, 1954. Cranston voted to become a city in 1910, and the town hall was renamed city hall. The city hall sported an antenna and was home to the Cranston Police Department. The building was eventually demolished, and the Knightsville gazebo at Itri Square was built on its site.

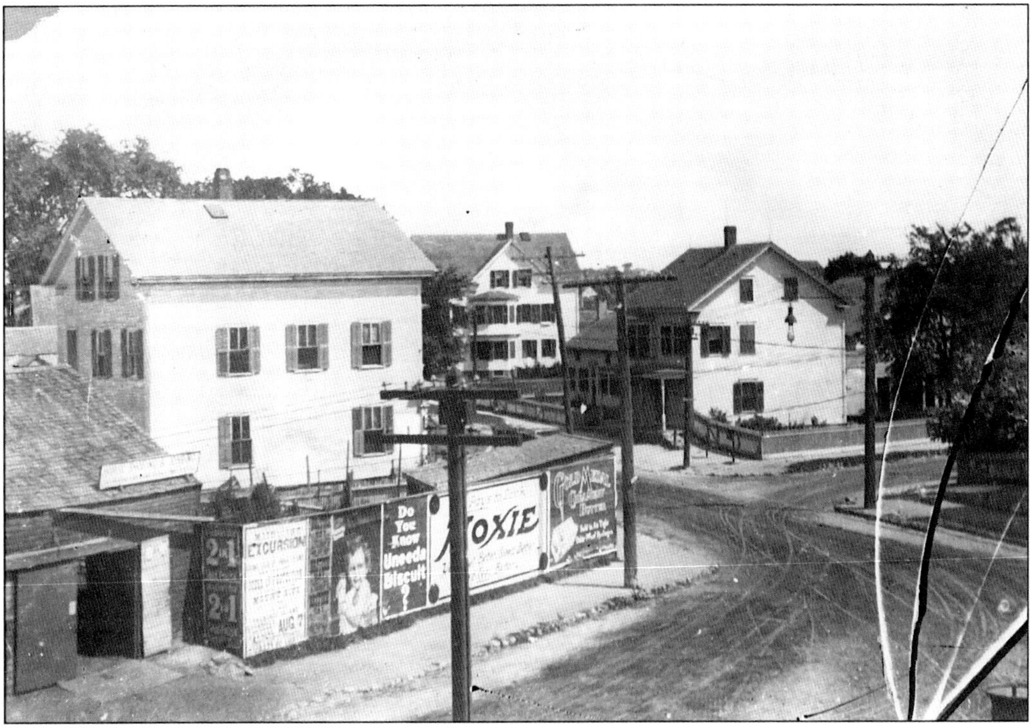

THE INTERSECTION OF CRANSTON STREET, PARK AVENUE, AND PHENIX AVENUE, C. 1910. A blacksmith shop is on the left of the picture. Across the street is a grocery store that was operated by George Hill. Note the wagon wheel tracks on the unpaved road. This picture was taken from a room in the old city hall.

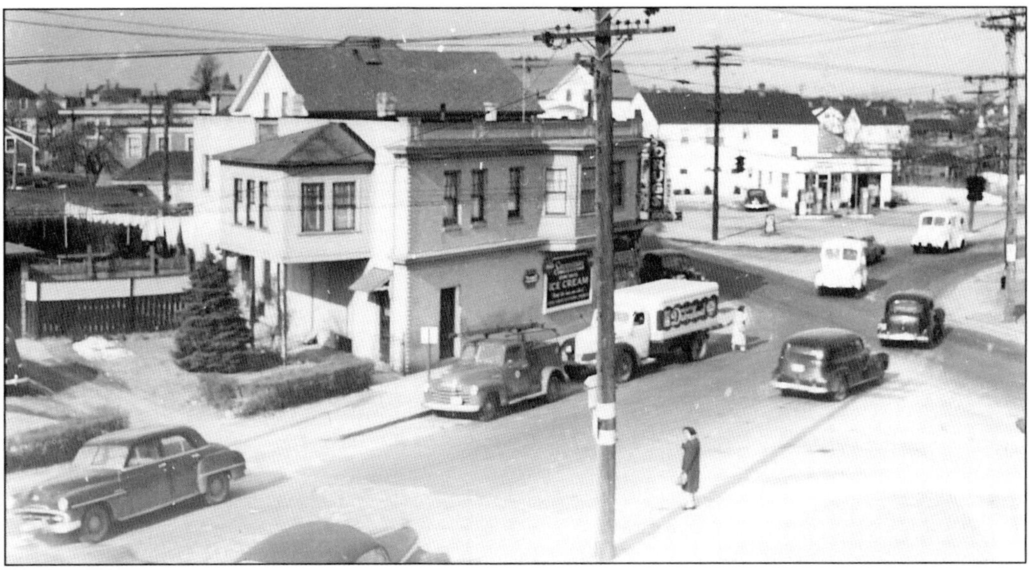

THE INTERSECTION OF CRANSTON STREET, PARK AVENUE, AND PHENIX AVENUE, C. 1950. The street has been widened and paved to accommodate the increase in automobile traffic.

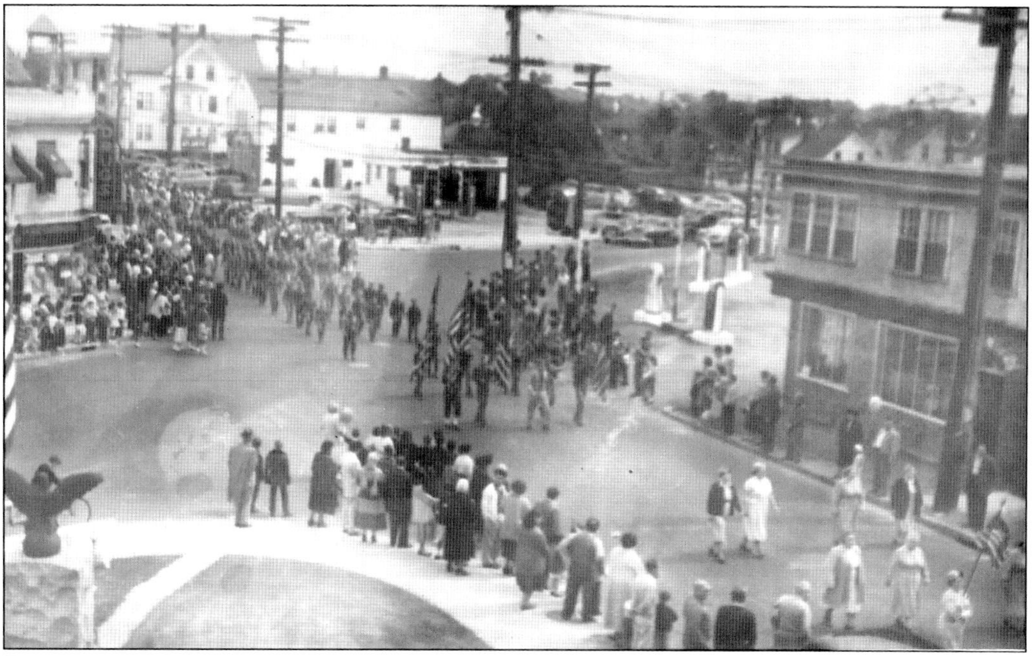

The Intersection of Cranston Street, Park Avenue, and Phenix Avenue, c. 1950. This photo, taken from a room in the old city hall, shows a parade heading south on Cranston Street.

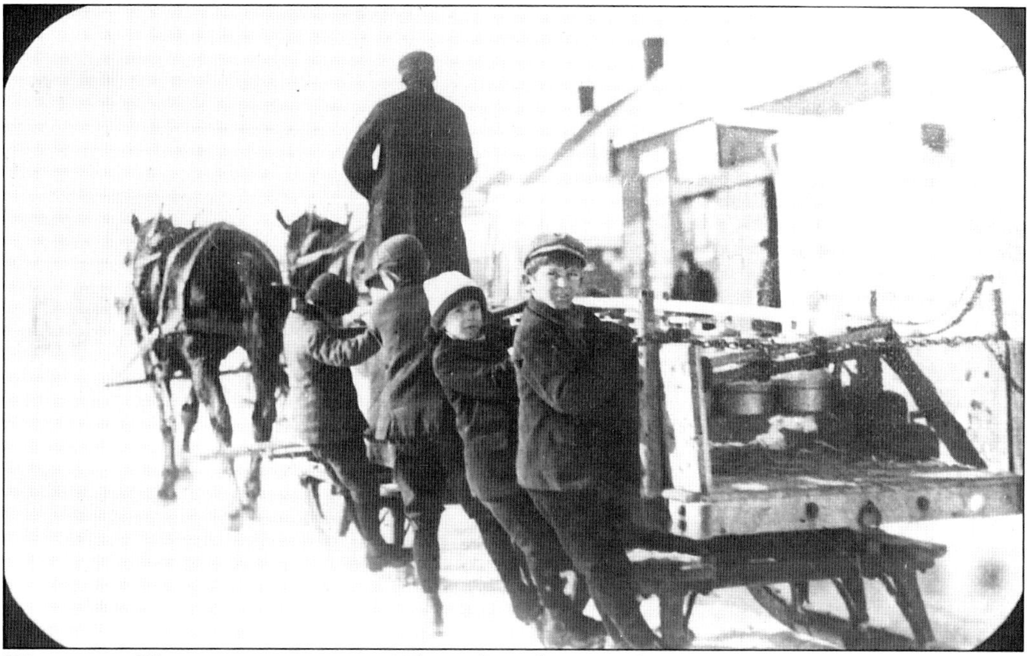

Winter in Knightsville, 1917. When this photograph was taken by Reverend Wilfred E. Stone in front of the old city hall police headquarters, motor vehicle owners had not yet begun to demand the streets be plowed immediately. John McLean's blacksmith shop is visible in the background.

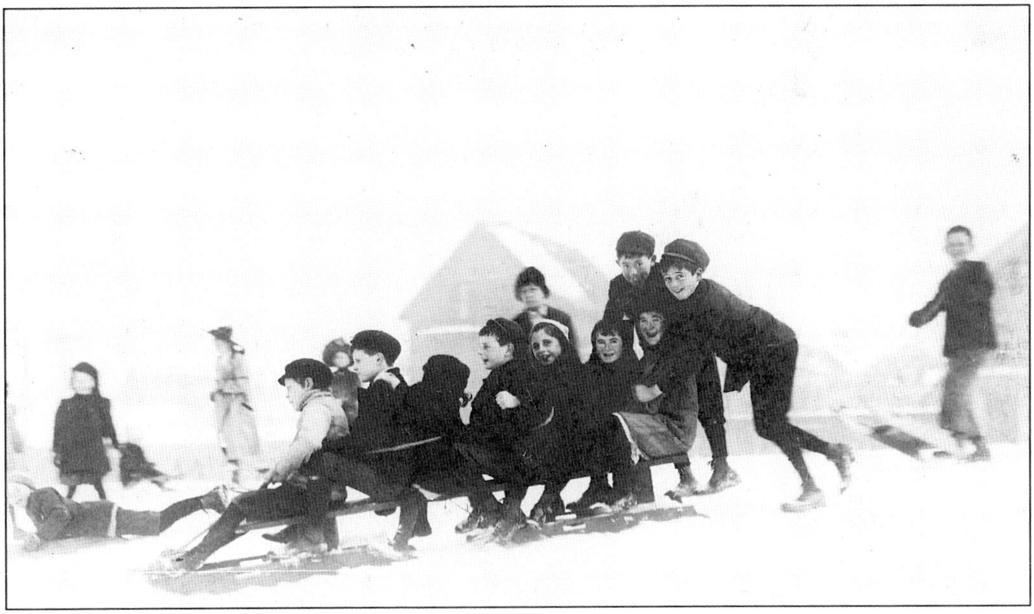

Winter in Knightsville, 1914. Wilfred Stone photographed these children on a hill in Knightsville taking advantage of the last boy, who has to push the sled to get it going. The girls, even while playing, wore skirts.

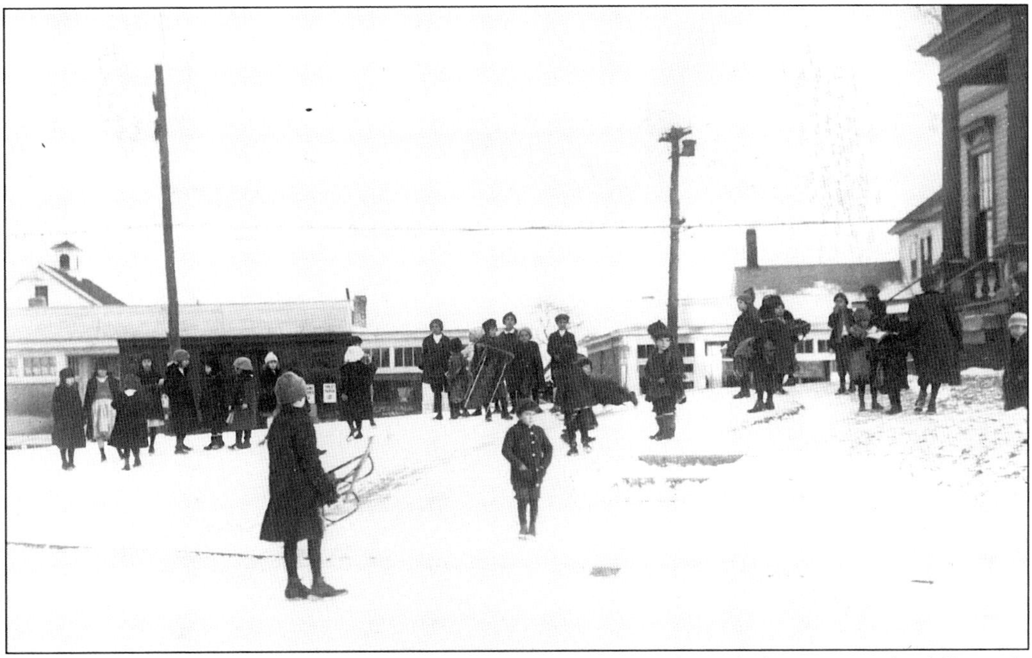

City Hall, Phenix Avenue, c. 1914. This was an era when sleds were made differently for boys and girls. Girls' sleds, called cutters, had decks that sat high on a framework above the runners. Cutters were built so that girls could ride sitting up, which prevented their undergarments from showing. Boys' sleds, called clippers, were low to the ground and good for racing.

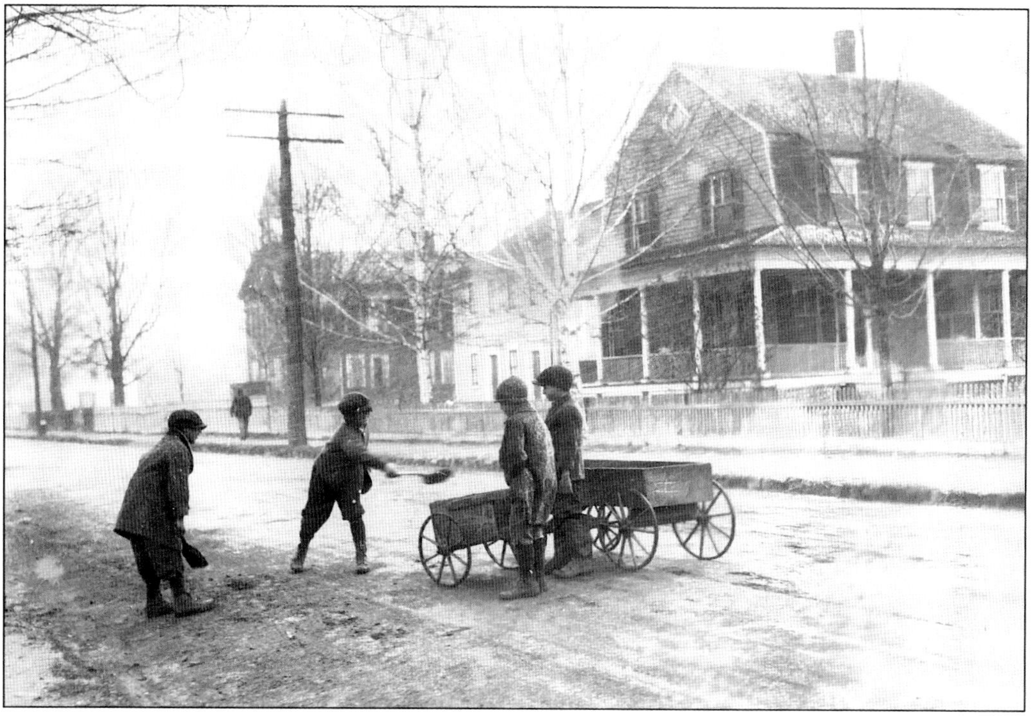

A Salvage Operation, c. 1914. Times weren't always fun for children back then. Some had unpleasant chores to attend to, and others even had jobs like this one—cleaning up after a horse on Phenix Avenue.

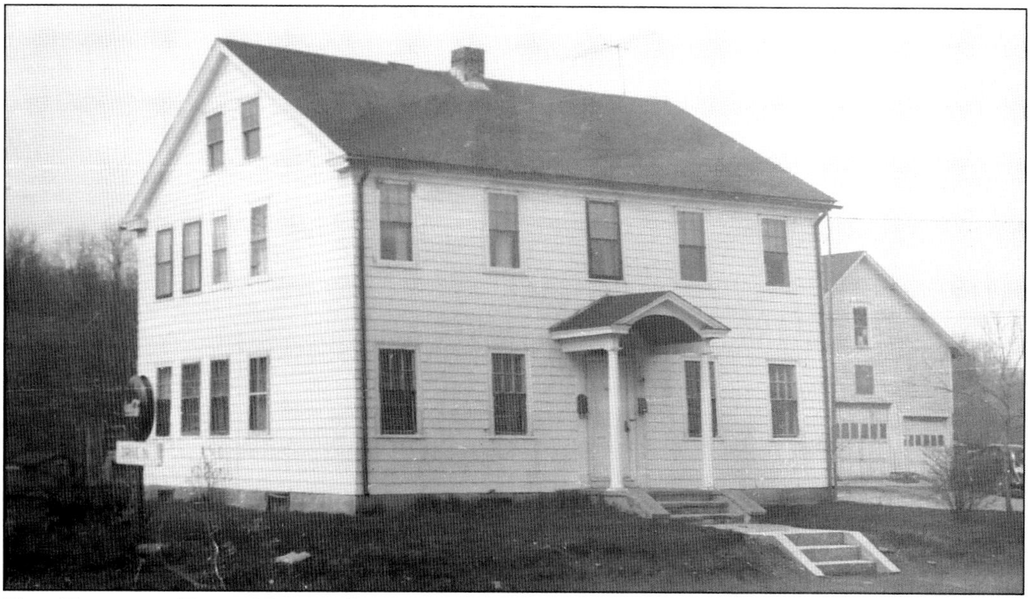

The Cranston Bank House, Corner of Scituate and Phenix Avenues, c. 1950. An old English custom required that the money of the bank be kept in a safe, under guard at the home of the cashier, so a vault with a heavy iron door was installed at the home of the Cranston Bank cashier Jeremiah Knight. The bank's starting assets in 1818 were $37,500. The house is still standing today.

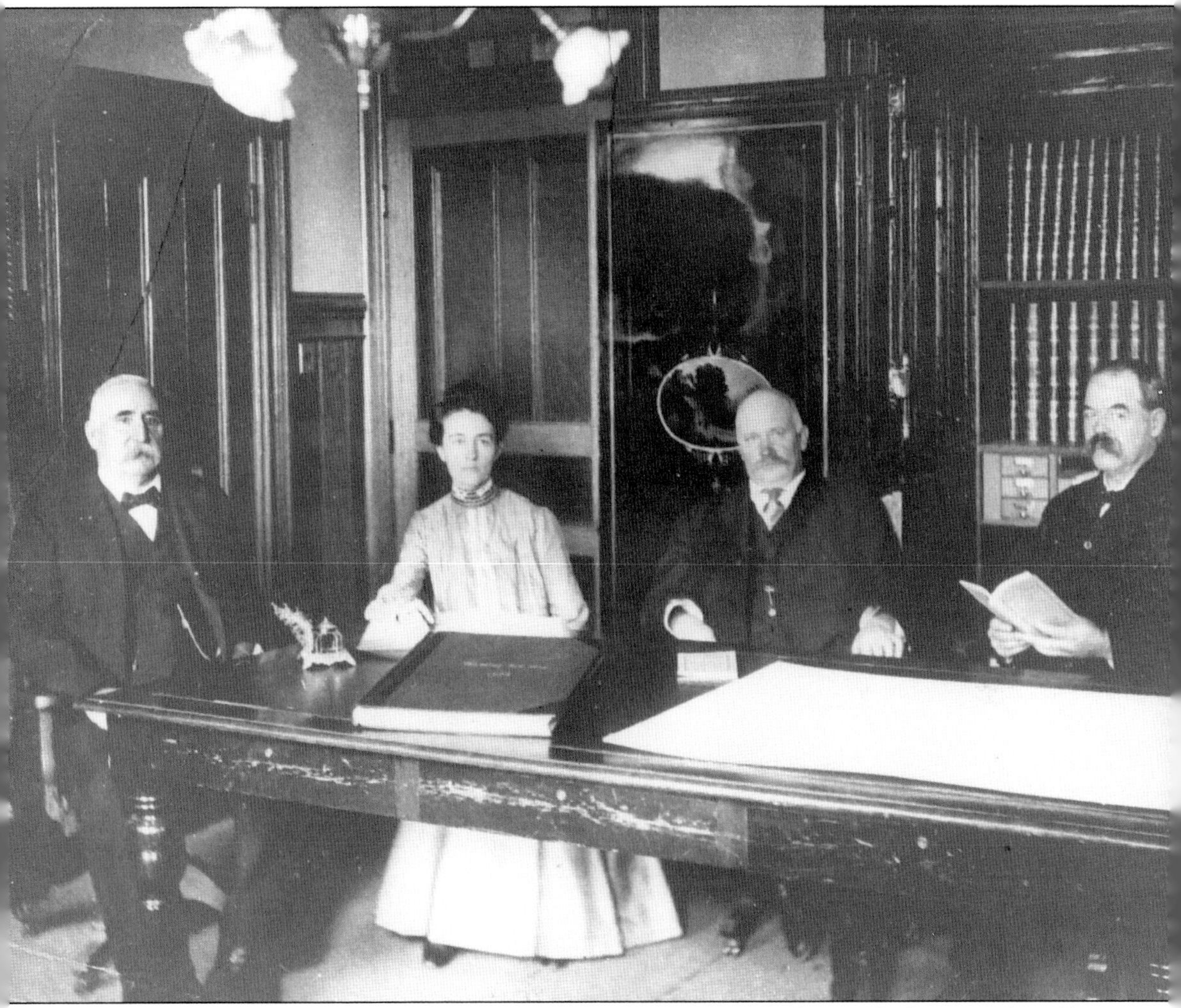

The Town Tax Assessors' Office, c. 1904–1906. Inside the old town hall in Knightsville, waiting to serve citizens, were the town tax assessors. From left to right are Mr. Edward Stanley (assessor from 1893 to 1910), Mrs. Mabel Williams (a clerk, one of the first women to work in town government), Mr. Frederick P. Hunt (assessor from 1903 to 1906), and Mr. William W. Bloomer (assessor from 1904 to 1920).

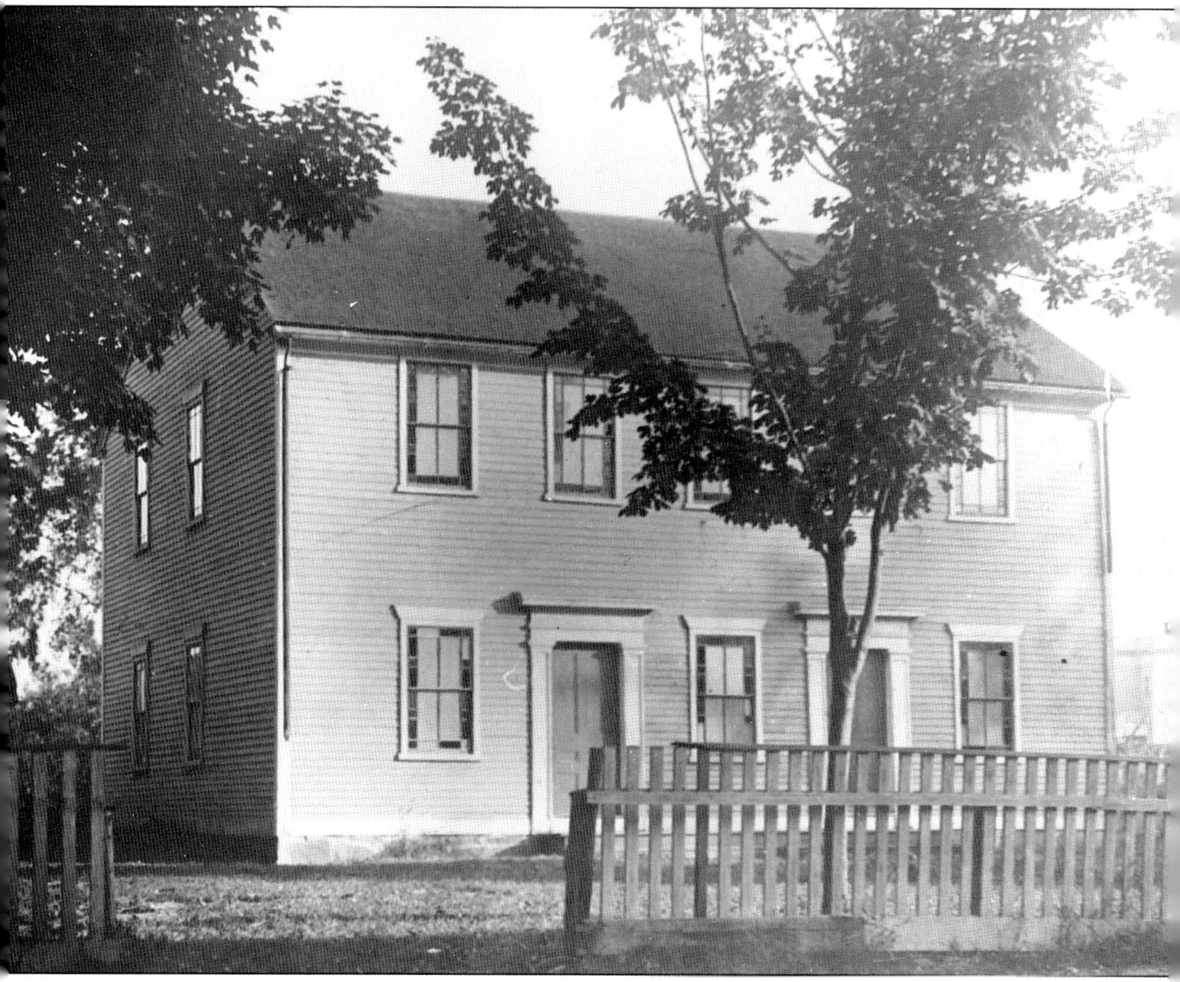

The Knightsville Meeting House, 67 Phenix Avenue, c. 1940. In 1806, the Benevolent Baptist Society sold $4 tickets to raise funds to build a meetinghouse on a quarter acre of land donated by Andrew Knight. Joseph Searle, a sawmill owner and member of the society, was chosen to build the structure, which was used by the Baptists on the first day of the week and was available for other denominations upon request at other times. Town meetings were held here for some 50 years.

After Andrew Knight died in 1812, his son set aside land behind the meetinghouse for a burial ground. Fittingly, Andrew Knight was the first to be buried there. The church is the only Baptist church in Cranston to have an accompanying cemetery. Still standing, the Knightsville Meeting House is Cranston's oldest public building.

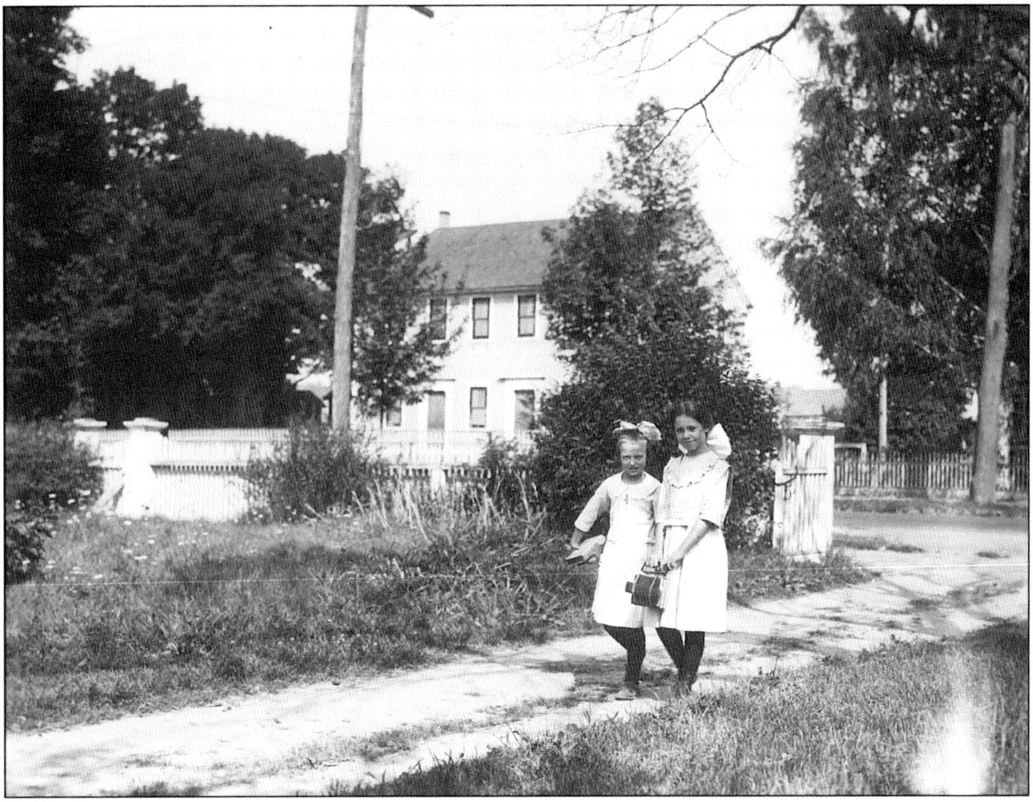

THE KNIGHTSVILLE MEETING HOUSE, C. 1900. Dressed in their Sunday best and carrying books, perhaps Bibles, these two young ladies are returning from afternoon Sunday school services at the Knightsville Meeting House. The Knightsville Mission Sabbath School began at the Meetinghouse in 1864. Miss Mary Holland was the first teacher of the primary class.

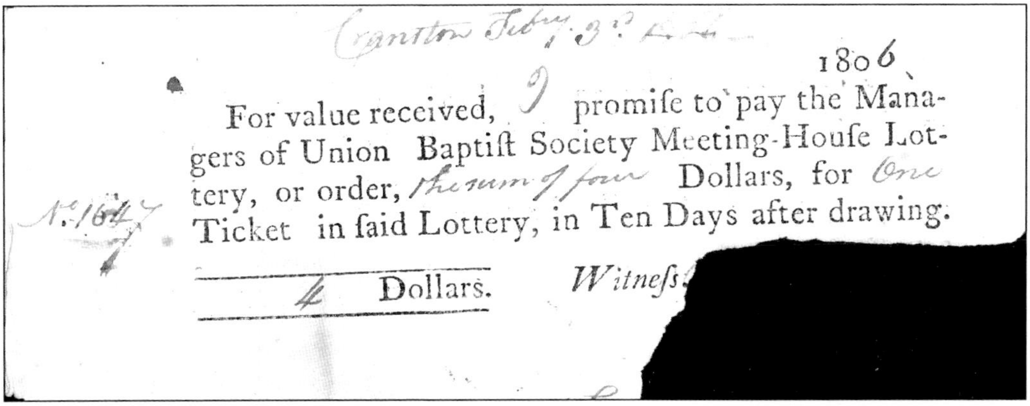

Canton Feby 3d

1806

For value received, I promiſe to pay the Managers of Union Baptiſt Society Meeting-Houſe Lottery, or order, the sum of four Dollars, for One Ticket in ſaid Lottery, in Ten Days after drawing.

No. 1647

4 Dollars. Witneſs

A KNIGHTSVILLE MEETING HOUSE LOTTERY TICKET, FEBRUARY 3, 1806. This ticket is only slightly tattered for being nearly 200 years old. Someone ripped the name off it, so the owner's identity has been lost for all time, but one thing is certain—the $4 helped support the building of the Meetinghouse.

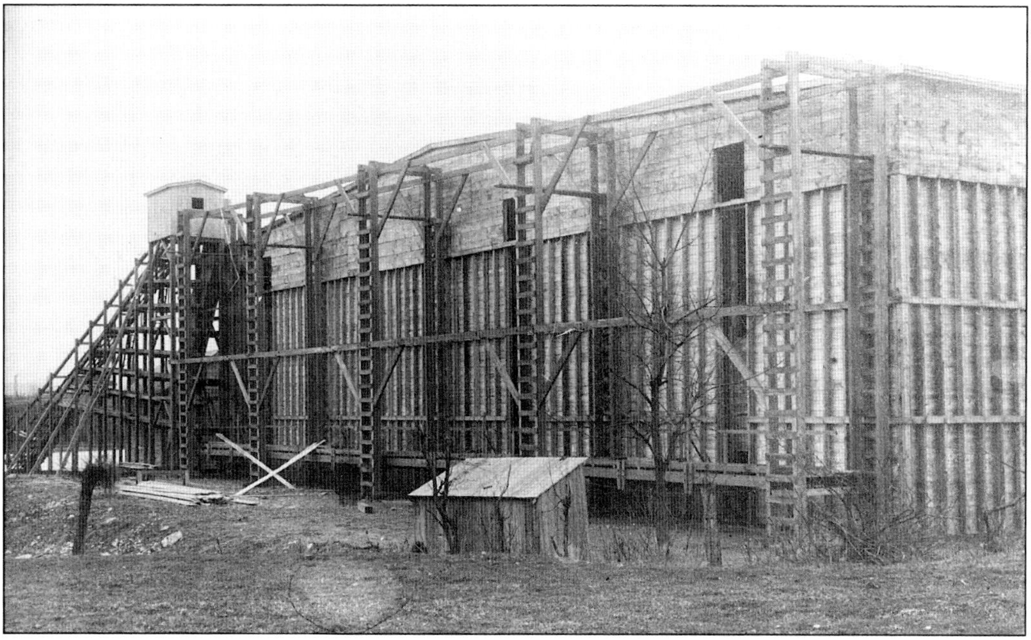

An Ice House at Randall's Pond, c. 1890s. Great ice houses sprang up along every pond in the town after Grocer Earl Carpenter started a new trend by selling his homemade beer cold in 1822. Stephen Mathewson built this ice house on Randall's Pond. In 1909 the price for a wooden ice box was $4.98. Add 12¢ for the melting pan.

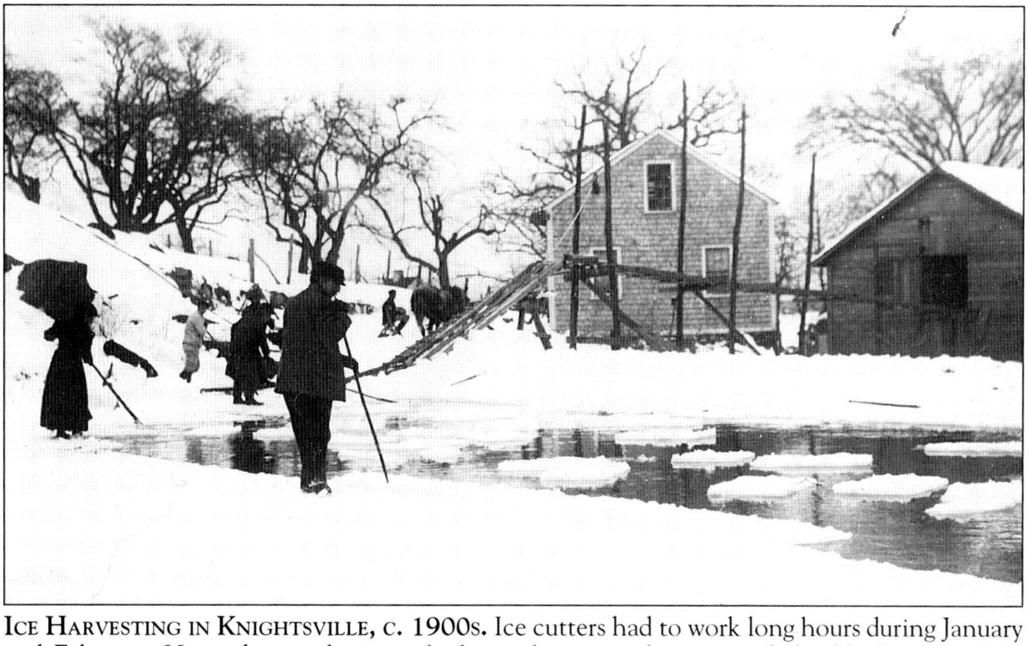

Ice Harvesting in Knightsville, c. 1900s. Ice cutters had to work long hours during January and February. Horse-drawn plows marked out the ice to be cut, and the blocks were then harvested using 6-foot saws. Packers inside the ice house stacked the ice between layers of sawdust and straw until the house was full.

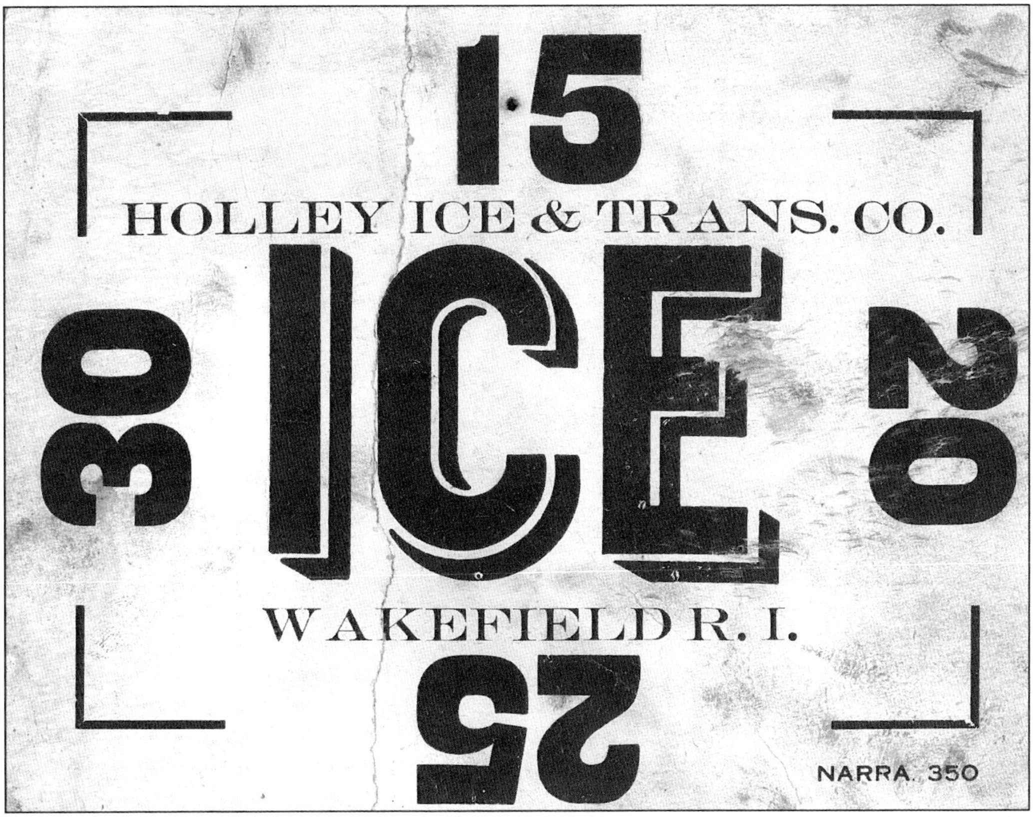

AN ICE SIGN, C. 1900. This sign was typical of those given to customers to display in the windows of their homes and businesses. The amount of ice needed was indicted by placing the number of pounds at the top. The iceman then knew how much to leave without having to knock on the door. (Lydia Rapoza Collection.)

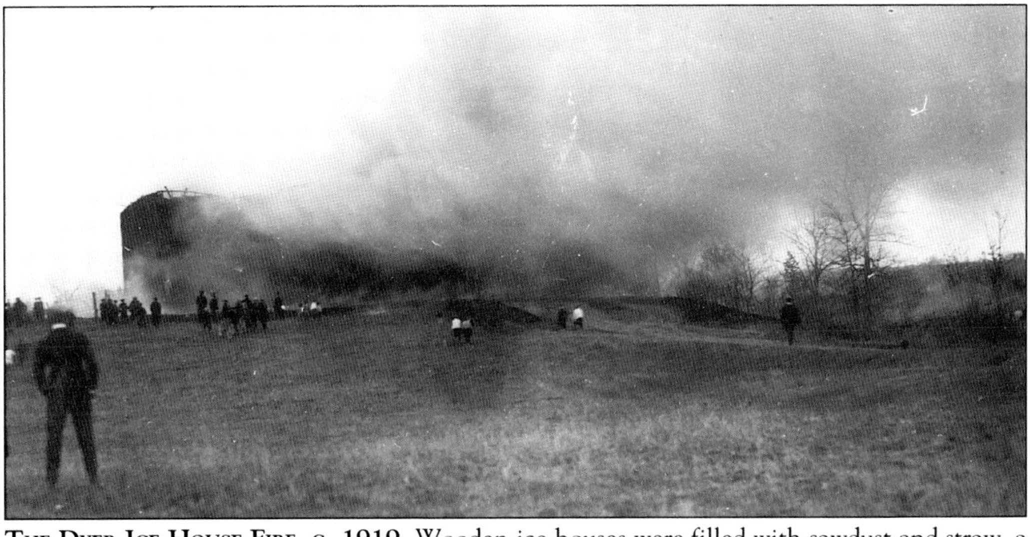

THE DYER ICE HOUSE FIRE, C. 1919. Wooden ice houses were filled with sawdust and straw, a deadly combination that often resulted in disastrous fires. Most of the ice houses in Cranston ended up sharing the same fate as the Dyer Ice House.

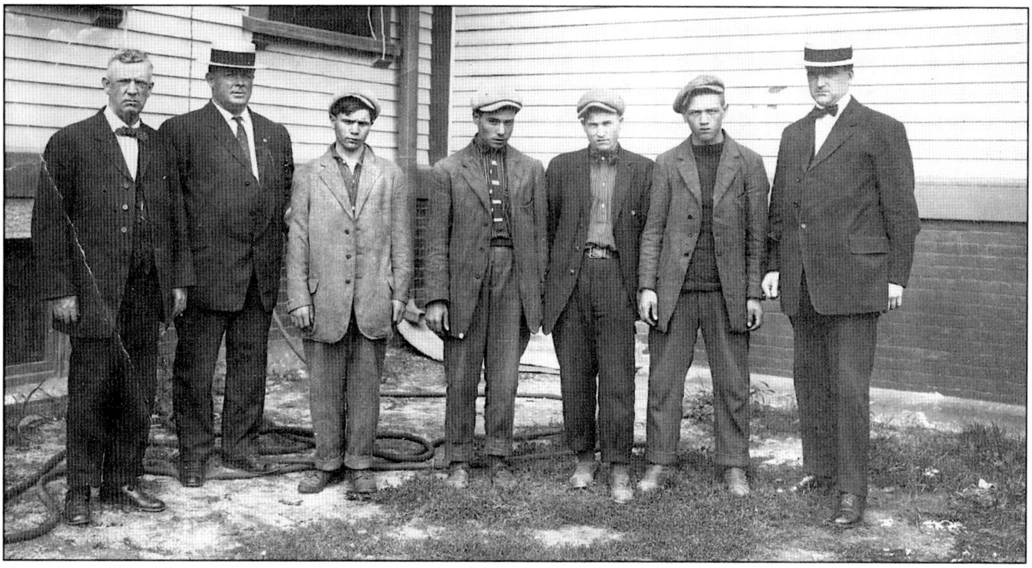

CRANSTON POLICE OFFICERS, C. 1912. Standing by the old city hall police station in Knightsville are, from left to right, Chief Daniel Kernan, James Miller (later to be appointed police chief), four unknown men, and policeman William Maher. Chief Kernan was appointed by Mayor Sullivan and served from 1912 to 1915.

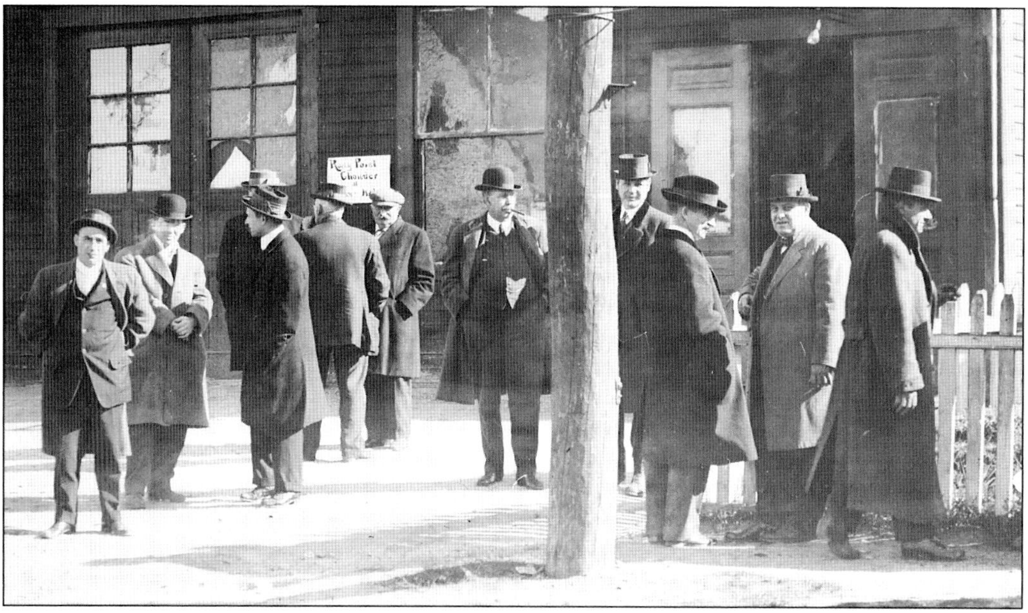

POCASSET HALL, CRANSTON STREET, C. 1914. The Pocasset Hose Company was created in 1895 at a meeting of the Knightsville Improvement Society when it was discovered that the section of Cranston known as Knightsville had the largest number of residents in town with no fire protection. The first foreman of the fire company was Leroy Whitman. John A. Yeaw was named assistant foreman.

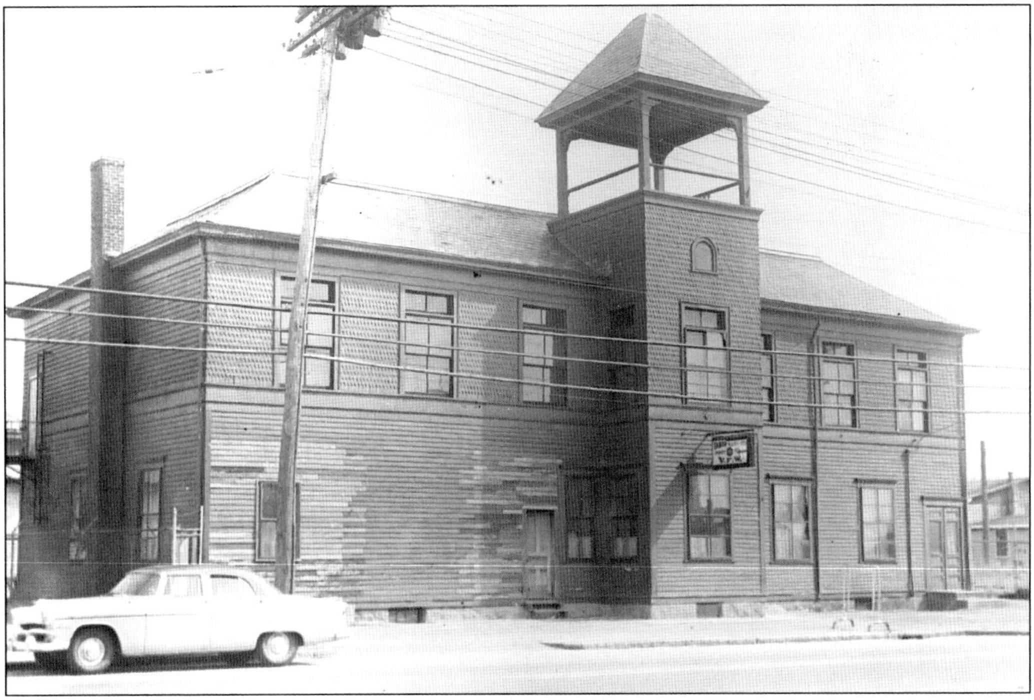

The Pocasset Volunteer Fire Hall, Cranston Street, c. 1954. The building was finished in July 1897 and became the social meeting place in the western part of Cranston. It hosted dancing classes, gala bazaars, and balls. The Knightsville Grammar School held many of its graduation exercises here.

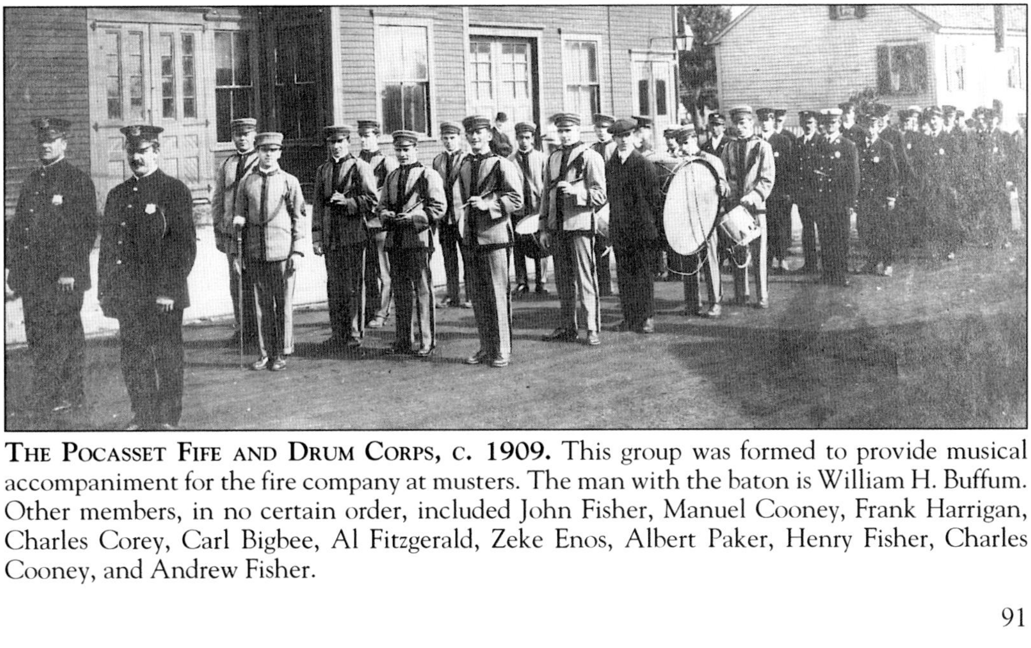

The Pocasset Fife and Drum Corps, c. 1909. This group was formed to provide musical accompaniment for the fire company at musters. The man with the baton is William H. Buffum. Other members, in no certain order, included John Fisher, Manuel Cooney, Frank Harrigan, Charles Corey, Carl Bigbee, Al Fitzgerald, Zeke Enos, Albert Paker, Henry Fisher, Charles Cooney, and Andrew Fisher.

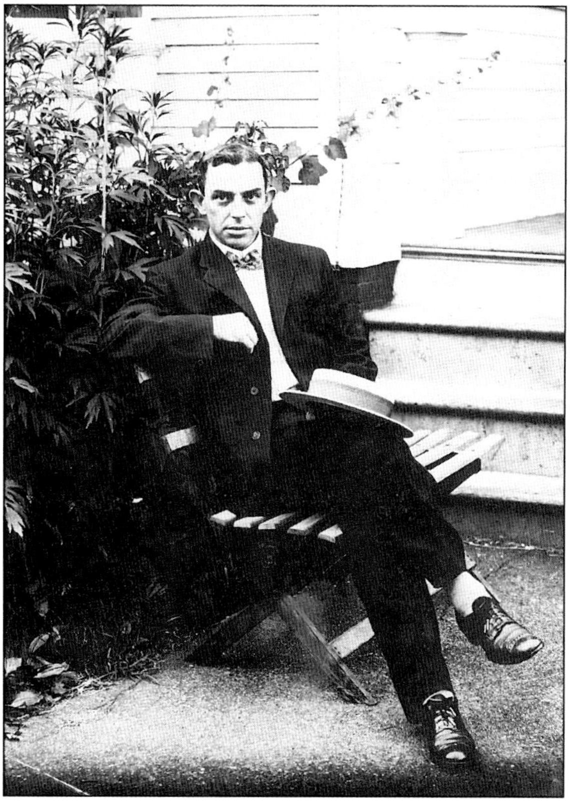

WALTER B. HAVEN, TREASURER OF THE POCASSET VETERAN FIREMEN'S ASSOCIATION, C. 1910. Haven Avenue off Cranston Street is named in his honor.

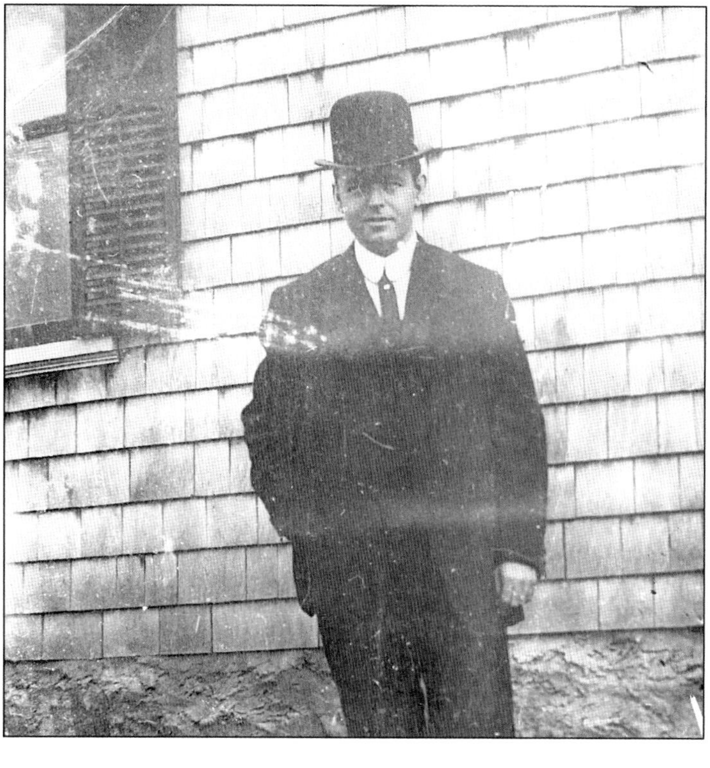

MAYOR EDWARD SULLIVAN, C. 1910. A classmate of Walter Haven at the Knightsville School, Edward Sullivan's studies led him to be Cranston's first mayor in 1910. He was elected to a second term, defeating Republican Dr. Daniel Latham, and a third, defeating future mayor John Horton.

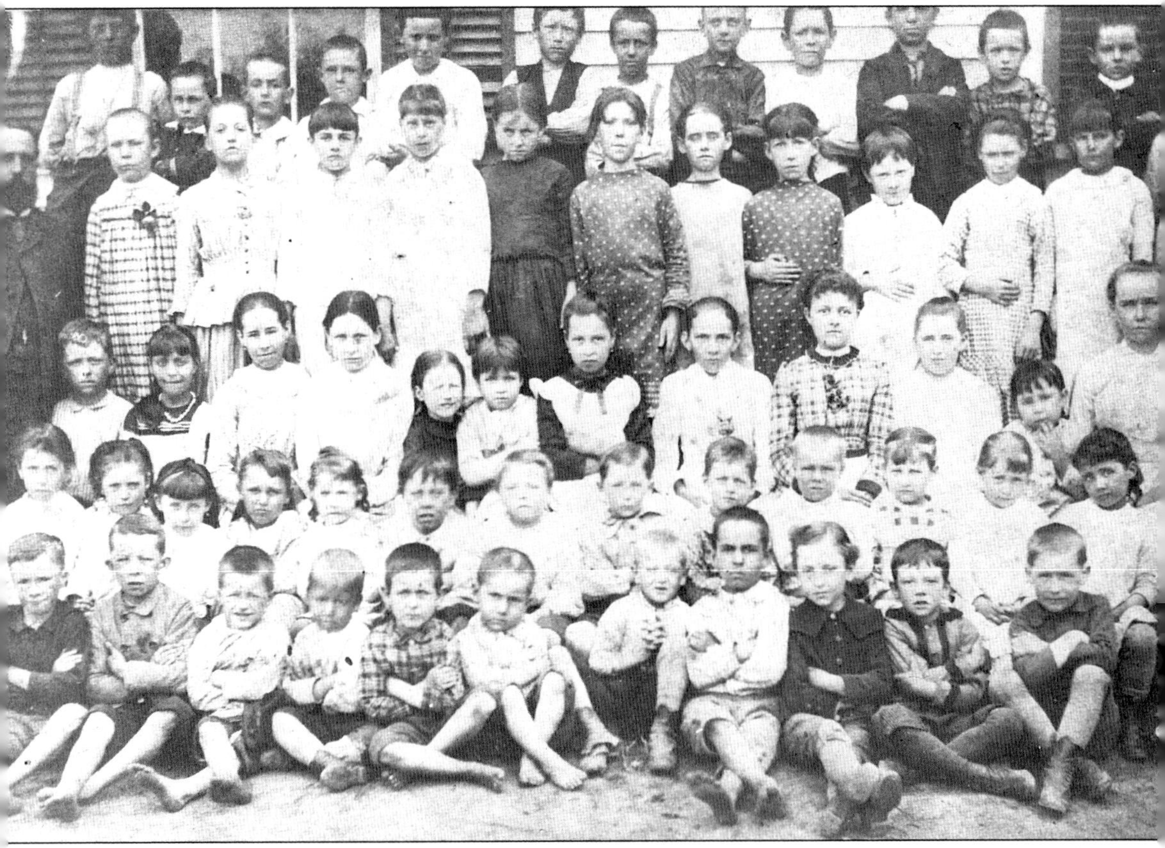

THE PHENIX AVENUE SCHOOL, KNIGHTSVILLE, 1885. A future mayor of Cranston, Edward Sullivan, is in this class, as is Walter Haven. Shown here are, from left to right, as follows: (front row) Henry Palmer, unknown, unknown, Frank Sullivan, six unidentified students, and Kate Sullivan; (second row) five unidentified students, ? Aimed, four unidentified students, Edith Platt, unknown, and Fanny Angell; (third row) unknown, Lizzie Logan, Alice Quigley, Velna Yeaw, four unidentified students, Josephine Aimed, Carrie Knight, Nellie Flanders, Sadie Arnold, Maggie Riley, and Miss Mary Richardson (teacher); (fourth row) Mr. James Earle (teacher), Geneva Warburton, Maude Boutelle, Rose McCarron, Alice Wood, Fanny Riley, Mary Gorman, unknown, Reggie Gorman, Sadie Pierce, Annie Logan, unknown, and Nanna Ball; (back row) three unidentified students, George Congdon, Hanley Carvey, unknown, William Flanders, unknown, unknown, Edward Sullivan, Walter Haven, and unknown.

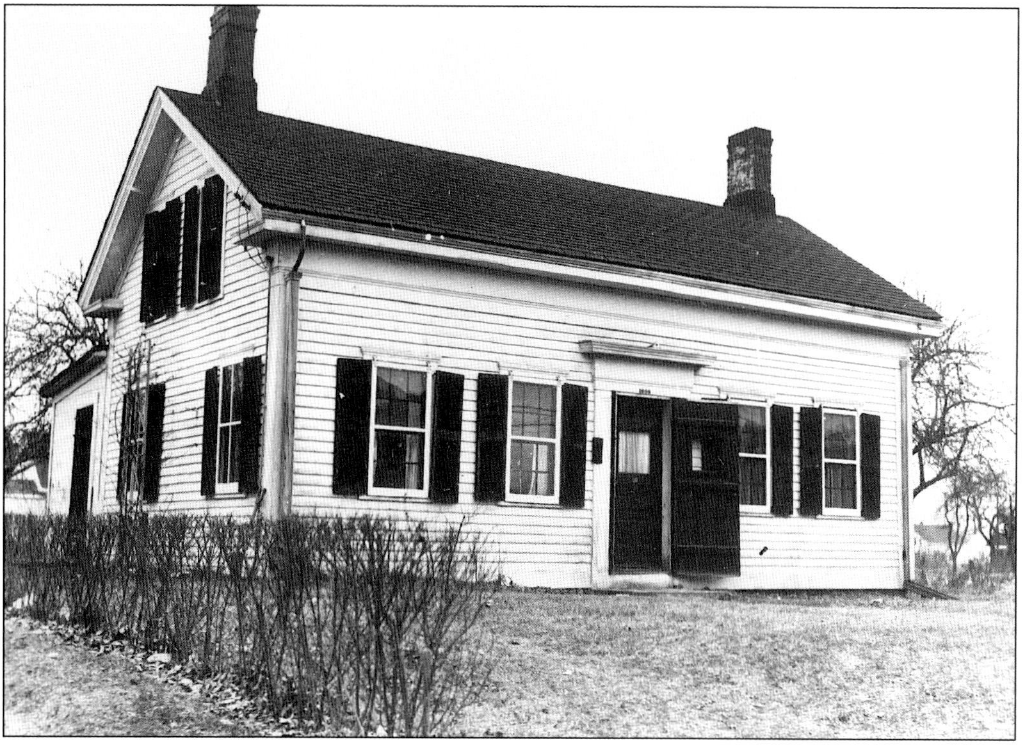

The Warburton House, 1609 Cranston Street, c. 1952. This building, the lifelong home of Geneva A. Warburton, contained a small wooden cupboard that once served the town as the first post office. Postmaster Fairbanks owned the house before the Warburtons purchased it sometime in the 1870s.

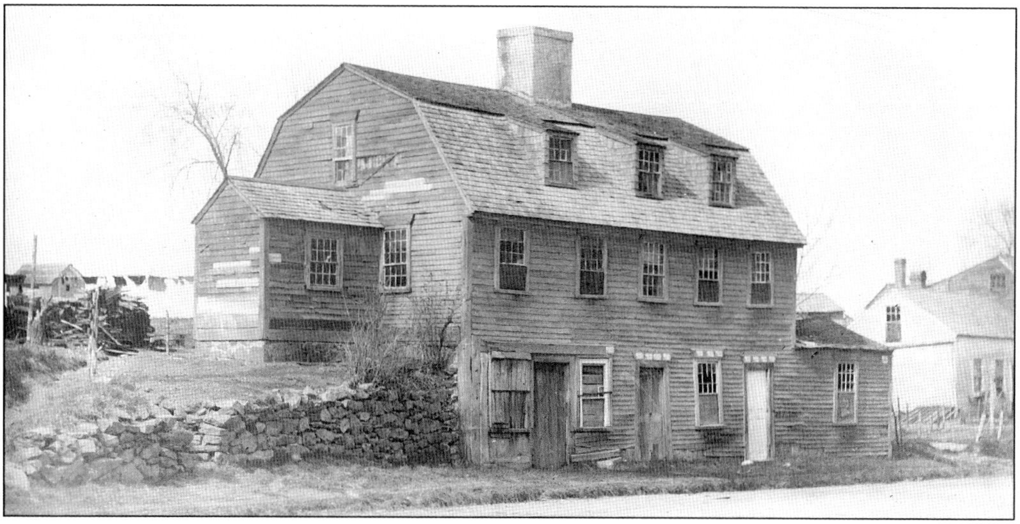

The Caleb Arnold Tavern, 227 Phenix Avenue, c. 1920. Eleven days after the city of Cranston was incorporated in 1754, John Burton, Zuriel Waterman, Jonathan Randell, Captain William Stone, and Benjamin Potter Jr. conducted the first town meeting at the tavern. Arnold's Tavern was destroyed in April 1943. All that remains of the building is a piece of the wooden mantle that is on display at the Governor Sprague Mansion.

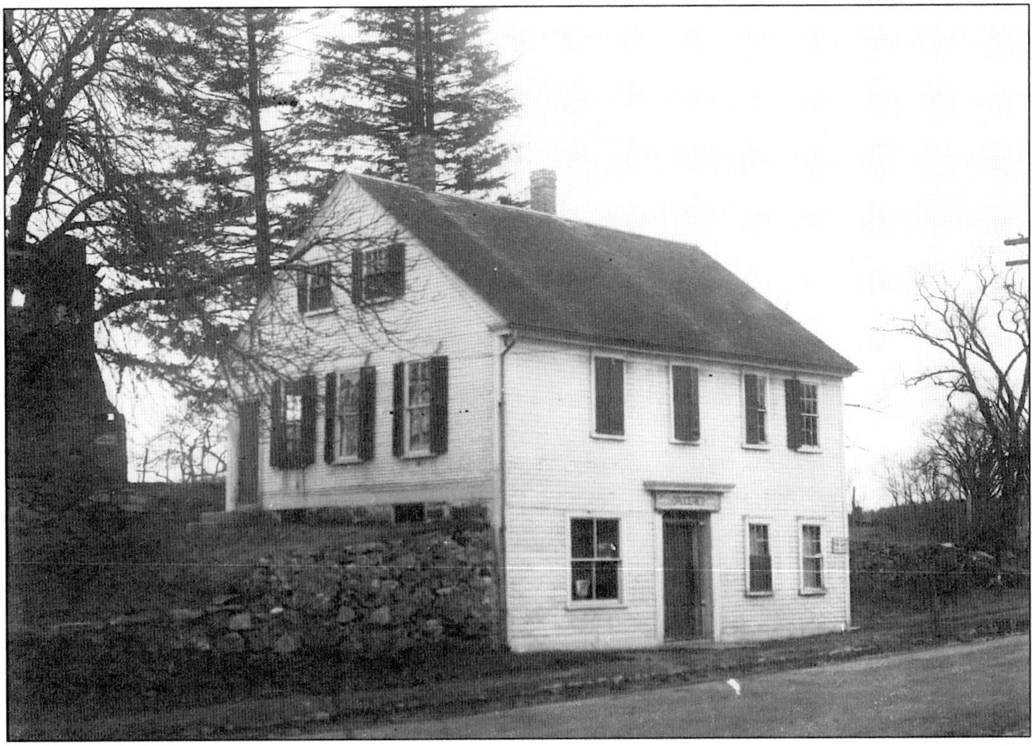

The Birthplace of Governor Henry Howard, c. 1940. Henry Howard was born in this simple house on Phenix Avenue on April 12, 1826. He was elected in 1857 and 1858 to serve as the representative to the Rhode Island General Assembly from Coventry, and was elected governor of Rhode Island in 1873 and 1874. He died at the age of 70 on September 22, 1905.

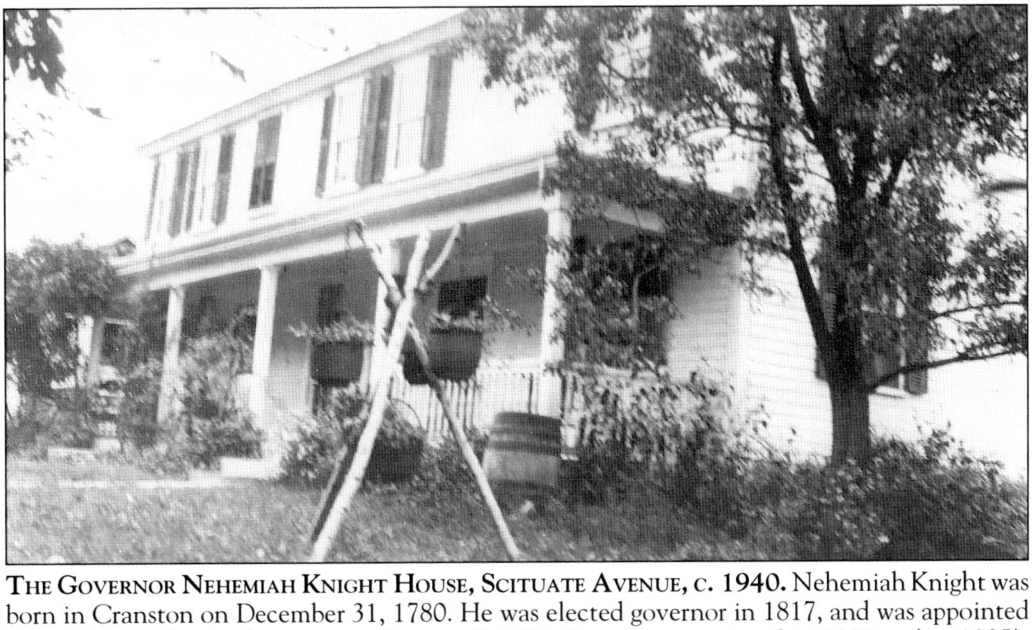

The Governor Nehemiah Knight House, Scituate Avenue, c. 1940. Nehemiah Knight was born in Cranston on December 31, 1780. He was elected governor in 1817, and was appointed to the Senate for the first time on January 9, 1821 (he was reappointed in 1828 and in 1835). Knight died on April 18, 1854. This house was demolished quite awhile ago.

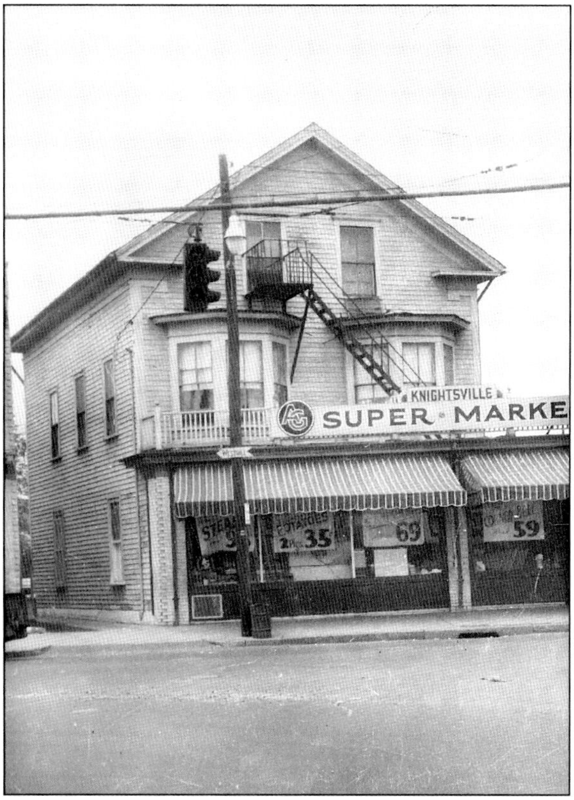

Pratt's General Store, c. 1940. During the early 19th century this supermarket used to be the general store of Thomas Pratt on Cranston Street just down from the old city hall. General stores like Pratt's were the hub of the community. They were used as a meeting place for the locals to chat about the topic of the day. Home deliveries were made by horse-drawn wagons.

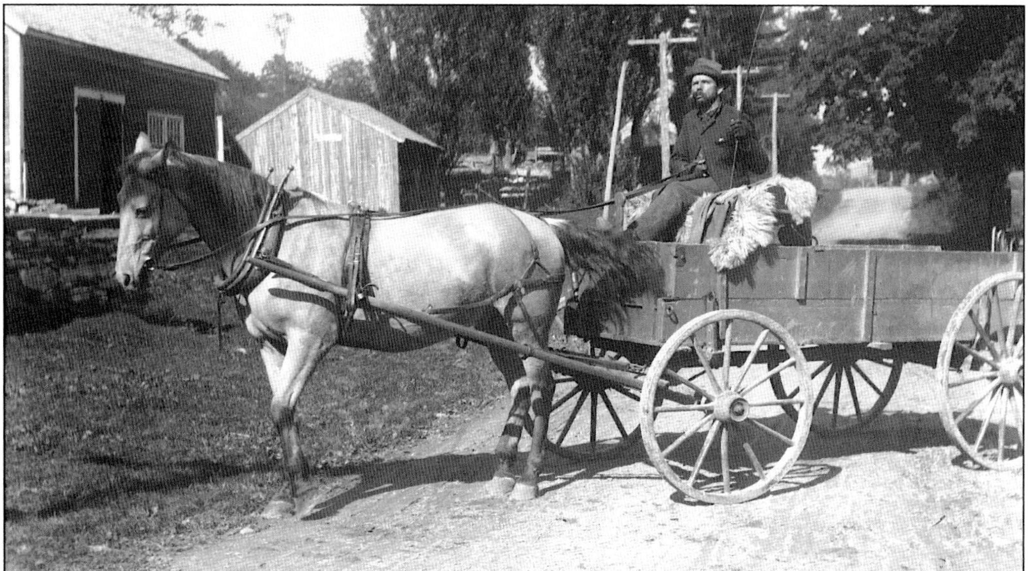

A Ragman during the Great Depression. The cry of "rags" was a familiar one during the Depression as ragmen with their horses and wagons went about the city, trying to earn a few dollars for their families. In 1933, the Red Cross set up a "share your clothes" relief station at the Brick Store for the needy. They also passed out bags of flour from their headquarters at the Brick Store.

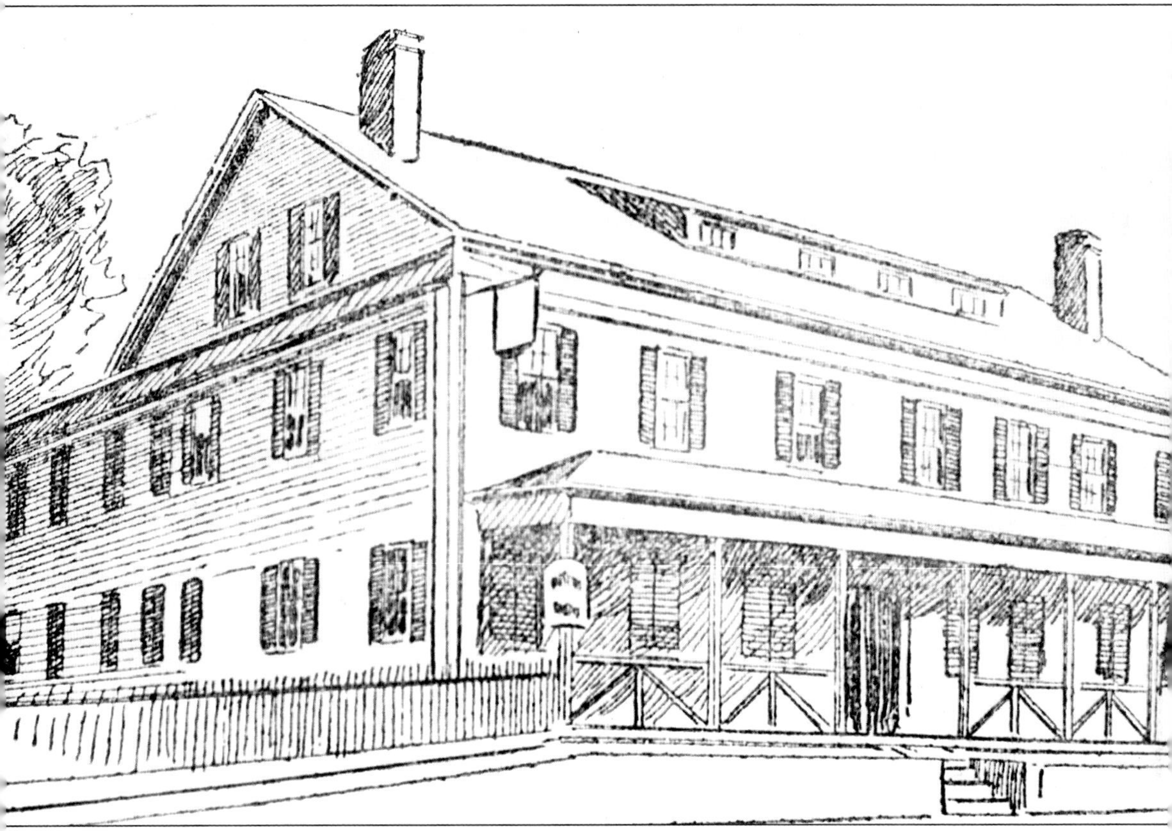

THE OLD NARRAGANSETT HOTEL, PARK AVENUE AND CRANSTON STREET, C. 1840. Once known as Wilbur's Tavern, this building was a gathering place for the town locals. William Sprague III made daily visits here that may have resulted in his being appointed to the Senate in 1842. The railroad men of the Hartford, Providence & Fishkill Railroad made Wilbur's Tavern their headquarters. Job Wilbur leased his tavern to Samuel Parker in 1856 when he moved to Oak Lawn. Parker renamed the tavern the Knightsville Hotel. William Ross bought the property in 1861. When Amasa Sprague II built the Narragansett Trotting Park in Spragueville, Ross renamed the hotel the Narragansett. Horsemen with events at the Narragansett Trotting Park would room at the hotel. A fire in 1903 left only the ground floor of the hotel standing. Another fire in 1930 completely destroyed the building.

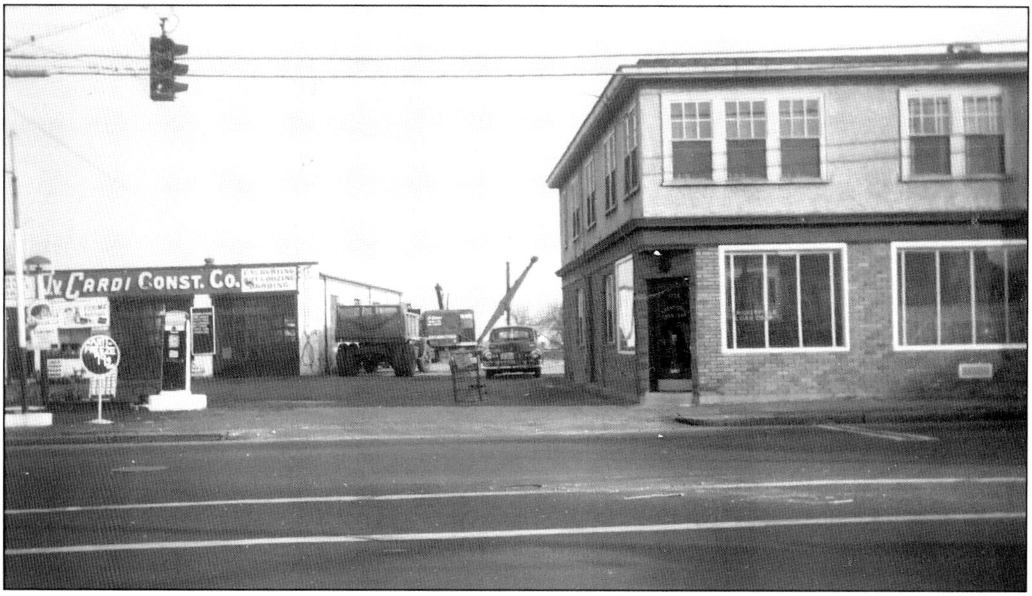

THE SITE OF THE NARRAGANSETT HOTEL, C. 1952. By this time the Knightsville Loan Company and Cardi Construction occupied the corner of Park Avenue and Cranston Street, the former location of the Narragansett Hotel.

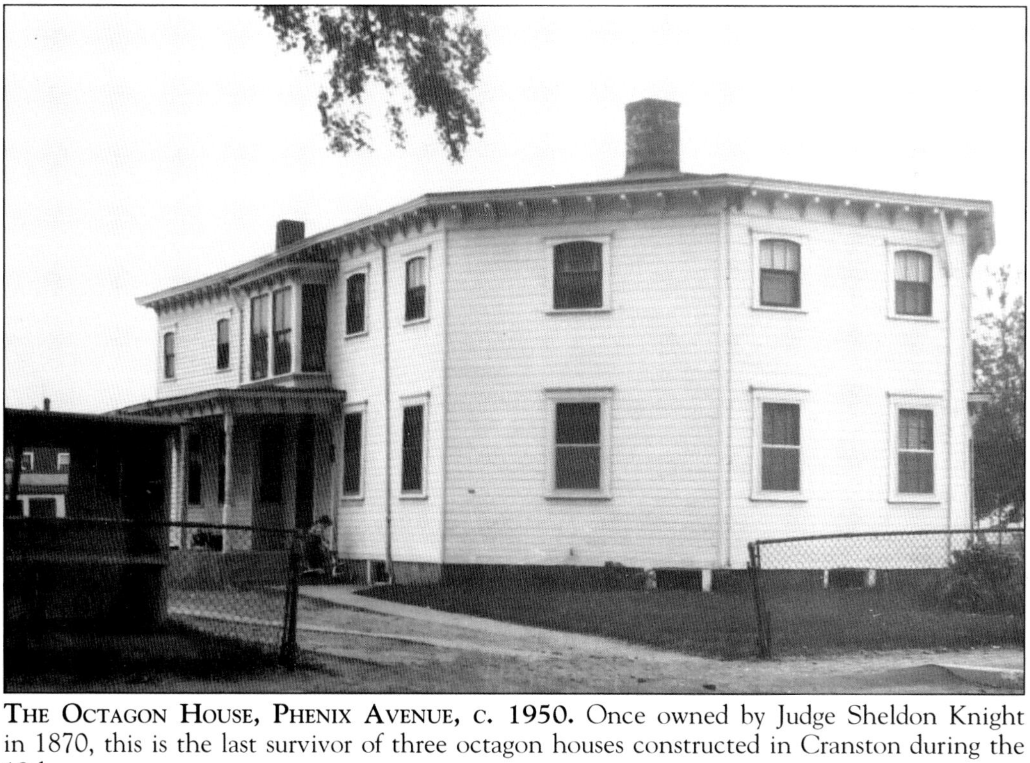

THE OCTAGON HOUSE, PHENIX AVENUE, C. 1950. Once owned by Judge Sheldon Knight in 1870, this is the last survivor of three octagon houses constructed in Cranston during the 19th century.

ST. MARY'S CATHOLIC CHURCH, 1525 CRANSTON STREET, C. 1935. In 1921 there were 3,000 more Italian immigrants in Cranston than Irish immigrants. The Italians attended St. Ann's and other churches until they formed their own parish and had St. Mary's Church built in 1935.

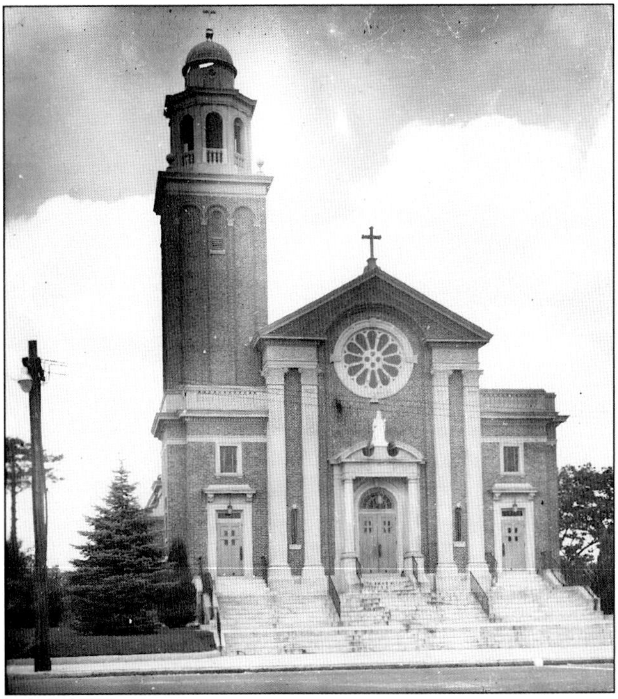

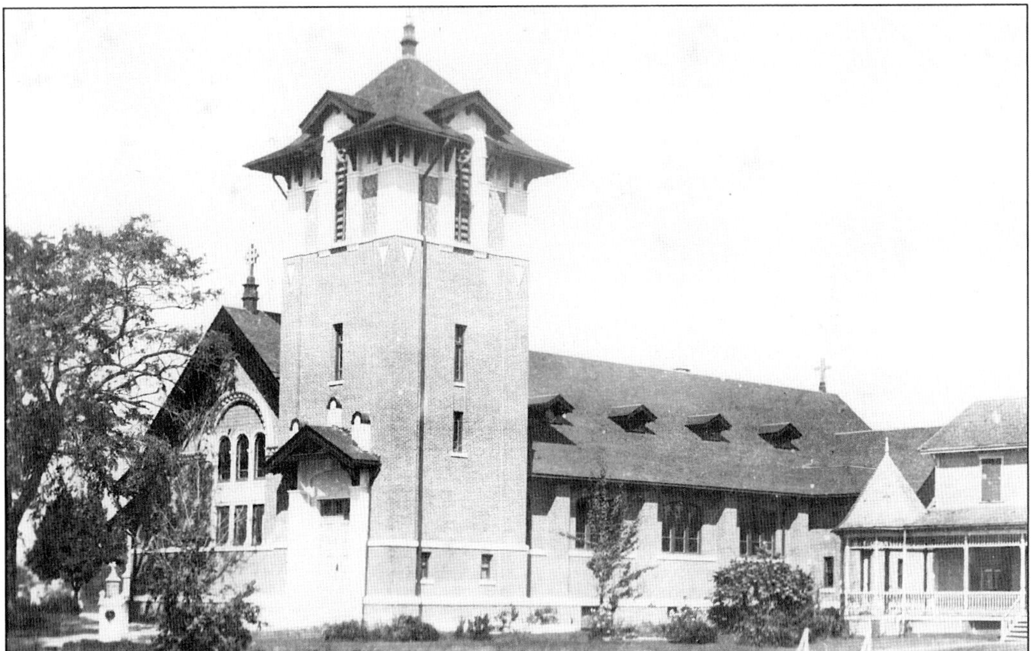

ST. ANN'S CATHOLIC CHURCH, 1493 CRANSTON STREET, C. 1907. This Italian Romanesque church is built approximately on the site that housed Nicholas Gordon's grocery store and small bar. After the execution of John Gordon for the murder of Amasa Sprague, the Irish workers at the A&W Sprague Company were filled with bitterness. Father John Quinn arrived in 1853 to serve the needs of the Irish workers. In 1858 a small wooden building was erected to serve 500 parishioners. St. Ann's became the first Catholic parish in Cranston in 1863.

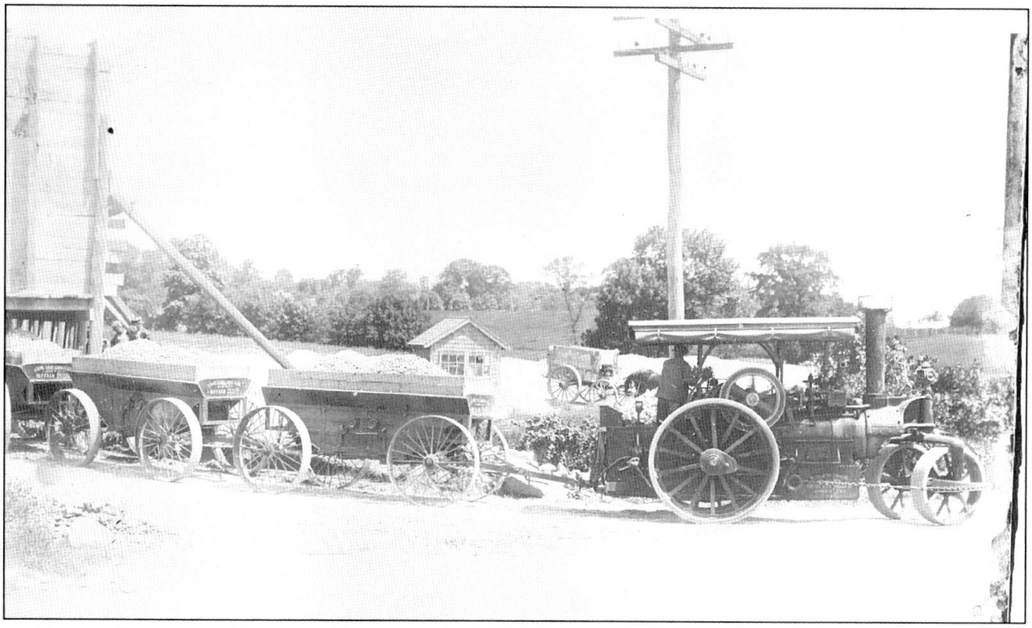

A Steam Tractor Pulling Dumpcarts of Stone, c. 1913. The city voters approved a $40,000 bond issue to rebuild Cranston Street into Knightsville. Each dumpcart held about 5 tons of stone. This rig hauled the stones from the stone crushing plant on Wayland Avenue to where they were needed.

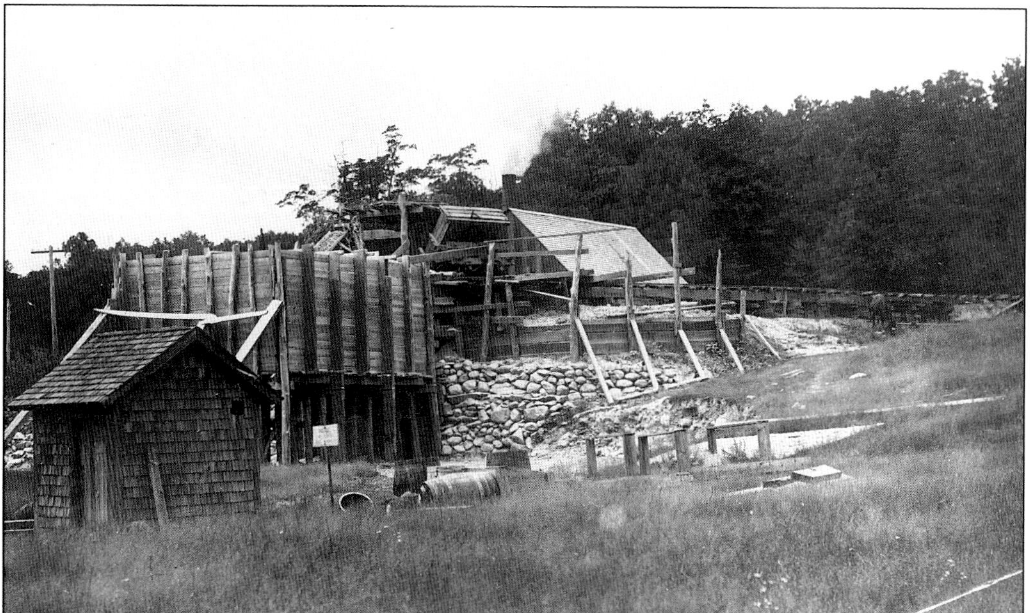

The Stone Crushing Plant on Wayland Avenue, c. 1913. The plant bought loads of stones from local farmers who were clearing their land. The average price for a ton of stone hauled to the stone crushing plant was 40¢. The crushing plant was later located on Phenix Avenue.

Seven

Oak Lawn

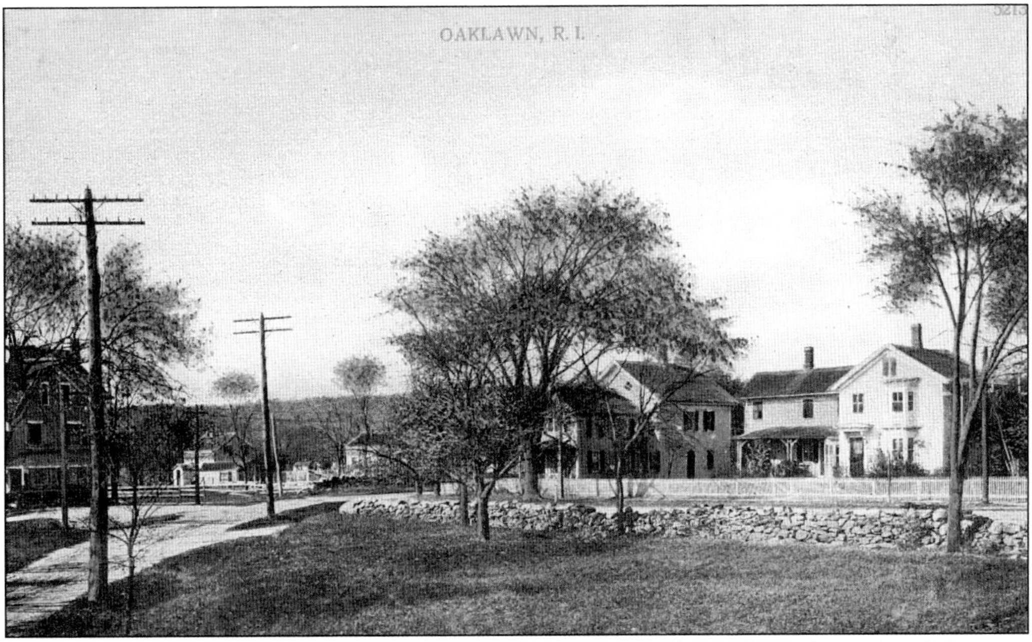

Oak Lawn, c. 1908. At the bottom left of the picture is the path to the railroad depot, a short distance from Wilbur Avenue. Exchange Street runs in front of the houses on the right. Oak Lawn was at the end of the longest 5¢ trolley ride in the state when passengers boarded in Providence.

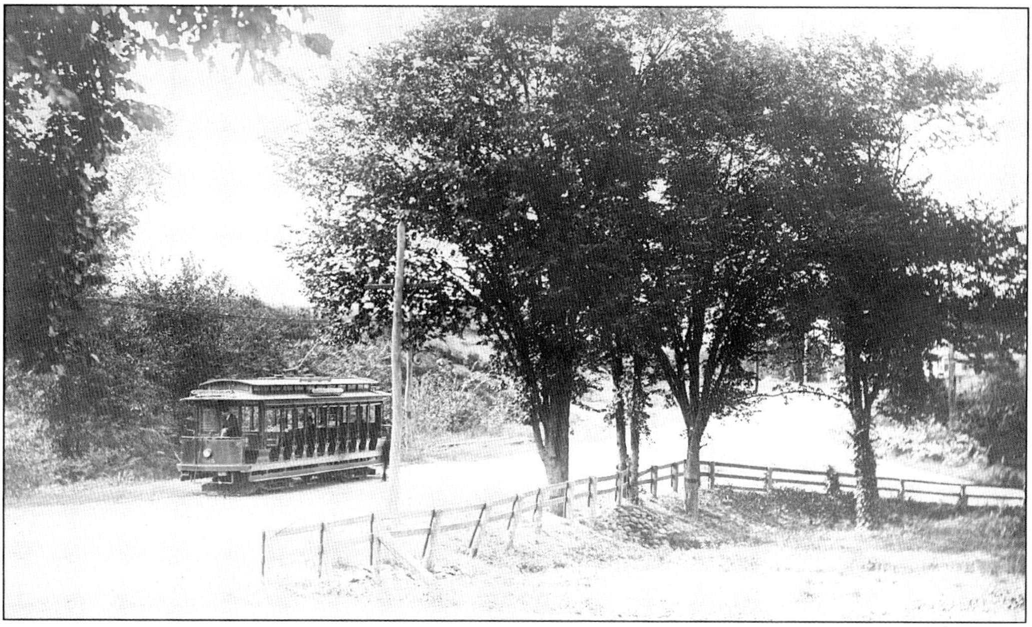

An Oak Lawn Trolley on Wilbur Avenue, c. 1901. In 1901 the trolley line finally arrived in Oak Lawn. Trolley tracks ran along the east side of Oak Lawn Avenue and ended by the side of a wooded lot on Brayton Avenue. The trolley in this picture is an open car called a "bloomer."

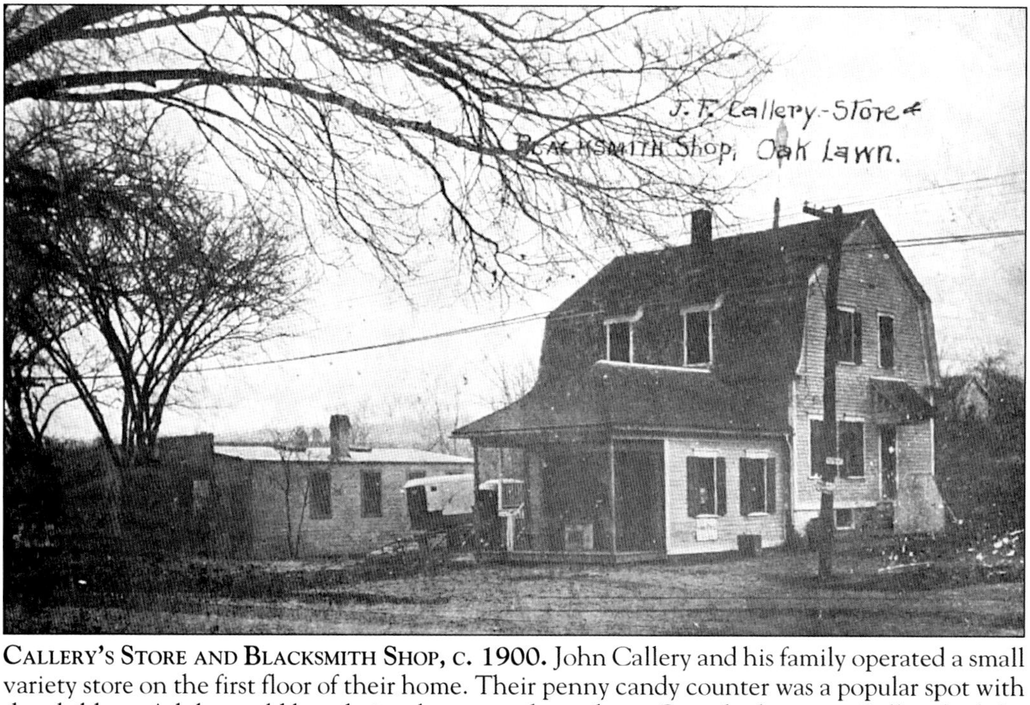

Callery's Store and Blacksmith Shop, c. 1900. John Callery and his family operated a small variety store on the first floor of their home. Their penny candy counter was a popular spot with the children. Adults could buy their tobacco products there. Outside the store, Callery had the only gasoline pump in town.

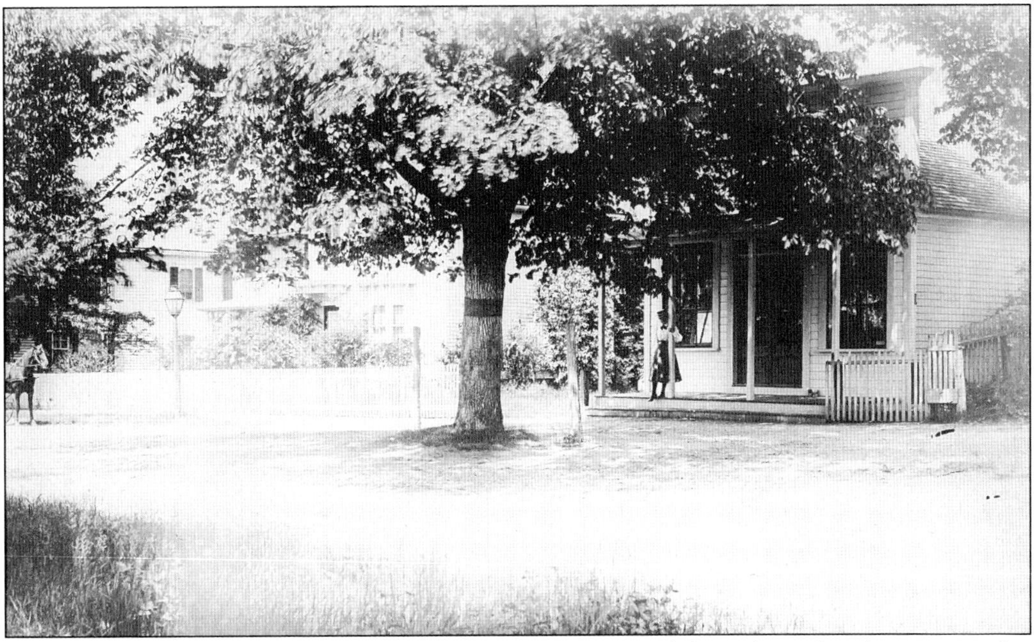

Edwin Searle's Store, c. 1884. The post office was moved from the railroad station to this store and then back to the railroad station when Frank Fowler became postmaster. The store was started by Crawford Williams and later run by Edwin Searle and William Leach.

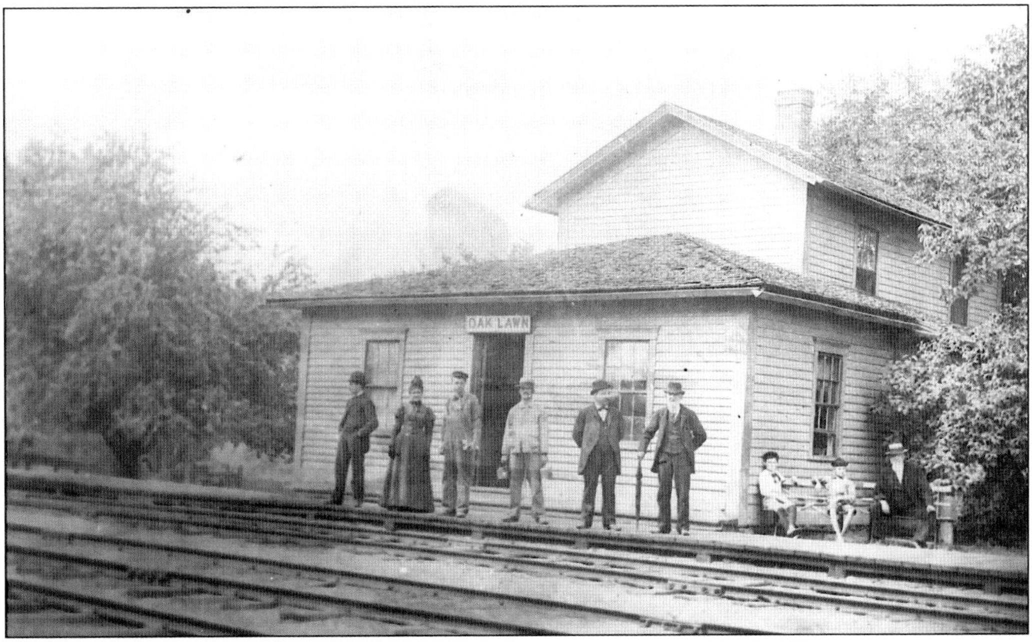

The Oak Lawn Railroad Station, Exchange Street, c. 1900. This station originally housed the post office. Mr. Mayo was the first stationmaster, and Francis Turner was the first postmaster. Frank Fowler later assumed both positions. Trains brought supplies and materials used at the state institution into the Oak Lawn Station.

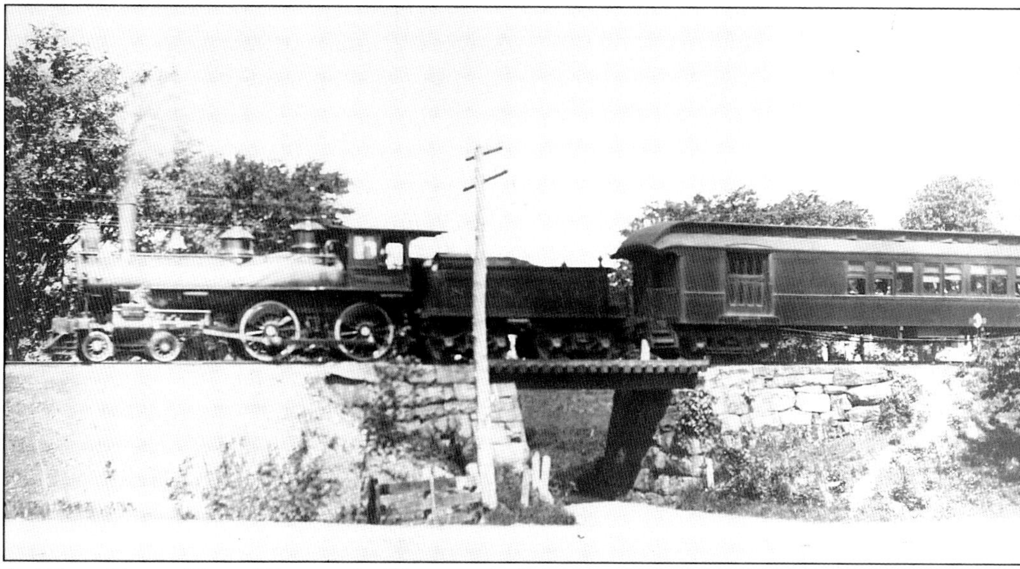

A NEW YORK, NEW HAVEN & HARTFORD RAILROAD TRAIN ON THE WILBUR AVENUE OVERPASS AT ROUTE 5, C. 1901. Known as the Hartford, Providence and Fishkill Railroad in the 1850s, this was the fourth major railroad to run through Rhode Island. It ran along the Pawtuxet River, stopping at the four Sprague Mills located on the river and the Cranston Print Works. This was no coincidence since the Sprague brothers were also owners of the railroad company.

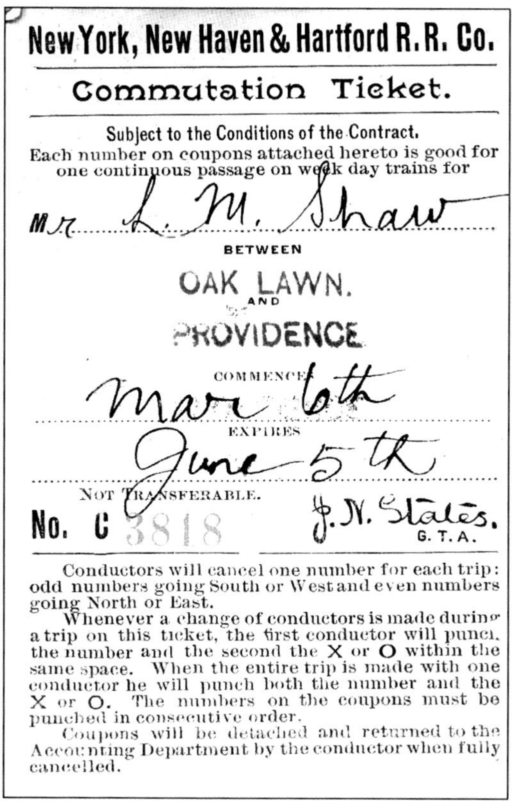

New York, New Haven & Hartford R. R. Co.

Commutation Ticket.

Subject to the Conditions of the Contract.
Each number on coupons attached hereto is good for one continuous passage on week day trains for

Mr L. M. Shaw

BETWEEN

OAK LAWN.
AND
PROVIDENCE

COMMENCES
Mar 6th

EXPIRES
June 5th

NOT TRANSFERABLE.

No. C 3818 J. N. States. G. T. A.

Conductors will cancel one number for each trip: odd numbers going South or West and even numbers going North or East.

Whenever a change of conductors is made during a trip on this ticket, the first conductor will punch the number and the second the X or O within the same space. When the entire trip is made with one conductor he will punch both the number and the X or O. The numbers on the coupons must be punched in consecutive order.

Coupons will be detached and returned to the Accounting Department by the conductor when fully cancelled.

A NEW YORK, NEW HAVEN & HARTFORD RAILROAD TICKET BOOK, 1901. This ticket book was good for a month's worth of fares on the train from Oak Lawn to Providence. The train made five stops between Auburn and Providence—Roger Williams Park, Webster Avenue, Plainfield Street, Atwells Avenue, and Union Station—all for 7¢.

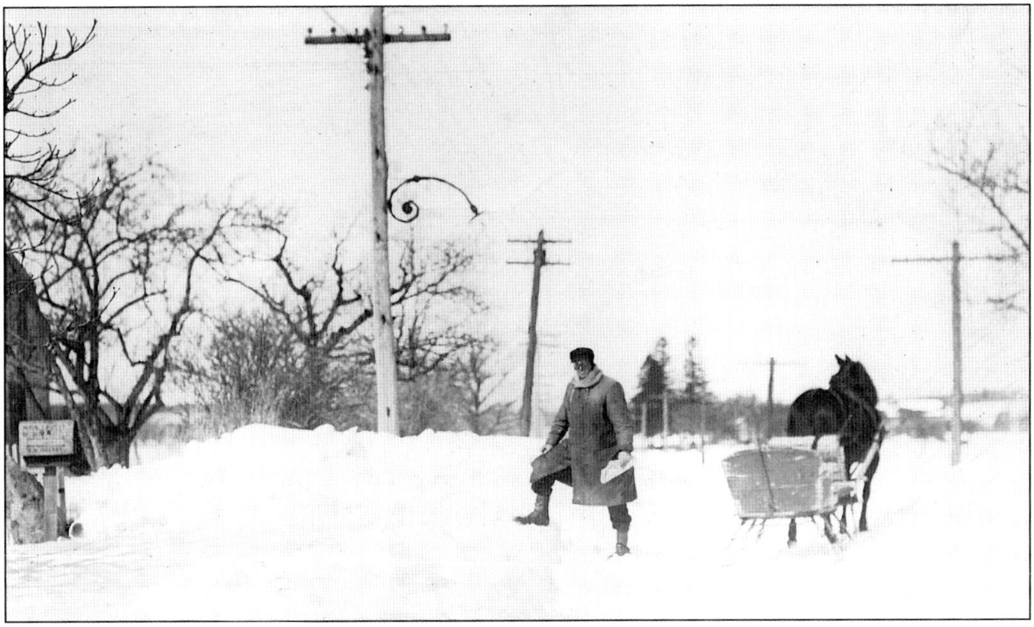

CHESTER SEARLE, MAIL CARRIER, C. 1905. The mail had to get through, and mail carriers could not always wait for a snow plow. Searle delivered mail by horse and sleigh in some of the worst Rhode Island weather. Mail carriers certainly earned their money, as they had to deliver mail twice daily. If homeowners needed to know what was going on in the area, the mail carrier was the one to ask.

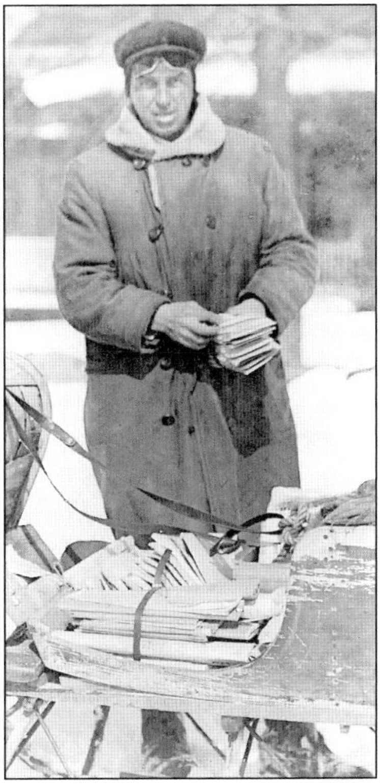

CHESTER SEARLE, C. 1905. Searle was an active member of the Oak Lawn Grange and attended the Oak Lawn Grammar School. He later owned one of the first motor vehicles in Oak Lawn, a 1908 Orient Buckboard. It had one cylinder, four horsepower, and one forward speed. He used it for his mail route and found it "very satisfactory."

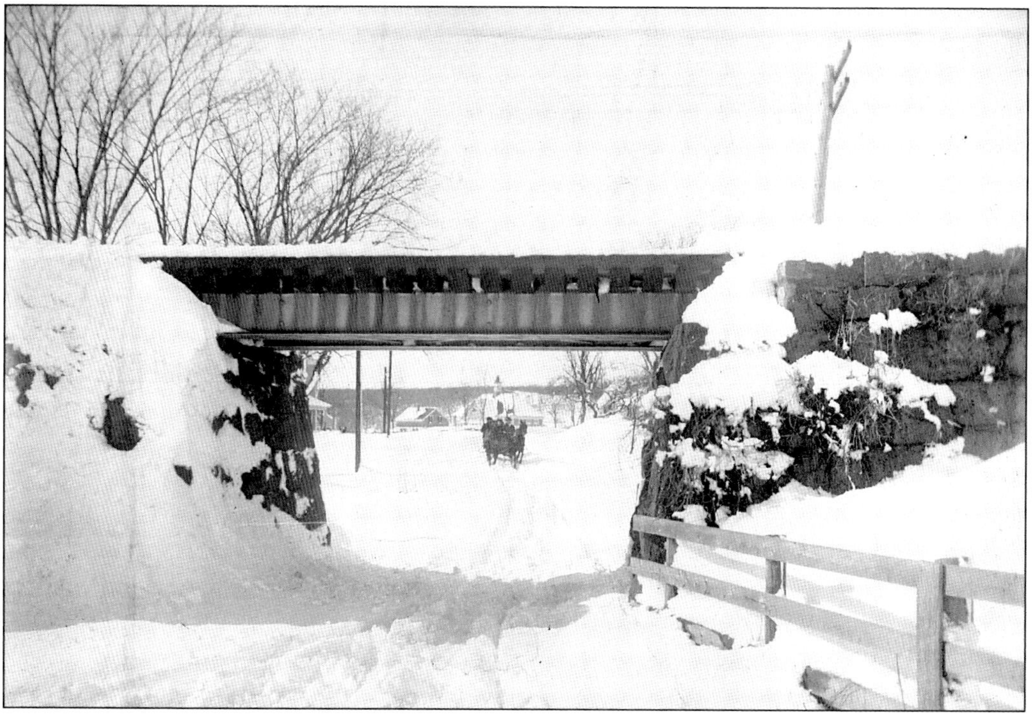

WINTER IN OAK LAWN, WILBUR AVENUE, C. 1900. On a snowy day the best way to get around was the old-fashioned way—by a horse and sleigh.

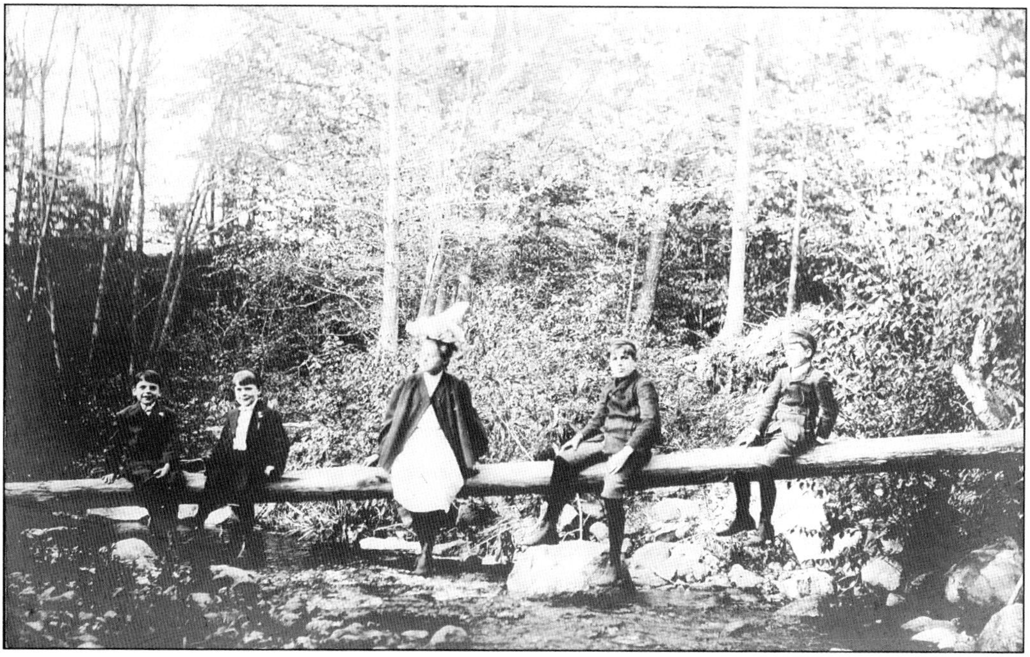

SUMMERTIME IN OAK LAWN, C. 1897. Oak Lawn was a quiet rural community where kids could have fun playing on log bridges spanning a brook. These children, apparently dressed in their Sunday best, were caught in action by a photographer. Did they ever make it to Sunday school that day?

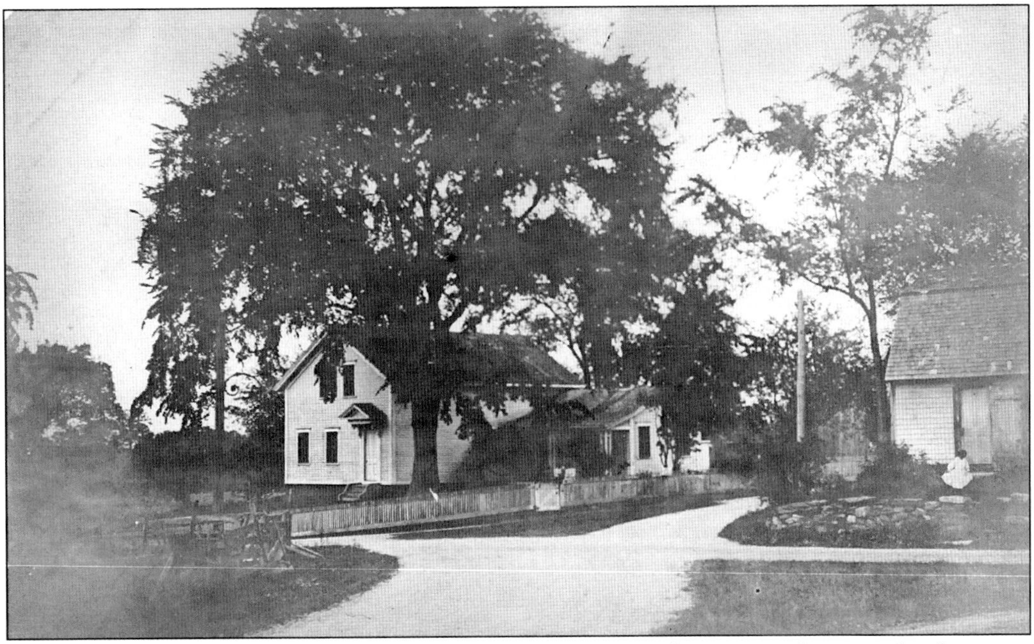

Brightman's Store, Wilbur Avenue, c. 1900. A general store was kept in this house at one time. Across the street from the store was a blacksmith shop. The house to the right was a tavern. The flat wall in front of the tavern had rings in it for hitching horses, and across from the tavern was the town pound.

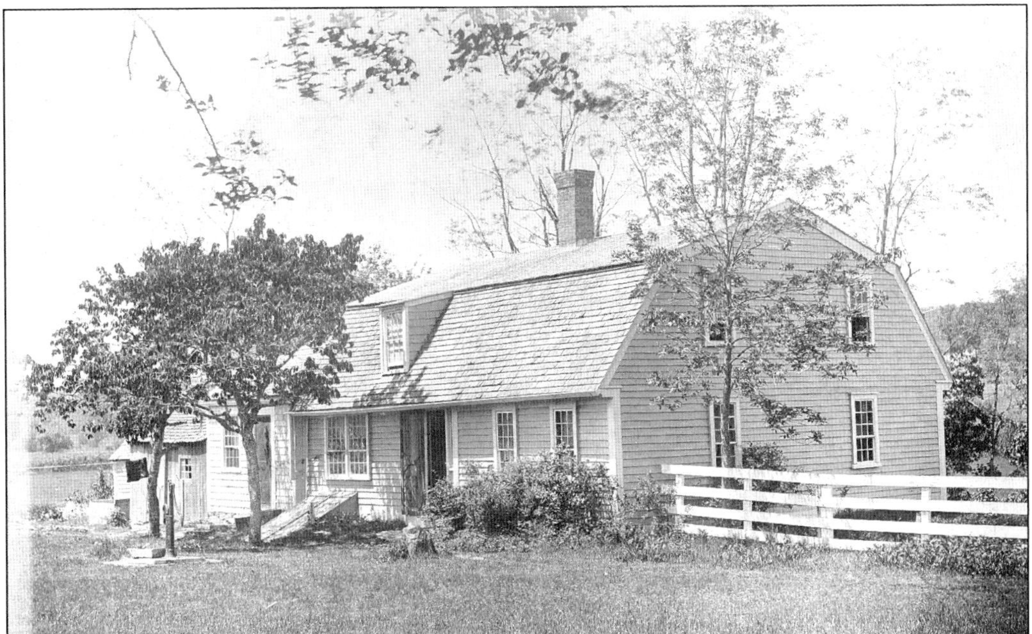

The William Burton House, c. 1900. Built in 1720, this was the home of William Burton, the first town clerk of Cranston. He was also the first justice of the peace. The town records were kept here in the 18th century. This house, known as Rose Cottage, was demolished to allow the construction of the Route 295 overpass.

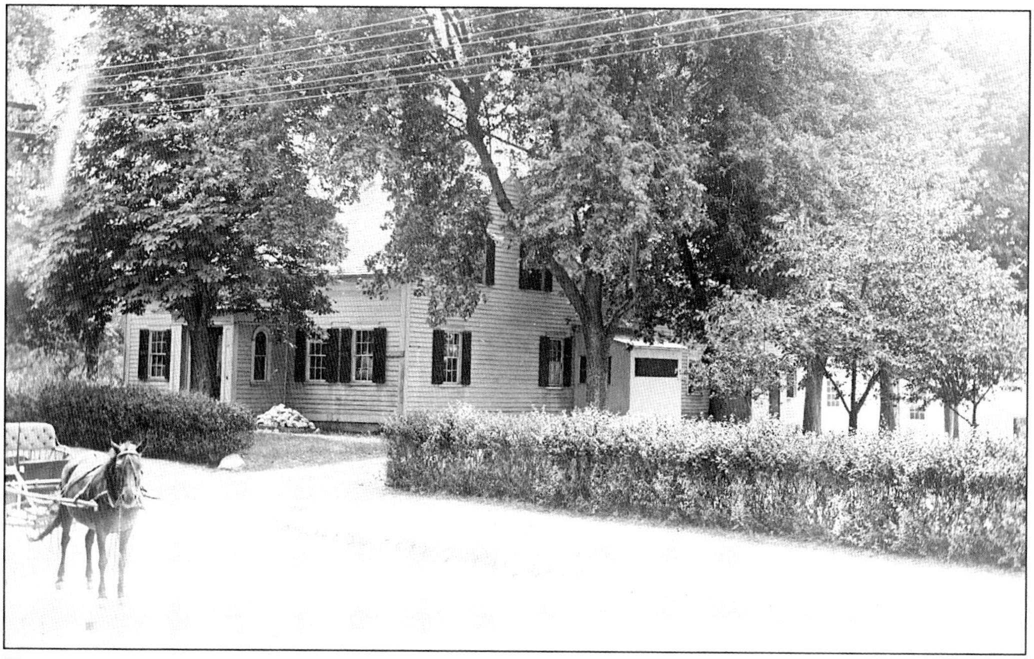

The Job Wilbur House on Wilbur Avenue, c. 1900. In 1867, Job Wilbur's wife, Roby, conceived the brilliant idea of having May Breakfasts as a way for the ladies of the Searle's Corner Benevolent Society to raise funds to build a new church. Her idea became a New England tradition that is still celebrated. Job Wilbur had the distinction of renaming Searle's Corner to Oak Lawn.

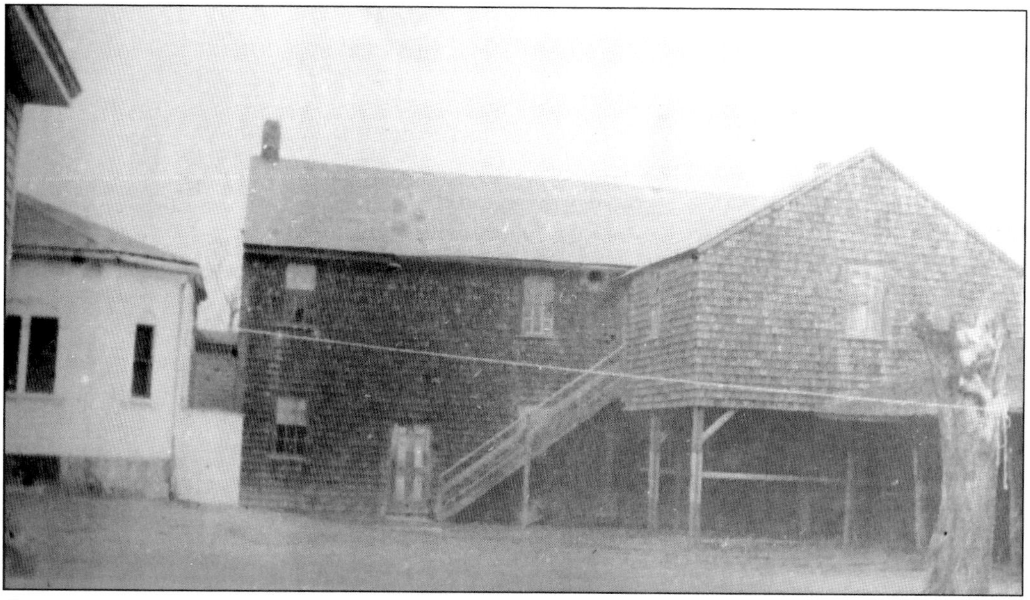

The Old Quaker Meeting House, c. 1940. The Quaker Meeting House was the first church of any kind to be built in Cranston. It was built by the Society of Friends in 1726 and remained in use until 1866. Later on the Baptists built a new church on the land, and the old meetinghouse was moved to the rear of the new church and used for May breakfasts and social gatherings. The building was torn down in the 1950s.

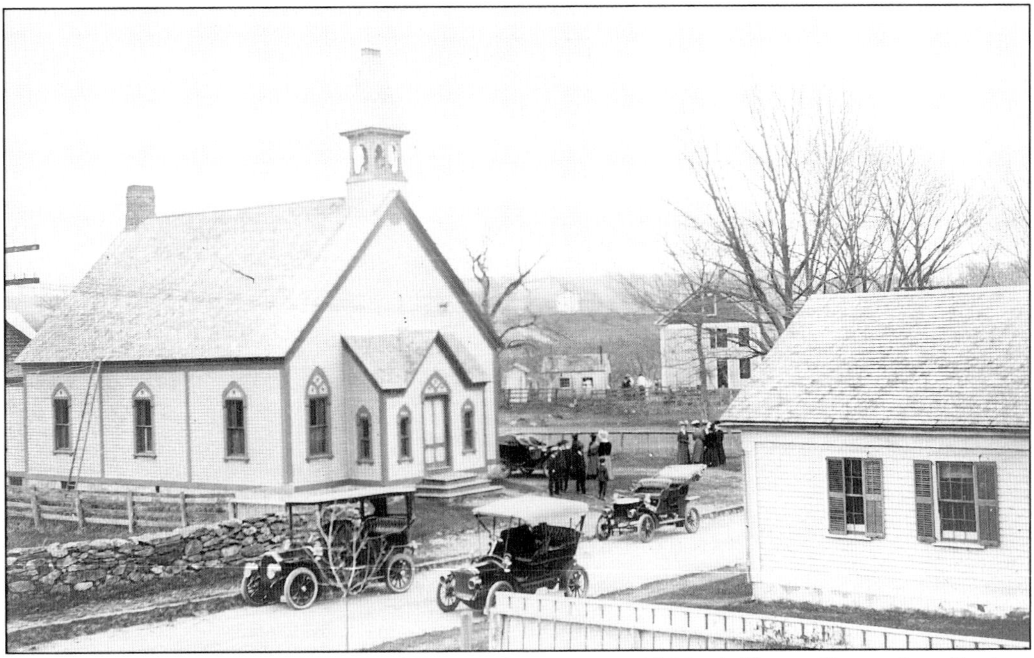

The Oak Lawn Baptist Church, Wilbur Avenue, c. 1900. A Union Benevolent Society was formed about 1866 in order to provide financial aid to build a church. In 1876 the church was organized with 18 members. H.S. Latham was the first pastor. This church was built in 1882.

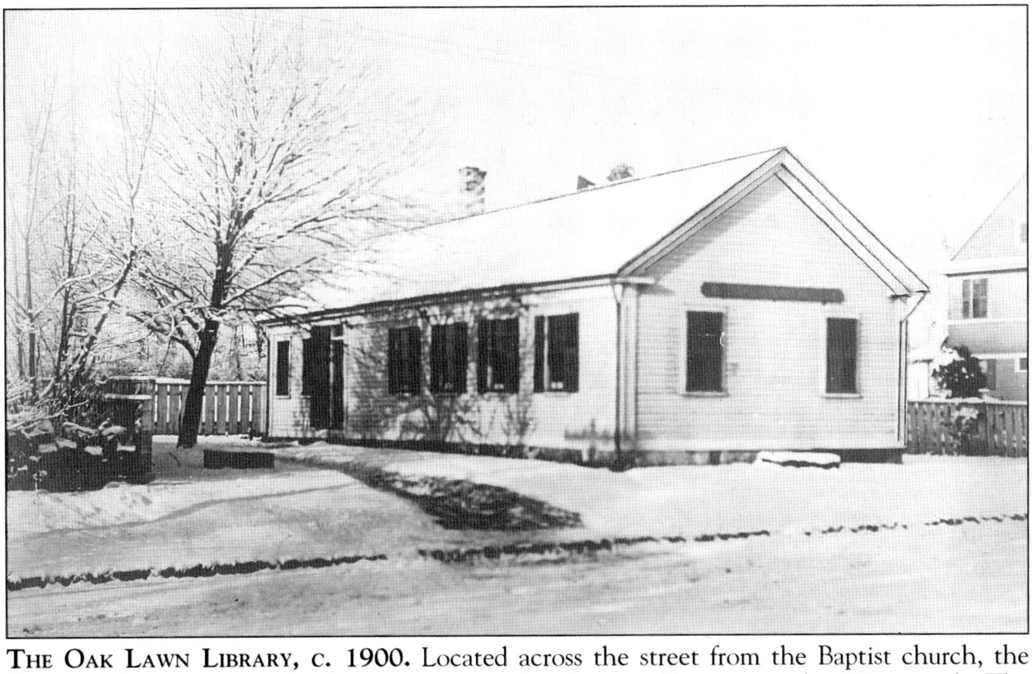

The Oak Lawn Library, c. 1900. Located across the street from the Baptist church, the library building served as a school until 1895. In 1913 the library owned 6,401 journals. The library extension truck was the bookmobile of its day, and in 1922 it loaned 100 books to the farmers of Oak Lawn.

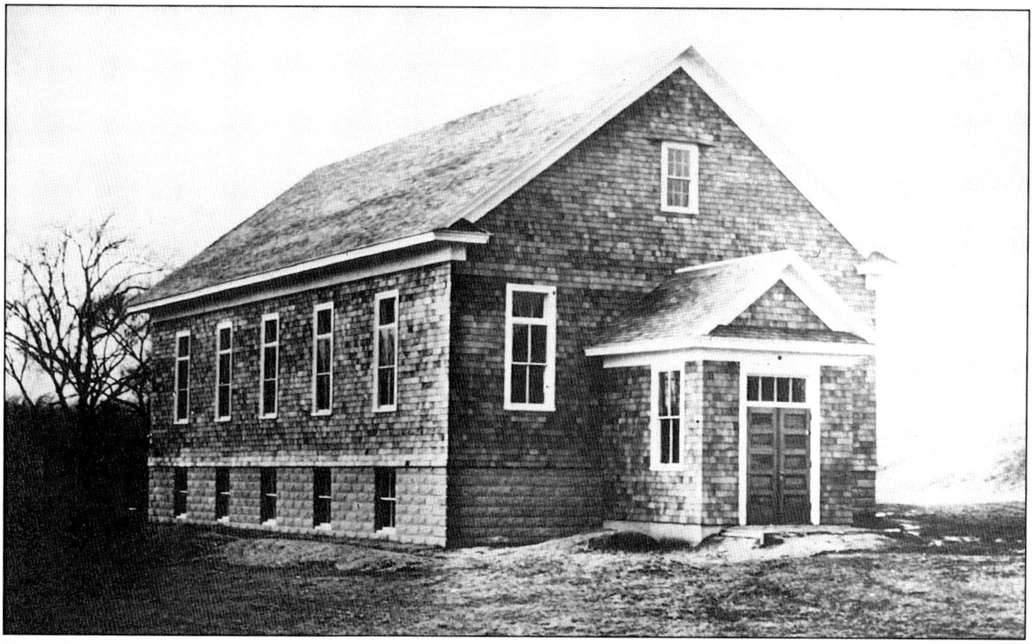

THE OAK LAWN GRANGE HALL. The members of the Oak Lawn Grange held their meetings at the church or at the homes of members before this hall was built. When it officially opened on June 4, 1914, Mayor Horton was one of the guest speakers. It was the cultural meeting place of Oak Lawn.

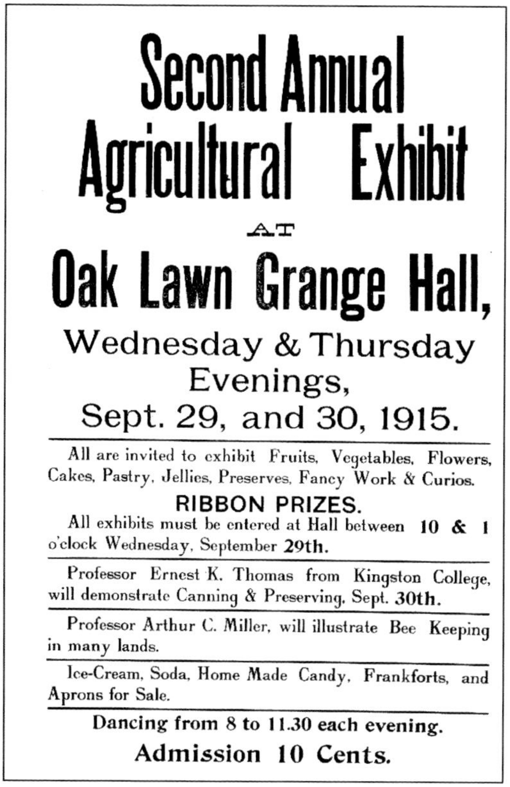

Second Annual
Agricultural Exhibit
AT
Oak Lawn Grange Hall,
Wednesday & Thursday
Evenings,
Sept. 29, and 30, 1915.

All are invited to exhibit Fruits, Vegetables, Flowers, Cakes, Pastry, Jellies, Preserves, Fancy Work & Curios.

RIBBON PRIZES.

All exhibits must be entered at Hall between 10 & 1 o'clock Wednesday, September 29th.

Professor Ernest K. Thomas from Kingston College, will demonstrate Canning & Preserving, Sept. 30th.

Professor Arthur C. Miller, will illustrate Bee Keeping in many lands.

Ice-Cream, Soda, Home Made Candy, Frankforts, and Aprons for Sale.

Dancing from 8 to 11.30 each evening.

Admission 10 Cents.

A 1915 GRANGE POSTER. All types of agricultural exhibits, barn dances, and social events were held at the grange. The price of admission to attend the second annual Agricultural Exhibit, where professors explained beekeeping, canning, and preserving, was 10¢.

THOMAS WALPA, C. 1925. Thomas Walpa was a captain in the Oak Lawn Volunteer Fire Company. He was born in Italy on May 30, 1895. As a teenager he left Italy and adopted Oak Lawn as his home. Known for his generosity, the local children especially liked him because he would slip them a spare nickel or dime in front of Brazil's store, where they could buy penny candy.

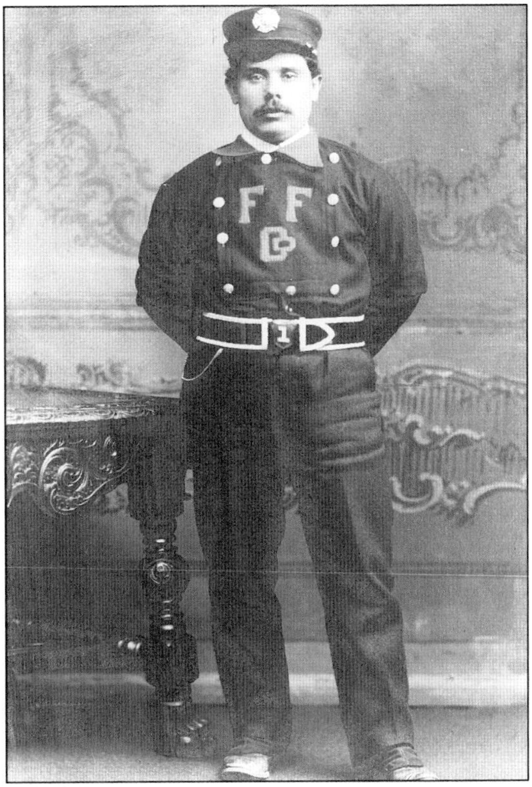

THE OAK LAWN VOLUNTEER FIRE COMPANY, C. 1930. The men of the fire company pose for a photograph with their c. 1923 pumper truck outside the fire station. They are, from left to right, as follows: (front row) unknown, Henderson, Harley Trice, and Curtis Albert; (on the truck) Thomas Walpa, unknown, Gilbert Brazil, Joseph Bettencourt, unknown, ? Montgomery, Earl F. Irons (with the white hat), and unknown.

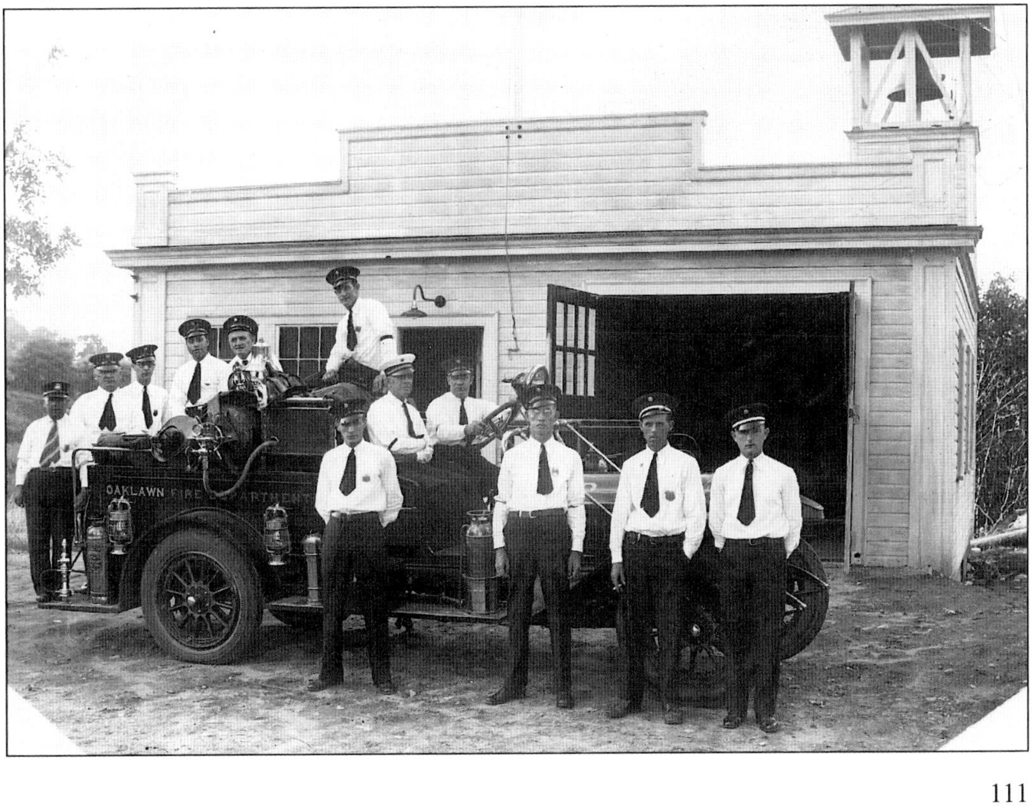

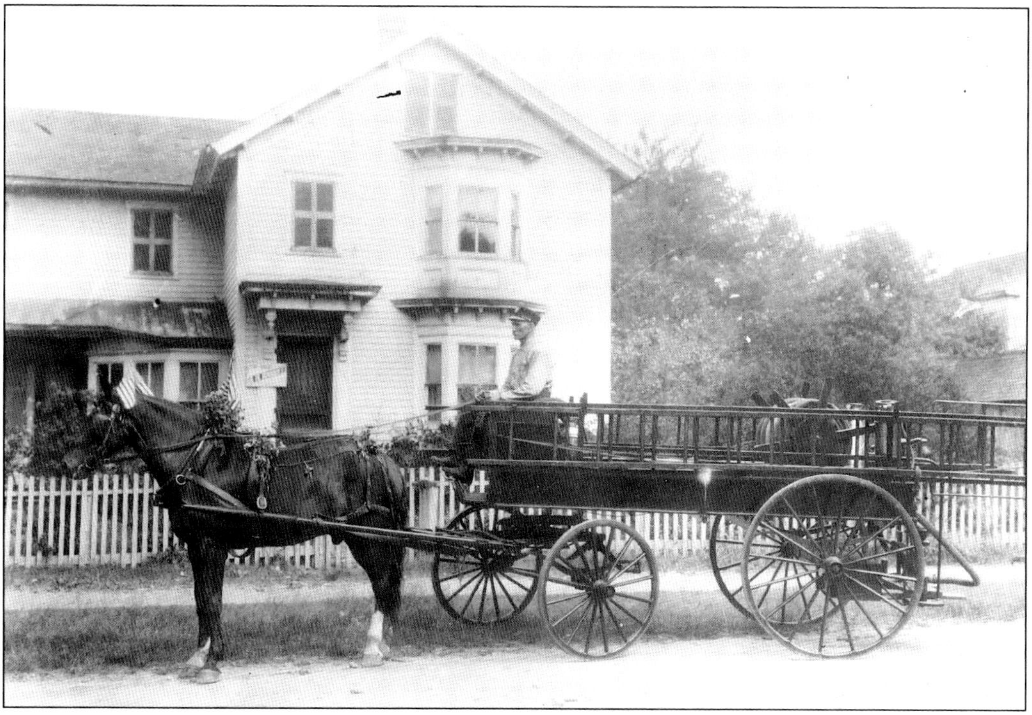

Early Fire Apparatus of the Oak Lawn Volunteer Fire Company, c. 1905. Captain Walpa may have started out his career at the fire company driving this ladder wagon.

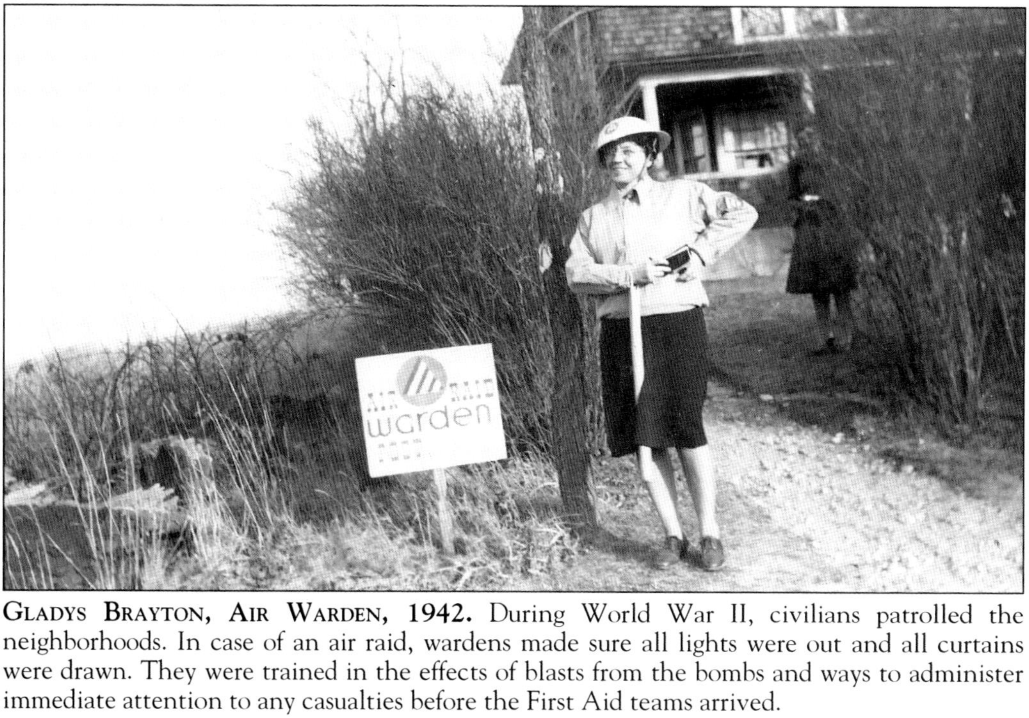

Gladys Brayton, Air Warden, 1942. During World War II, civilians patrolled the neighborhoods. In case of an air raid, wardens made sure all lights were out and all curtains were drawn. They were trained in the effects of blasts from the bombs and ways to administer immediate attention to any casualties before the First Aid teams arrived.

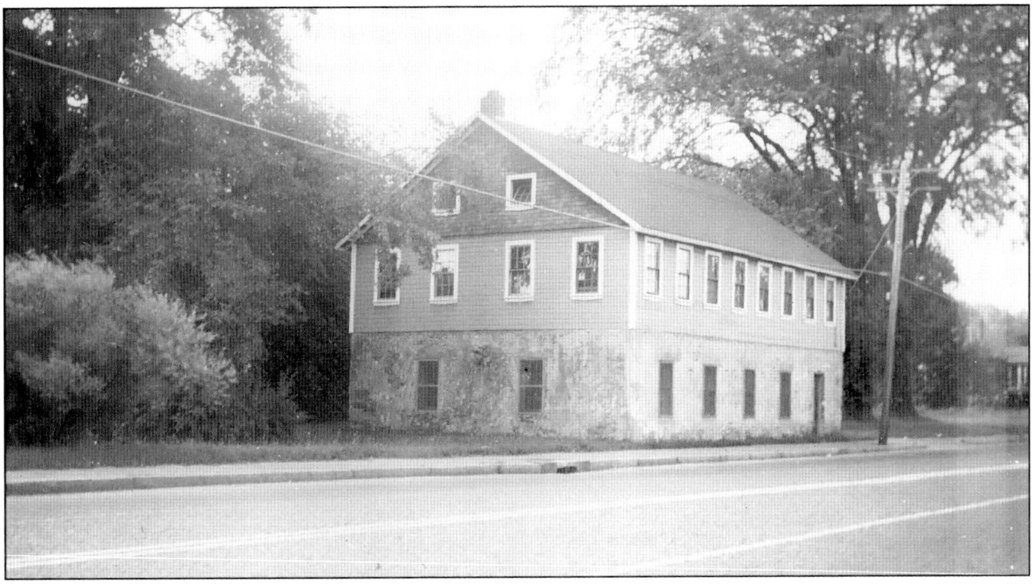

The S&S Turner Wading Mill, c. 1950. This building on Oak Lawn Avenue was originally a sawmill in 1822. It became a cotton mill in 1826, and is now the home of the Potter-Rathbun Organ Company. The wall of stone on the first story may be older than the rest of the mill. In the early 19th century, Stephen and Stuckley Turner started their company here, though they later moved to Olneyville.

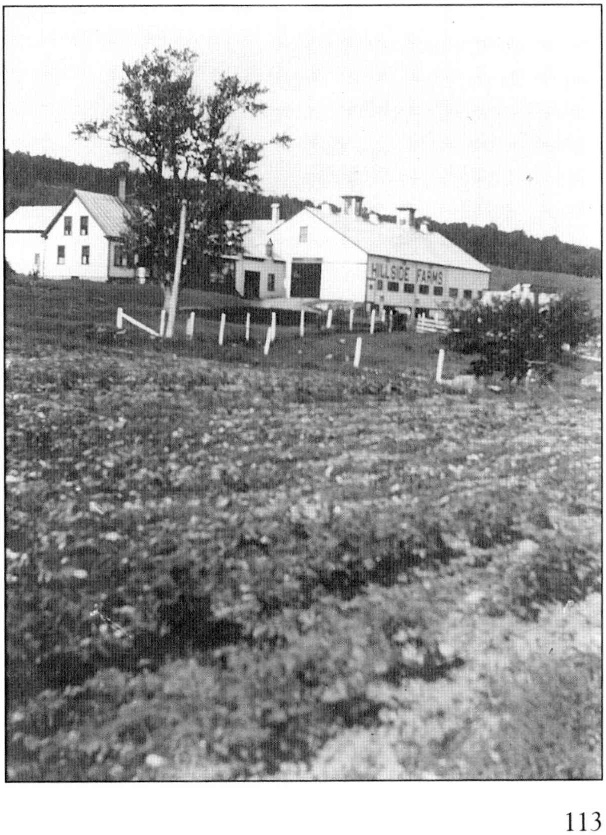

The Hillside Dairy Farm, 1308 Phenix Avenue, c. 1950. This dairy farm at one time had over 100 acres. The barn was recently made into a church and the pastures are now a plat filled with new houses.

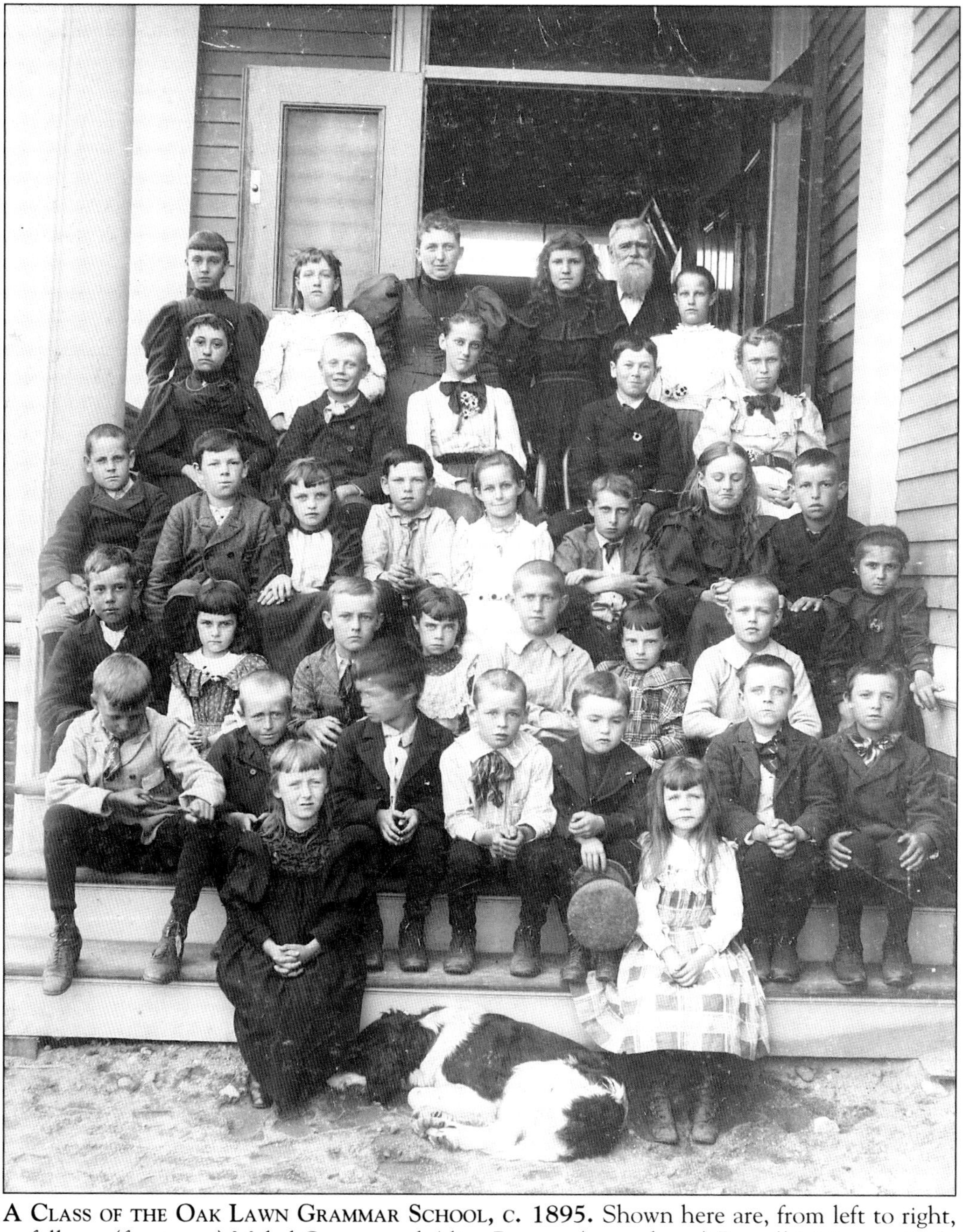

A CLASS OF THE OAK LAWN GRAMMAR SCHOOL, C. 1895. Shown here are, from left to right, as follows: (front row) Mabel Greene and Alice Bowen; (second row) Russell McIntyre, Earle Mathewson, Mickey Kelley, Clarke Smith, Harold Condgon, Nelson Borben, and unknown; (third row) Robert Brayton, Josephine Hines, Norman Robertson, Lena Bowen, Arthur Armstrong, Cora West, Arthur Kruger, and Mary Brazil; (fourth row) unknown, George Hines, Pearl Trainer, Henry Hines, Adelaide Shaw, Walter Mowrey, Bertha Robertson, and Chester Searle; (fifth row) Annie Andrews, unknown, Florence Armstrong, Leo Hines, and Marion Corey; (back row) Agnes Milliken, Annie Silva, Miss Hanson, unknown, Mr. Skinner, and Marjorie Shaw.

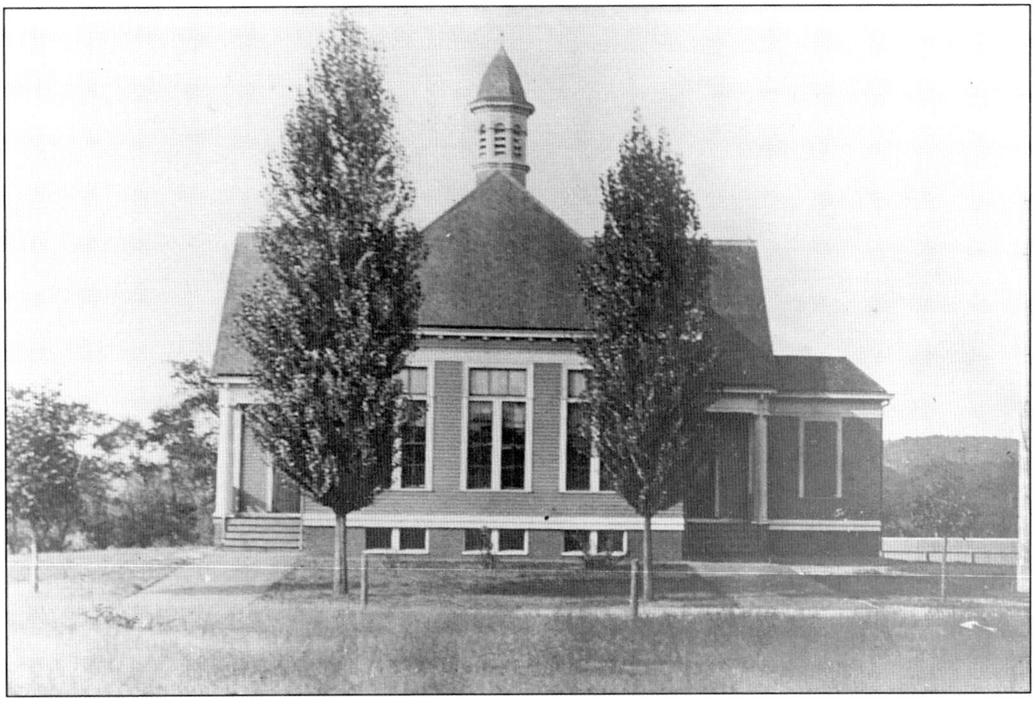

The Oak Lawn Grammar School, c. 1895. This school opened in the spring of 1895 at a cost of $6,232.69. The taxpayers certainly got their money's worth in those days.

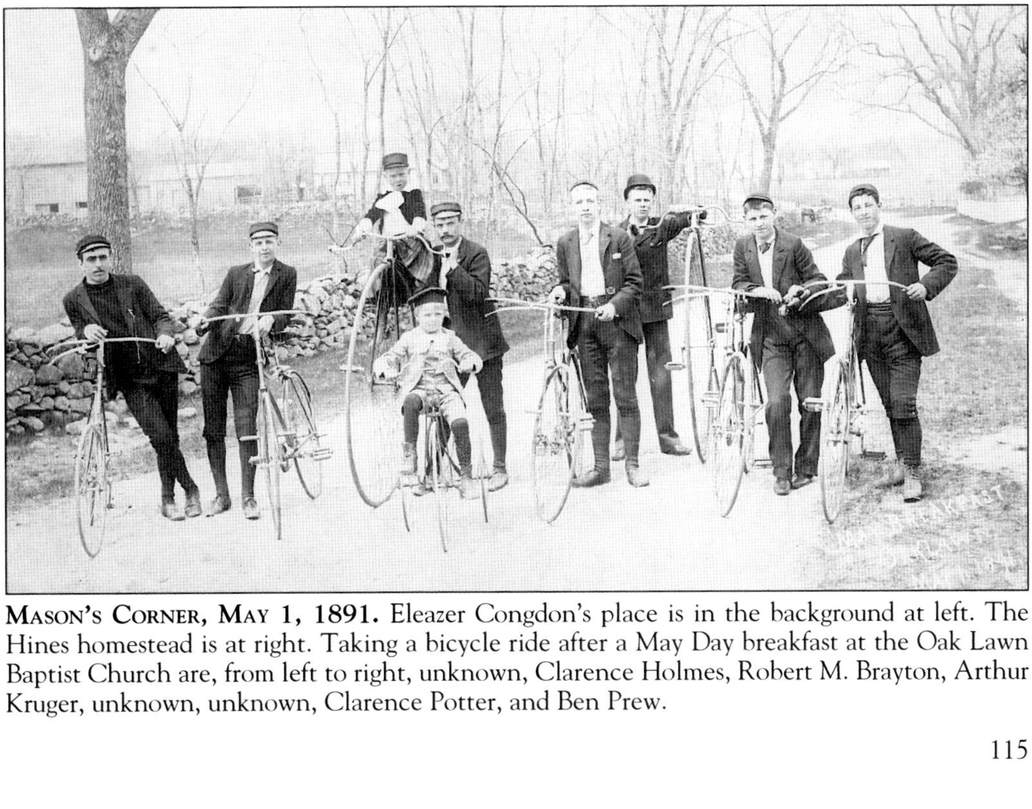

Mason's Corner, May 1, 1891. Eleazer Congdon's place is in the background at left. The Hines homestead is at right. Taking a bicycle ride after a May Day breakfast at the Oak Lawn Baptist Church are, from left to right, unknown, Clarence Holmes, Robert M. Brayton, Arthur Kruger, unknown, unknown, Clarence Potter, and Ben Prew.

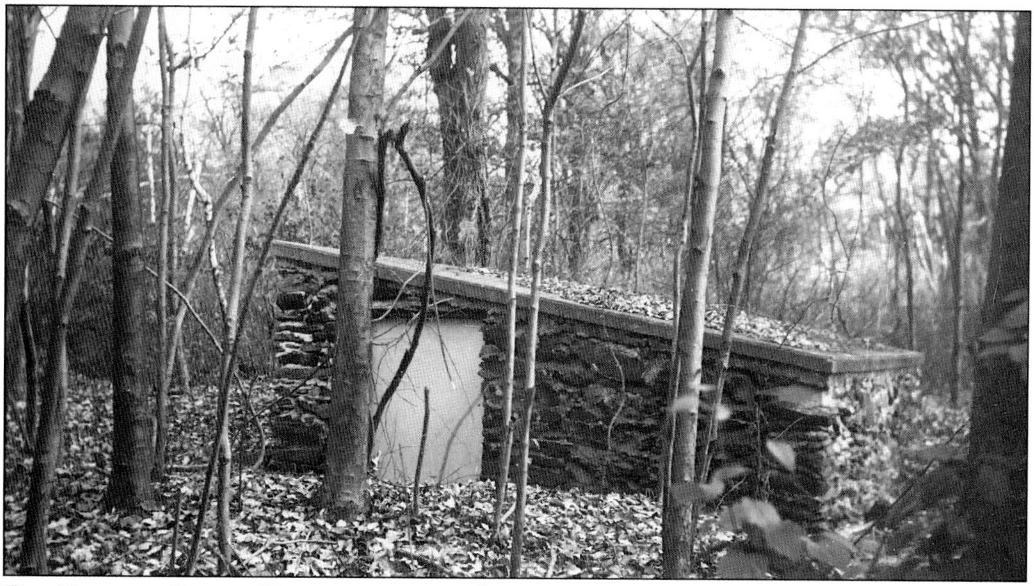

The Brayton Spring House, c. 1950. This stone house covered a spring on the Brayton property that gave Old Spring Road its name. Back in the 1900s, the Braytons sold bottled water from the spring, which never runs dry. (Bette Miller Collection.)

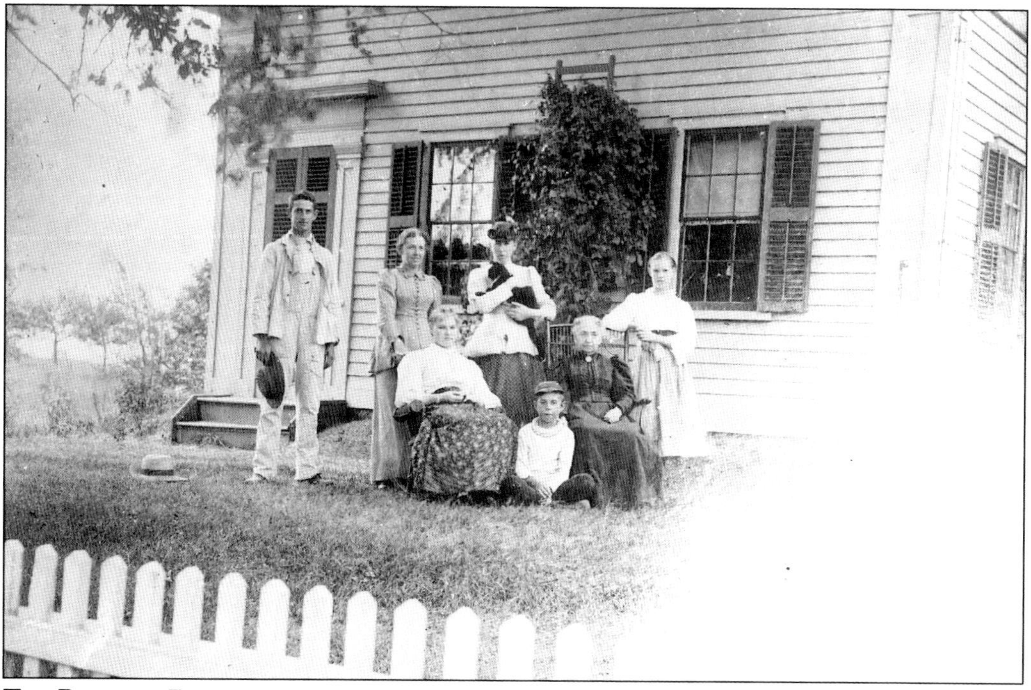

The Brayton Family in front of the Brayton Homestead, c. 1896. One of this book's authors, Bette Miller, is a member of the Brayton family, one of the oldest families in Oak Lawn. The little boy in the center of the picture is her father, Robert Brayton (also seen in Oak Lawn School group and in the old bicycle picture, p. 114 and p. 115). (Bette Miller Collection.)

Eight

THORNTON

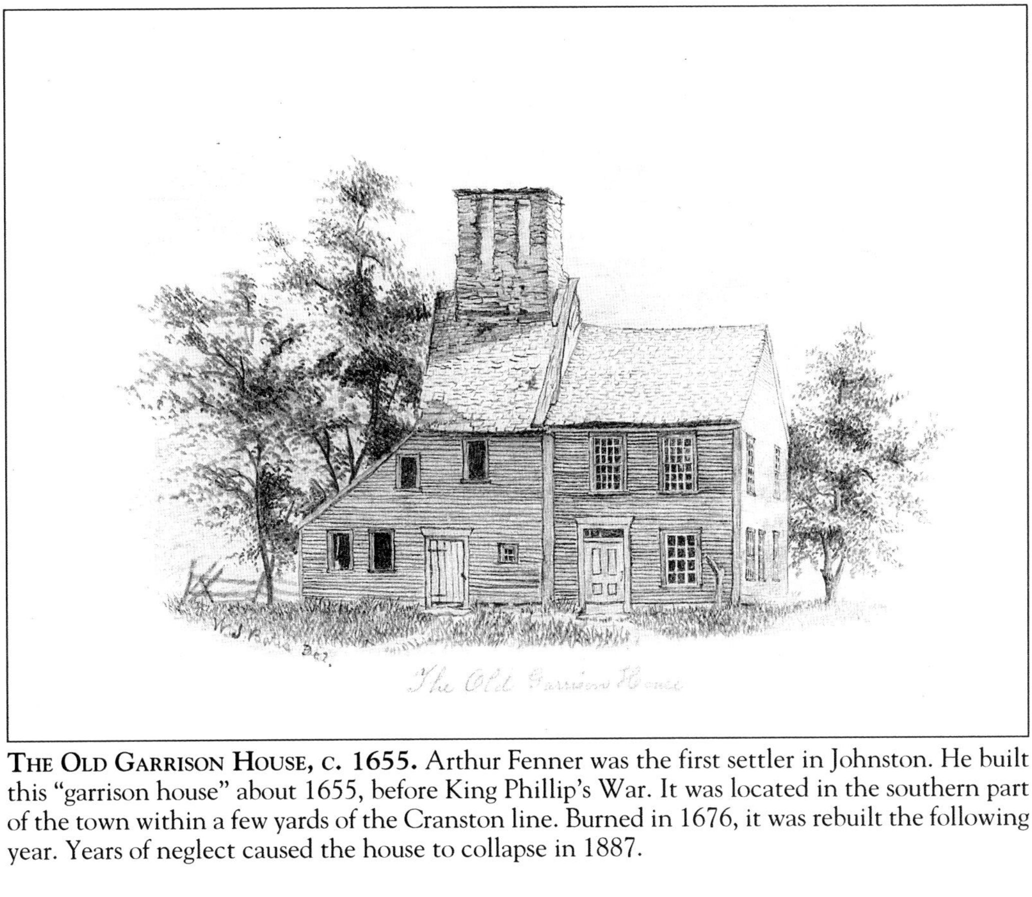

THE OLD GARRISON HOUSE, C. 1655. Arthur Fenner was the first settler in Johnston. He built this "garrison house" about 1655, before King Phillip's War. It was located in the southern part of the town within a few yards of the Cranston line. Burned in 1676, it was rebuilt the following year. Years of neglect caused the house to collapse in 1887.

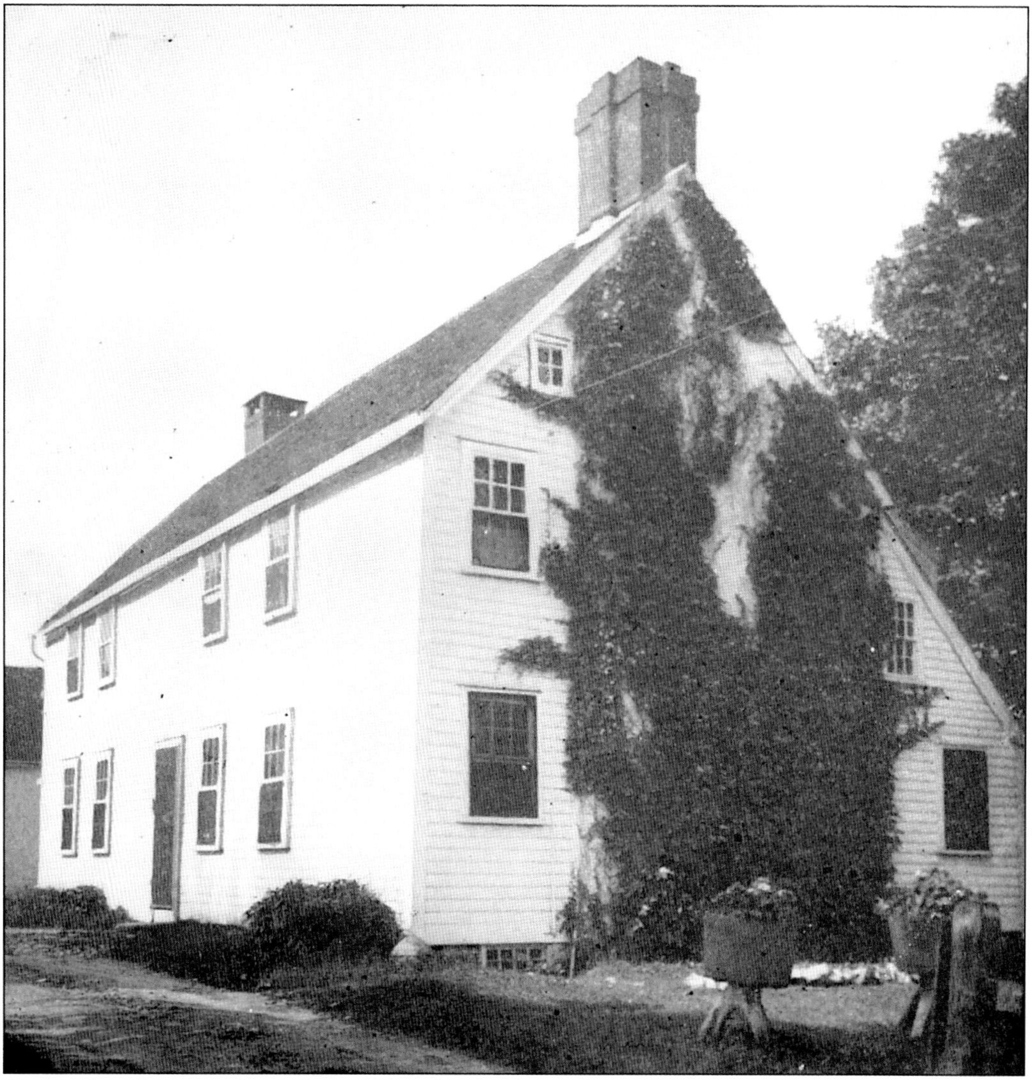

THE MAJOR THOMAS FENNER HOUSE. This homestead was built in 1667 by Arthur Fenner for his son Thomas following the wars with the Native Americans. When it was built it had only one room on the ground floor, one room on the second floor, and an unfinished attic. It was used as a tavern in the 19th century, and is a piece of Rhode Island history on Plainfield Pike.

Nine

Western Cranston

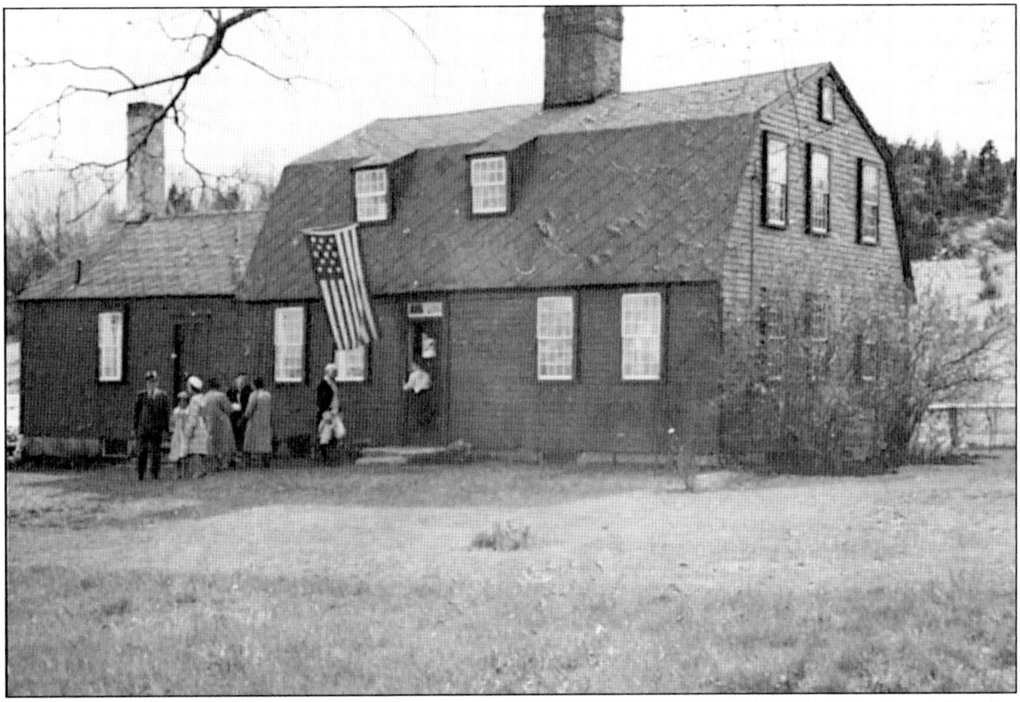

The Joy Homestead, 156 Scituate Avenue, c. 1976. Now owned and maintained by the Cranston Historical Society, the Joy Homestead is an example of 18th-century construction. It was home to three generations of the Joy family. Job Joy was a cobbler and farmer. This quaint house is one of the last remaining houses that were standing when Rochambeau's troops marched from Providence through Knightsville on the Monkeytown Road and along Scituate Avenue on the way to Yorktown, VA.

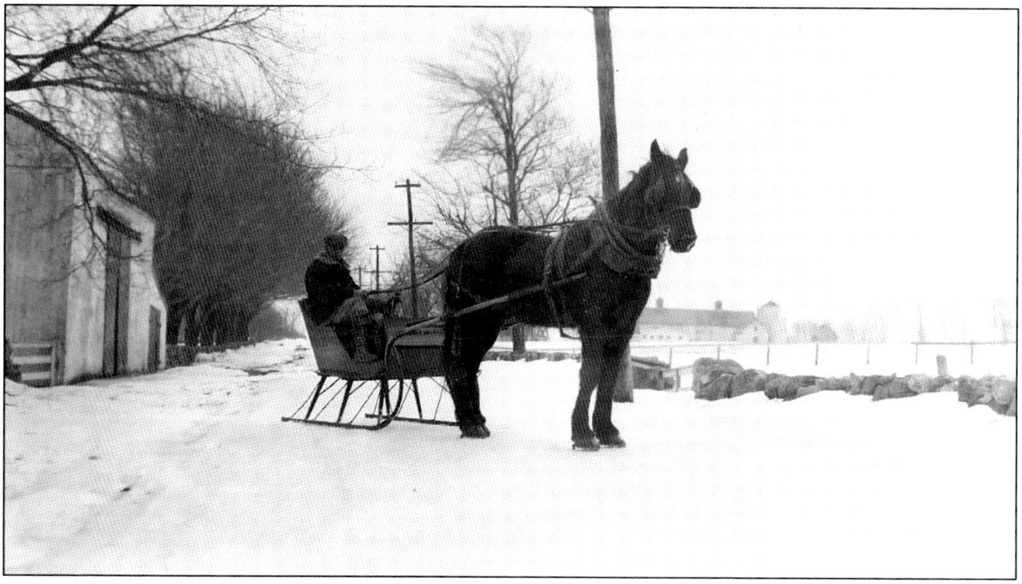

COMSTOCK PARKWAY, c. 1922. The hay barn pictured here on the road was blown down in the 1938 Hurricane. The big barn off in the distance burned in May 1930. Manuel Bettencourt, in the sleigh, is going for supplies. There was probably no better way to get around in winter then a one-horse sleigh.

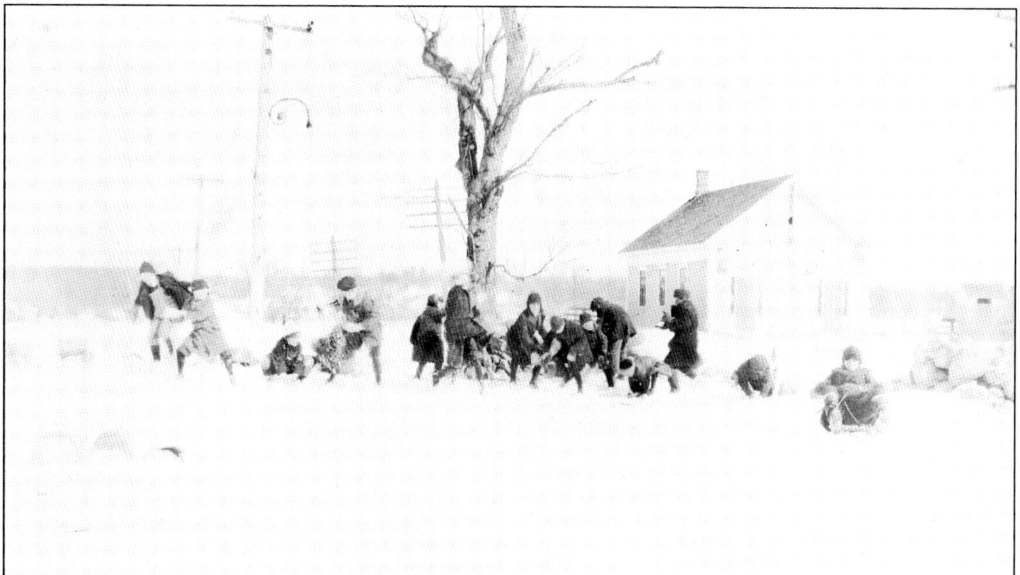

THE PIPPIN ORCHARD SCHOOL, NORTHEAST CORNER OF SCITUATE AVENUE AND PIPPIN ORCHARD ROAD, c. 1898. Students at recess acted the same way children do today when there is snow on the ground. They are having a snowball fight and sledding down the small hill.

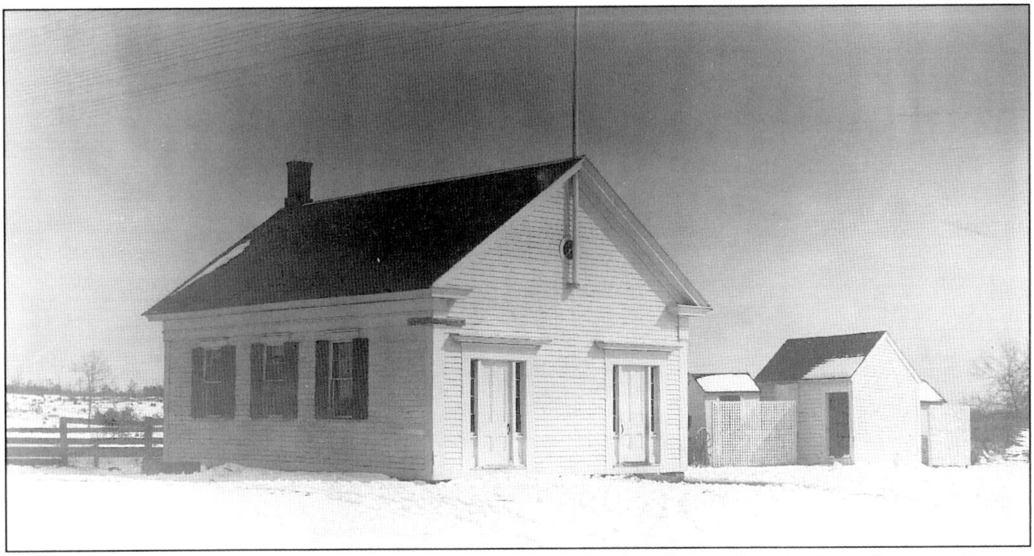

THE PIPPIN ORCHARD SCHOOL, C. 1898. The original school was closed when the new Pippin Orchard School was opened. In 1923 the old building was sold for $1 to Frank Knight, who had donated part of his property for the new schoolhouse. In the 1950s the old school was moved to the Knight Farm to be used as a garage.

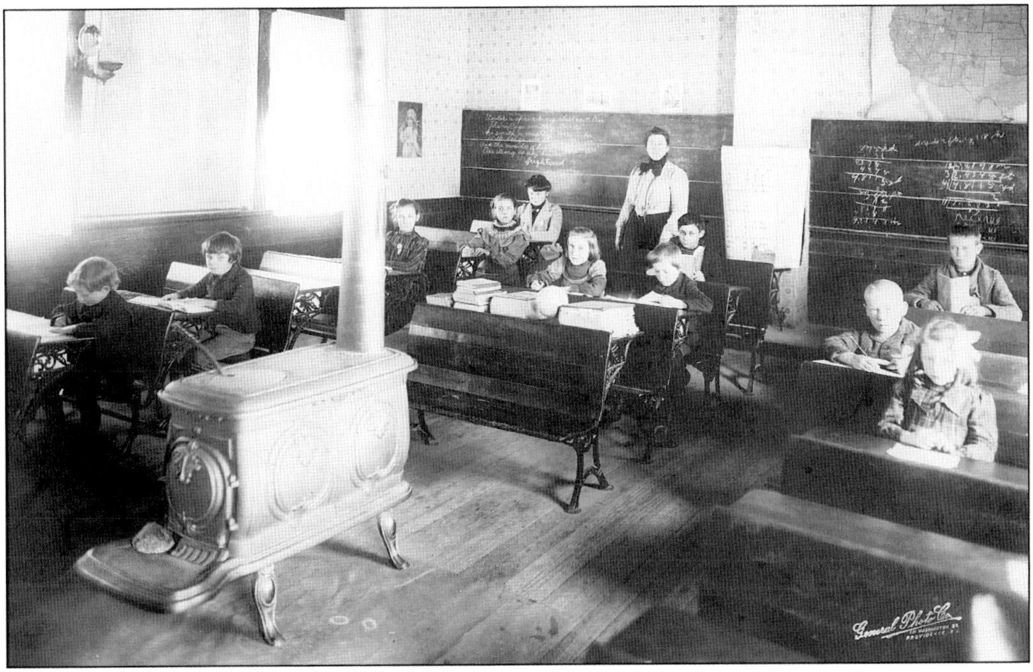

THE PIPPIN ORCHARD SCHOOL, C. 1900S. The teacher would choose one of the older boys to be in charge of getting the firewood and keeping the stove going. The student was paid 50¢ a week for bringing in the wood, and, of course, he had to be at school very early to start the fire in order to warm the room before the teacher rang the bell to begin the day's activities.

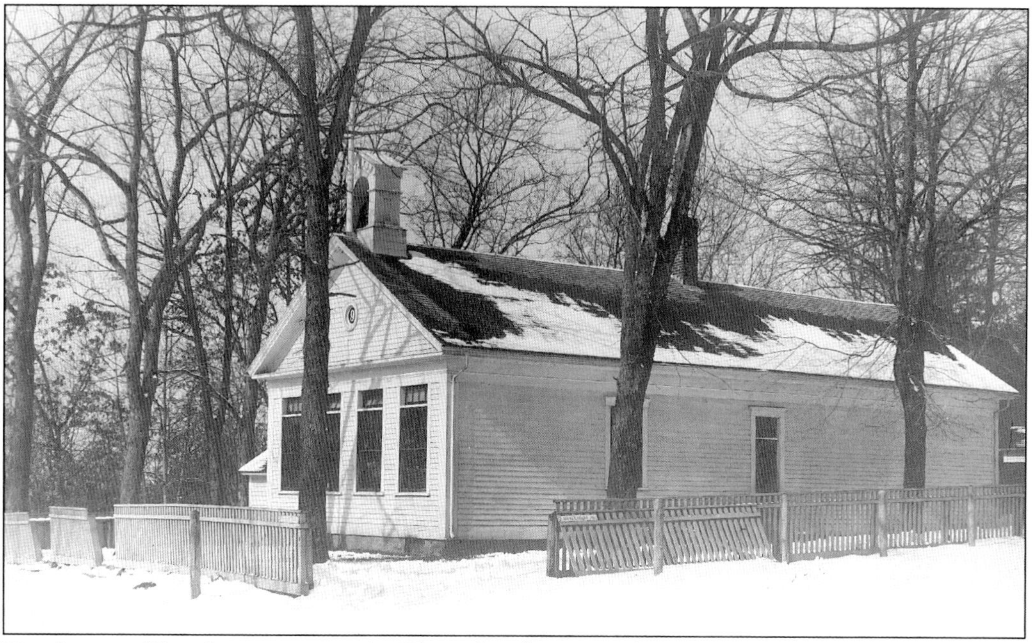

The Lippitt Hill School, c. 1958. This schoolhouse at the corner of Hope Road and Lippett Avenue closed its doors to students for the last time in 1958. Today it is a private home, and the owners retain much of the original schoolroom environment.

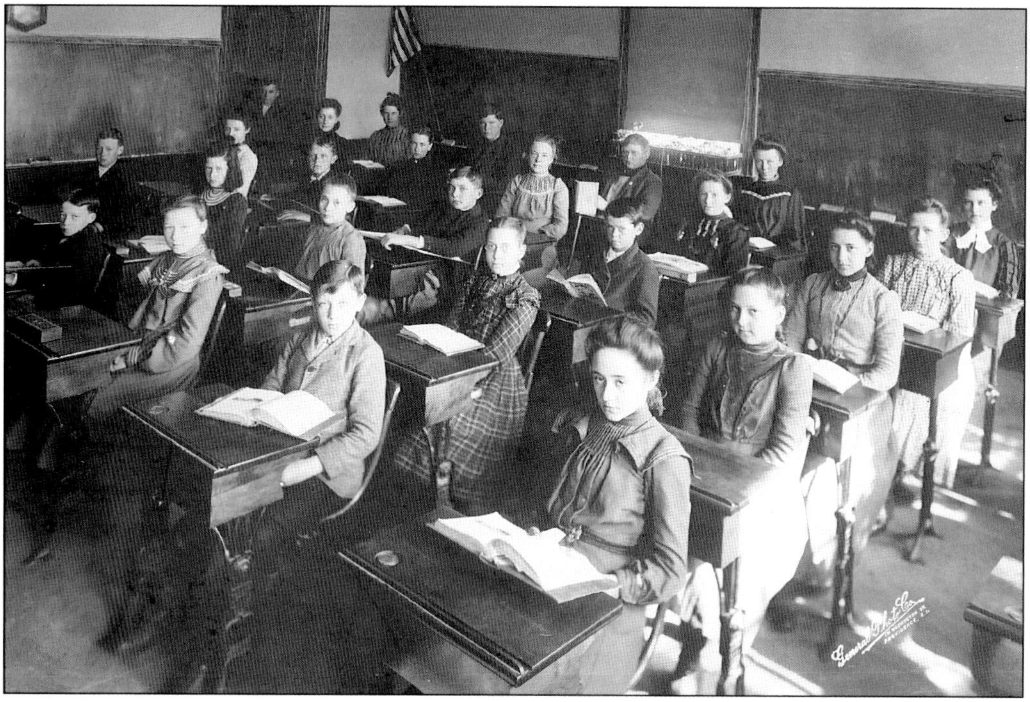

A Lippett Hill School Class, c. 1920. Do you recognize any of these serious scholars? If walls could speak, one can bet they would have some wonderful tales to tell of times in an old-fashioned schoolhouse.

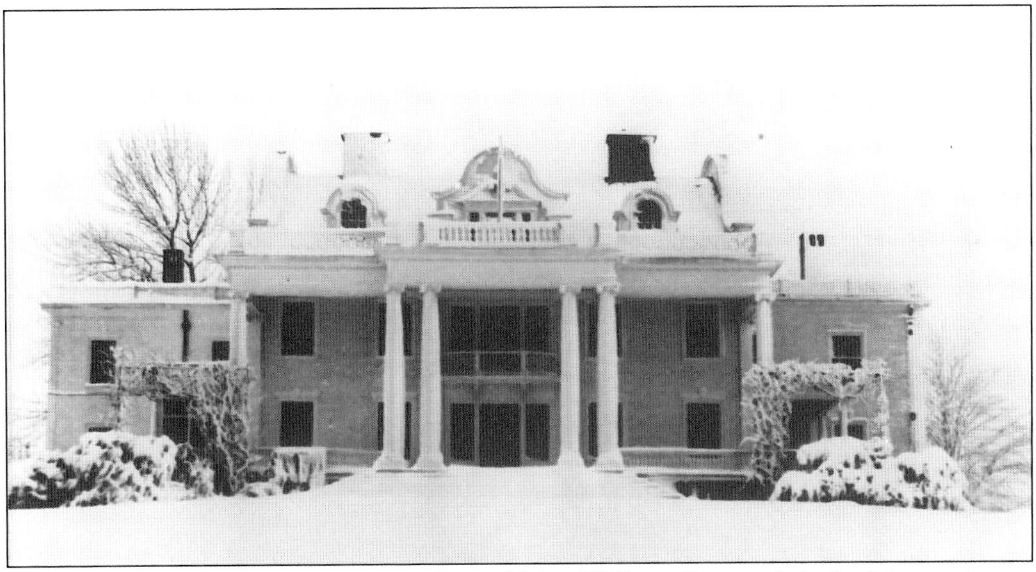

THE COMSTOCK MANSION, C. 1906. Mr. and Mrs. William Comstock built this mansion to reassemble a house that they saw at the 1904 St. Louis Exposition exhibition. The three-story house stood on Apple House Hill. It was one of the showplaces in the state.

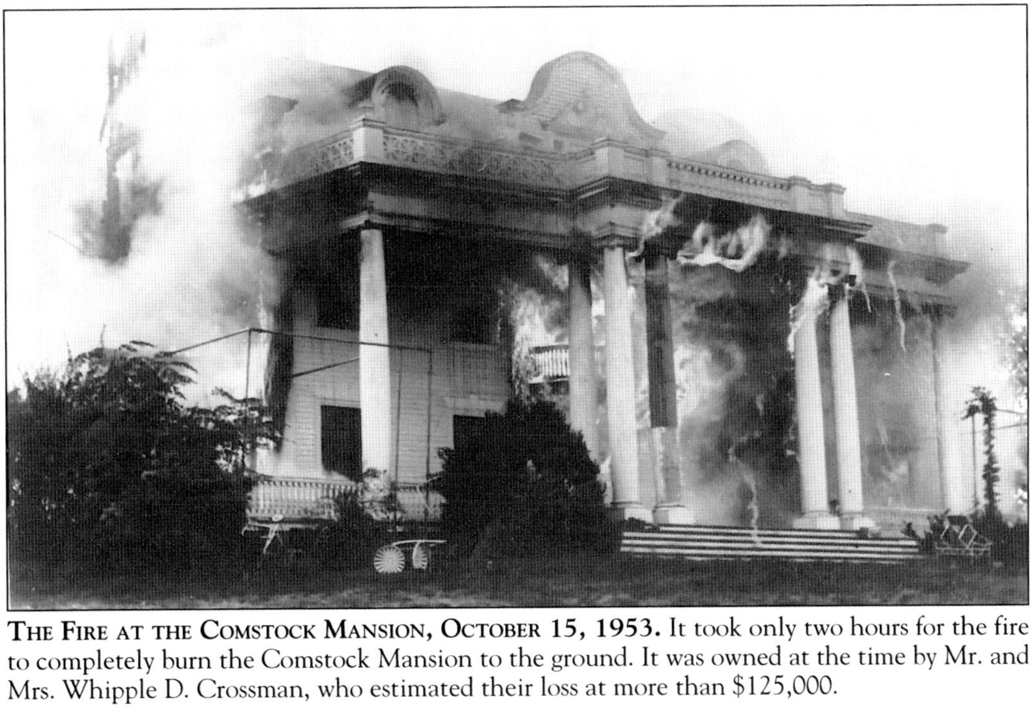

THE FIRE AT THE COMSTOCK MANSION, OCTOBER 15, 1953. It took only two hours for the fire to completely burn the Comstock Mansion to the ground. It was owned at the time by Mr. and Mrs. Whipple D. Crossman, who estimated their loss at more than $125,000.

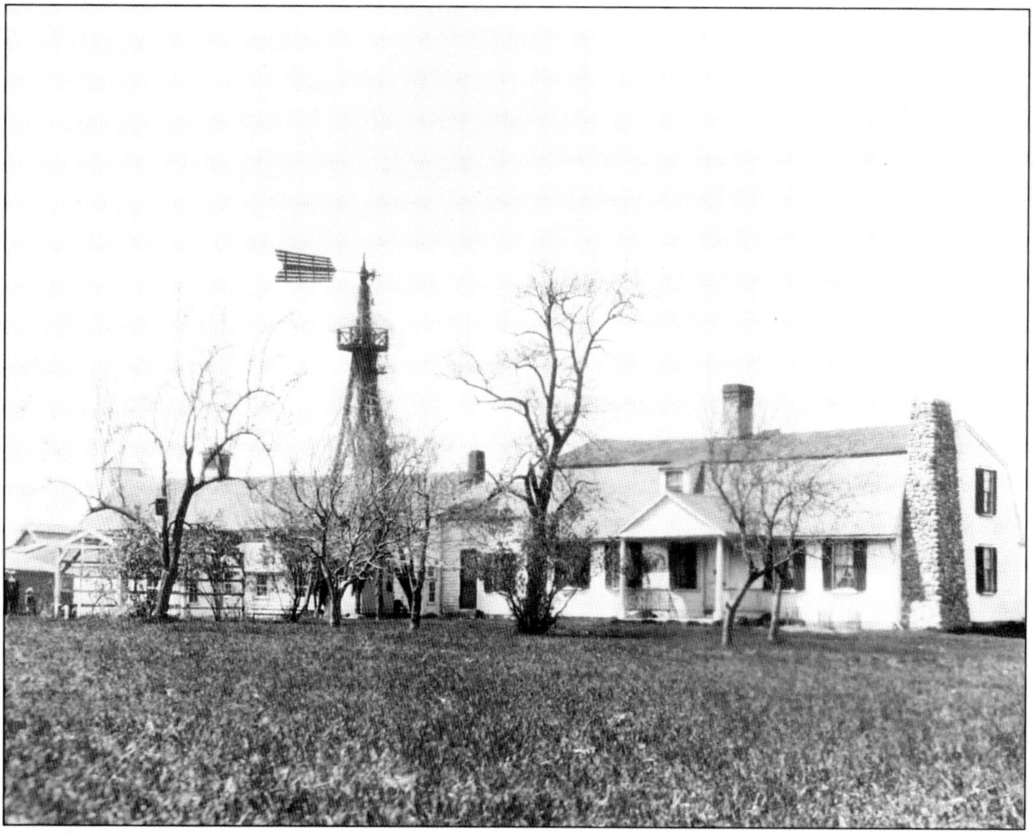

THE SQUIRE JOHN BURTON HOUSE, C. 1920. This house became the main building of the Cranston Country Club. The golf course opened for business on August 1, 1928. It was the longest nine-hole course in Rhode Island at that time. When the historic Burton Farm was first settled, the Meshanticut Indians still used the area for hunting. The home was saved from a fire in 1930 that destroyed a storage barn and an ice house.

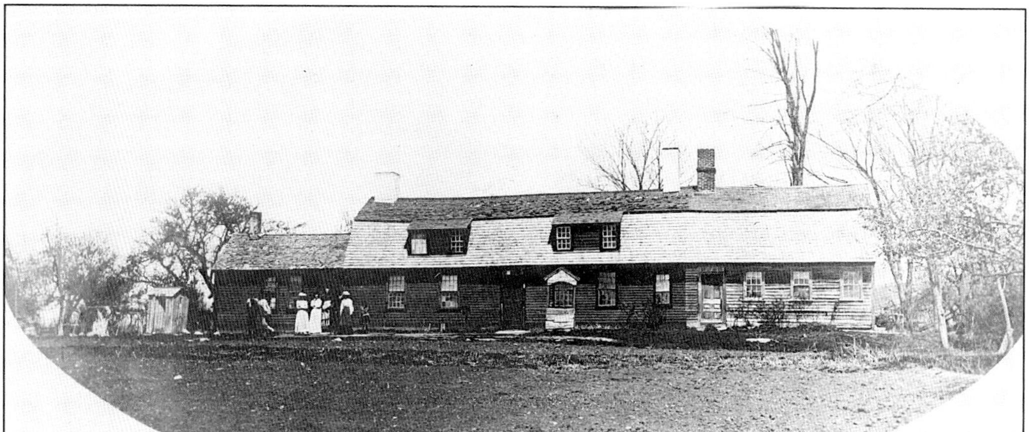

THE LONG HOUSE, C. 1900. This home was built by Edward Searle just before 1700. Located on the northeast side of Pippin Orchard Road in the vicinity of Herrod Brook, it was the only house left standing after King Phillip's War. It was torn down in 1946.

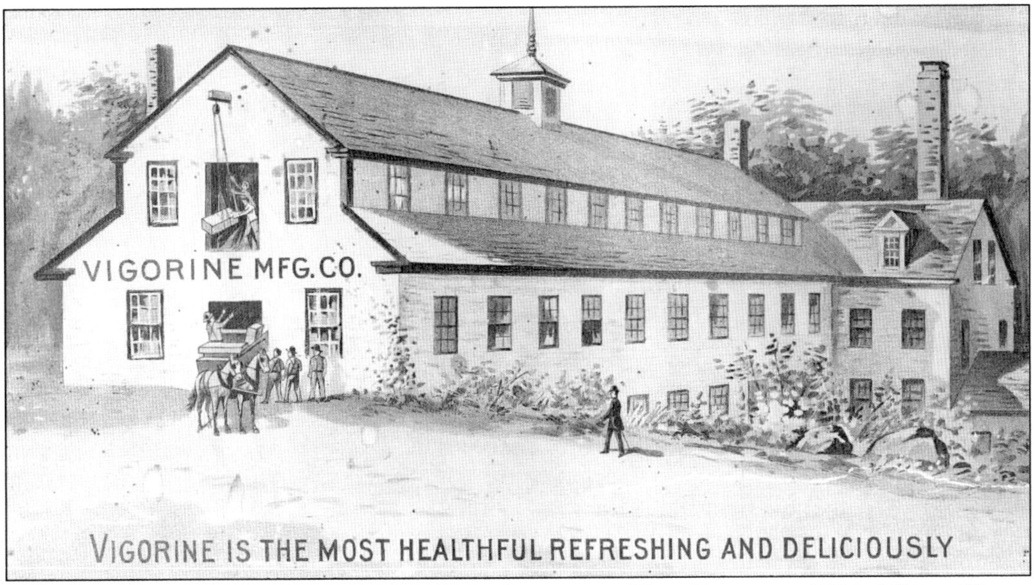

The Vigorine Manufacturing Company, Dugaway Hill Road, c. 1829. This mill was once the site of the Rhode Island Print Works. In the early 1900s, Charles Halstead opened the Vigorine Factory. Vigorine was marketed as a temperance beverage. It was a favorite of bicyclists because a drink of the beverage would give them a boost. It was no wonder they liked it—the alcohol content was 15 percent.

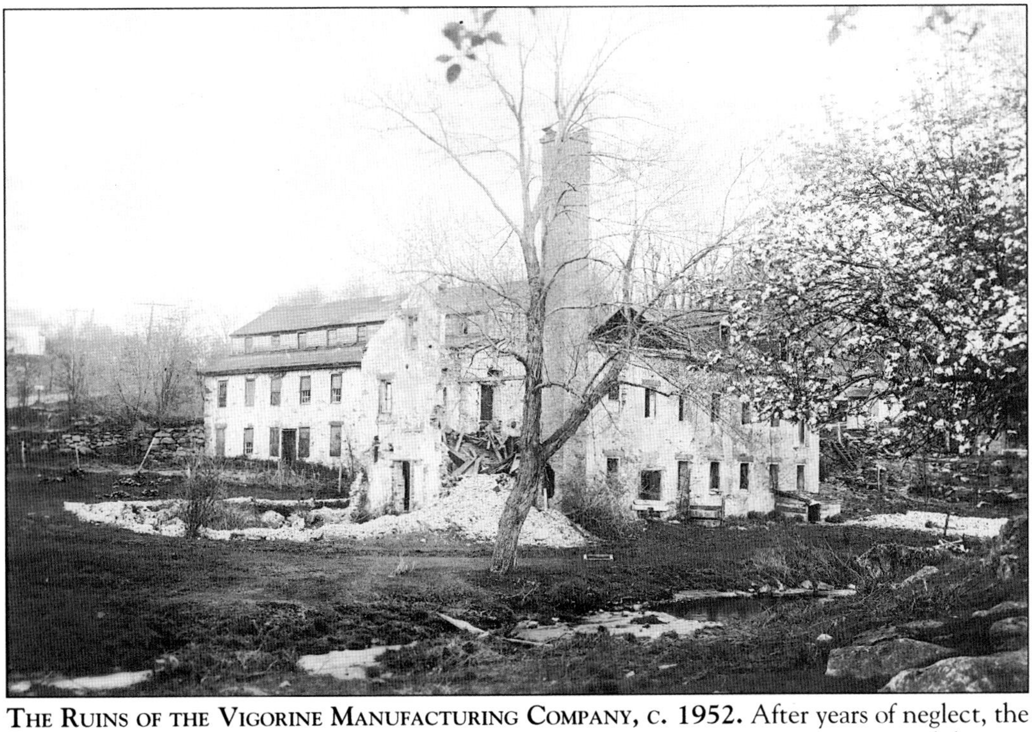

The Ruins of the Vigorine Manufacturing Company, c. 1952. After years of neglect, the Vigorine Mill at Dugaway Hill became a pile of ruins. In 1952, the Boy Scouts acquired the site, cleaned it up, and made a new camp site. It is now the Champlin Reservation.

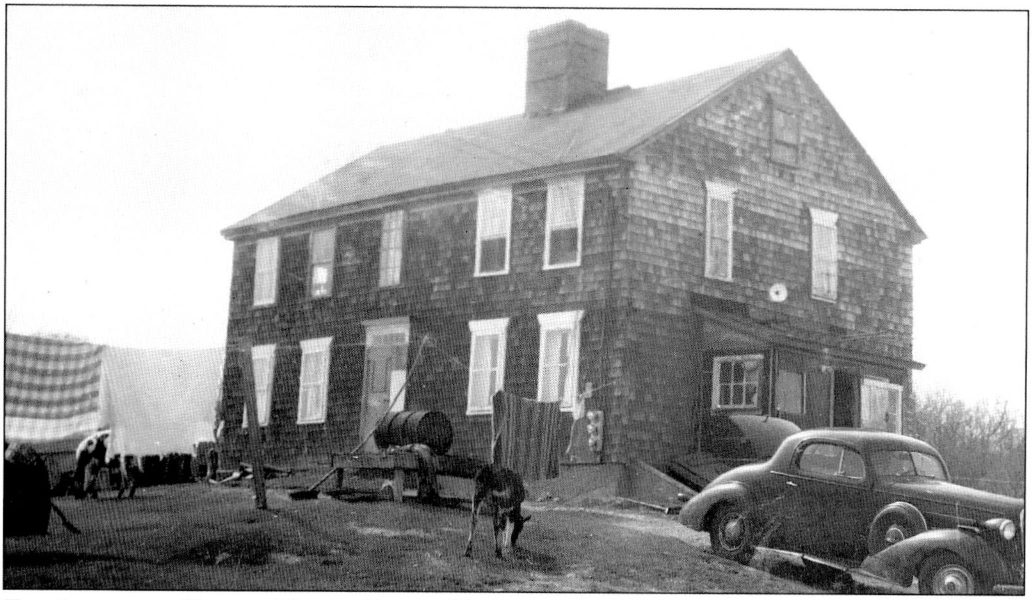

The Jonathan Knight House, Laten Knight Road, c. 1950. The Castle Hill Farm was constructed about 1785. Reverend Jonathan Knight served in several different units during the Revolutionary War, including stints on the frigate *Providence*. The farm remained in the Knight family until 1863, when it was sold to the Hudson family. Over the next 66 years the farm changed hands several times until Byron Lawton bought it in 1929.

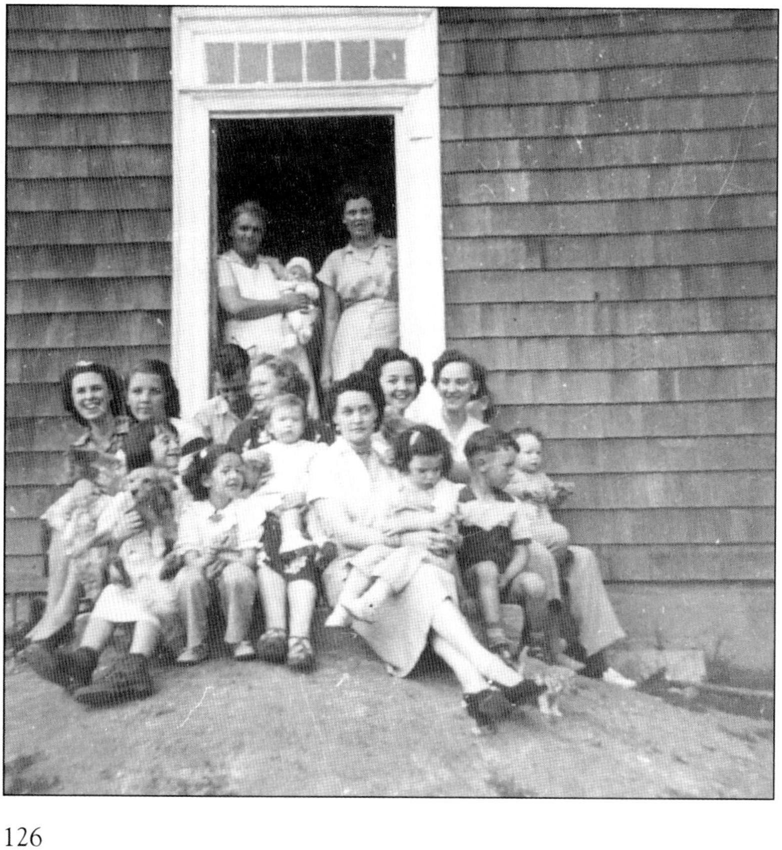

The Byron Lawton Family at the Jonathan Knight House, June 1951. From 1929 until 1997, Byron Lawton and his family worked the Castle Hill Farm. Byron and Evelyn raised 11 children, six of whom were born on the farm. During its peek, the Castle Hill Farm produced milk for much of Cranston and its surrounding communities. (Courtesy of Bierman family, Castle Hill Farm.)

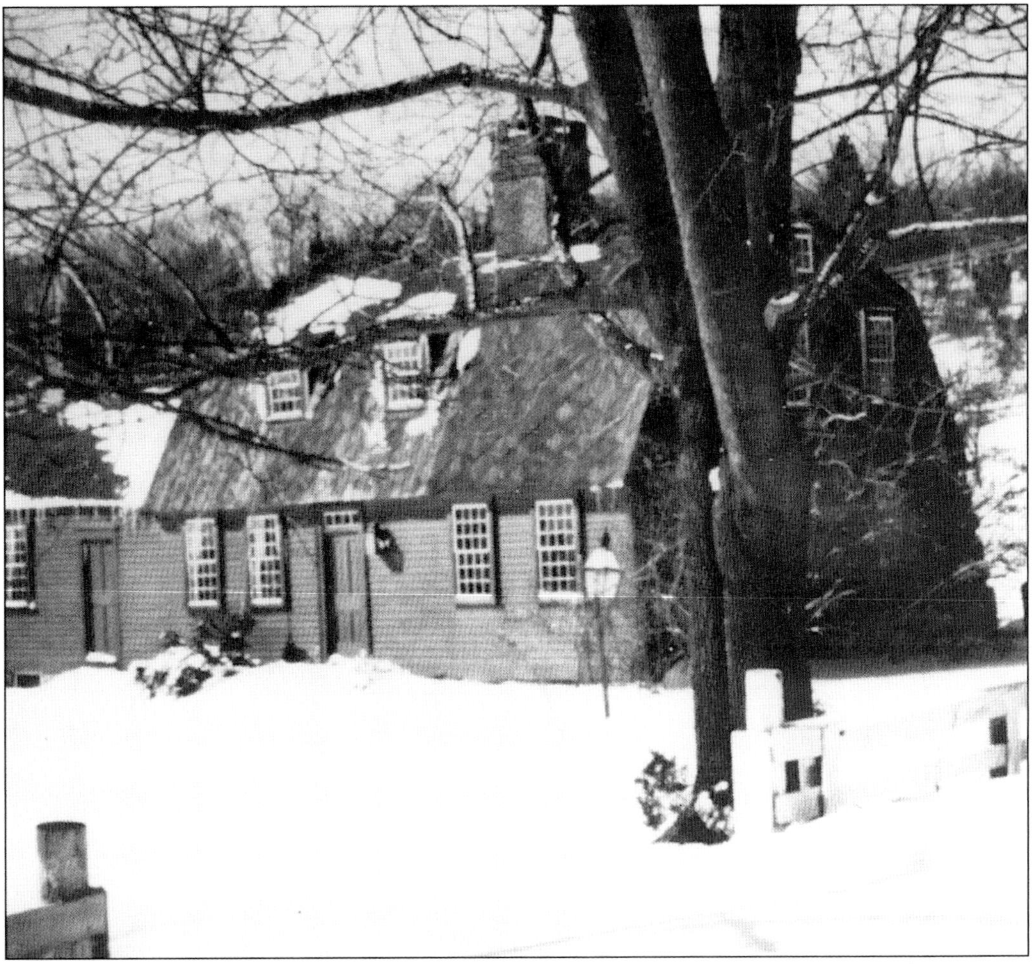

THE JOY HOMESTEAD, 156 SCITUATE AVENUE, C. 1976. The Cranston Historical Society is fortunate to own two pieces of historical property in Cranston. Each house embraces a different era and way of life. The Joy Homestead offers an example of simple but hard farm life in the 18th century. Job Joy was so poor he was excused by the town council from paying his taxes. In the 19th century, the Sprague Mansion was the center of a manorial paternalist system. The Sprague family was known for their wealth, not only monetarily but politically and socially. The Cranston Historical Society, celebrating 50 years of historic preservation in 1999, is proud to be able to enrich the lives of students who tour the Joy Homestead and Sprague Mansion through glimpses of the life styles of people from two different eras and social standings. Hopefully the young people of today will be the caretakers of history tomorrow.

Acknowledgments

The Cranston Historical Society offers sincere thanks and acknowledge our indebtedness to those in the past who have donated photographs and other historical memorabilia that have made the completion of this volume possible.

Gratitude is offered to Jeanne Grandchamp, Chair of the English Department at Bristol Community College in Fall River, Massachusetts, for her unwavering support and encouragement, for proofreading and suggestions, and for other efforts in support of this project.

A special thank you is extended to Cranston Historical Society President Herbert Zakrison, who, in addition to being a pillar of support to the Cranston Historical Society, has been a catalyst in the completion of this project.

Special thanks also go out to Alice Baxter, for her lifelong contributions to the Cranston Historical Society, and the Brock Bierman family of Castle Hill Farms, for information about the Jonathan Knight House.

A thank you to all who offered advice and encouragement.

Bibliography

Brayton, Gladys W. *Cranston Historical Society Newsletters*. 1968–1984.

Brayton, Gladys W. "The Old Dugaway Mill." *Cranston Herald*, January 3, 1952.

Brayton, Gladys, W. *Other Ways and Other Days*. East Providence, RI: Globe Publishing Company, 1976.

Byrnes, Garrett D. "The Sprague Murder Case." *Providence Evening Bulletin*, May 17– 23, 1933.

Coccia, Joseph A.A. "The Cranston Print Works—Its Economic Significance to the City of Cranston and Its Influence on the Political, Social and Industrial Life of the City and State of Rhode Island." M.A. thesis, Rhode Island College, June 1955.

Larned, Edward (Edwin) and William Knowles. "The Trial of John Gordon and William Gordon Charged with the Murder of Amasa Sprague, Before the Supreme Court of Rhode Island, March Term, 1844" Providence: Sidney S. Rider, 1884.

Miller, Bette. *Cranston Historical Society Newsletters*. 1984–1998.

Rhode Island Historical Preservation Commission. *Cranston, Rhode Island*. Rhode Island Historical Preservation Commission. 1970.

Sprague, Warren Vincent, M.D. *Sprague Families in America*. Rutland, VT: The Tuttle Company, 1913.

Wyss, Bob. "They Did Not Know What They Were Doing." *The Providence Sunday Journal Magazine*, July 19, 1981, pp. 24–26.